IMPRISONING RESISTANCE

Sydney Institute of Criminology Series No 25

Series Editors: Chris Cunneen, University of New South Wales
Mark Findlay, University of Sydney
Julie Stubbs, University of Sydney

Titles in the Series:

Aboriginal Perspectives on Criminal Justice Cunneen, C (ed) (1992)

Doing Less Time: Penal Reform in Crisis Chan, J (1992)

Psychiatry in Court Shea, P (1996)

Cricket and the Law Fraser, D (1993)

The Prison and the Home Aungles, A (1994)

Women, Male Violence and the Law Stubbs, J (ed) (1994)

Fault in Homicide Yeo, S (1997)

Anatomy of a French Murder Case McKillop, B (1997)

Gender, Race & International Relations Cunneen, C & Stubbs, J (1997)

Reform in Policing Bolen, J (1997)

A Culture of Corruption Dixon, D (ed) (1999)

Defining Madness Shea, P (1999)

Developing Cultural Criminology Banks, C (ed) (2000)

Indigenous Human Rights Garkawe, S, Kelly, L & Fisher, W (eds) (2001)

When Police Unionise Finnane, M (2002)

Regulating Racism McNamara, L (2002)

A History of Criminal Law in New South Wales Woods, G (2002)

Bin Laden in the Suburbs Poynting, S, Noble, G, Tabar, P & Collins, J (2004)

Global Issues, Women and Justice Pickering, S & Lambert, C (eds) (2004)

Aboriginal Childhood Separations and Guardianship Law Buti, A (2004)

Refugees and State Crime Pickering, S (2005)

Reshaping Juvenile Justice Chan, J (ed) (2005)

Interrogating Images Dixon, D (2007)

Recapturing Freedom Goulding, D (2007)

IMPRISONING RESISTANCE

LIFE AND DEATH IN AN AUSTRALIAN SUPERMAX

Bree Carlton

Sydney 2007
The Institute of Criminology Series No 25

Published by
Institute of Criminology Press
Sydney Institute of Criminology
University of Sydney Law School
173-175 Phillip Street Sydney 2000
www.criminology.law.usyd.edu.au

365.3
cat

Distributed by
The Federation Press
PO Box 45 Annandale 2038
www.federationpress.com.au

National Library of Australia Cataloguing-in-Publication

Carlton, Bree.
Imprisoning resistance : life and death in an Australian supermax.

Bibliography.
Includes index.
ISBN 9780975196755 (pbk.).

1. Pentridge Prison (Coburg, Vic.). Jika-Jika High Security Unit. 2. Pentridge Prison (Coburg, Vic.) - History. 3. Prison discipline - Victoria - Melbourne - History. 4. Prison violence - Victoria - Melbourne - History. 5. Prisons - Victoria - Melbourne - History. I. Title. (Series : Sydney Institute of Criminology monograph series).

365.641099451

© 2007 The Institute of Criminology

Cover design by Daniel Bryan
Front cover photograph by Bree Carlton 2006
Back cover photograph: Jika Jika interior of prisoner accommodation unit 1980. The Age Archives/Courtesy of *The Age*.
Typeset by The Institute of Criminology
Printed by Southwood Press Pty Ltd

This book is written in the memory of the men and women who died as a result of their imprisonment in Jika. It is also dedicated to the survivors of Jika; particularly those who continue to survive in prison, their families, friends and loved ones.

To all families and friends who have suffered the ordeal of losing loved ones in custody.

CONTENTS

Foreword by Phil Scraton   iii
Prologue   1
Introduction   13
   Modern High-Security in Australia   15
   Politics of Modern High-Security   19
   Disciplinary Power, Resistance and High-Security   22
   Cultures of Violence and High-Security   25
   Official Responses to Disorder, Death and Institutional Crisis   28
   Book Overview   30

Part One: Power and Resistance

Chapter One
   Polarisation, Power and Prisoner Resistance in the 1970s   33
   Introducing Power and Resistance in H Division   34
   Prisoner Representations of Violence and Resistance   37
   Politics of Maximum-Security Classification   40
   'H for Hell': Two Versions of H Division   43
   Jenkinson Inquiry and the Power of 'Official Truth-Making' 48
   1978 Prisoner Rebellion and The Ombudsman's Report   53
   Legacy of H Division   56

Chapter Two
   Official Beginnings of the Jika Jika High-Security Unit   59
   Psychological Control and Coercion   63
   Jika Jika High-Security Complex: Philosophy, Design, Structure   69
   The Official Opening   75
   Troubled Beginnings: Jika Jika and the Challinger Report   80
   Official Classification Procedures   82
   The Physical Impact   85
   Prisoner Management, Placement and Privileges   87
   Absence of Adequate Programs and Useful Work for Prisoners 91
   From Jika Jika to K Division: Concealing Institutional Fractures   93

Chapter Three
   Prisoner Accounts of Survival in the 'Pressure-Can'   97
   Experiencing Power: Prisoner Accounts   101
   Jika Jika: The 'Mind Games Capital of Pentridge'   106
   Sensation of 'Being Buried Alive': 'R&A' and Classification   114
   Exerting Physical Power and Discipline in the Jika Regime 120

Chapter Four
    'Rebelling Against the Dictatorial Regime in Jika'   125
    Conceptualising Power and Resistance as Institutional Text   126
    Conceptualising Resistance in Jika   130
    Transgression and Resistance in Jika   134
    Power Meets Resistance: A Crisis-Inducing Cycle   145

Part Two: Concealing Crisis

Chapter Five
    Deaths of John Williams and Sean Downie   149
    Reconstructing the Case Studies of Downie and Williams   151
    Flashpoint: Sean Downie 24 August 1987   152
    Sean Downie: An Official Summary of Events   153
    Prison Officer Representations   157
    Prisoner Representations   164
    Downie Family and Other Representations   173

Chapter Six
    Exonerating Institutional Liability   176
    Investigating Prisoner Deaths in Custody   180
    The Coronial Inquest as 'Public' or 'Official' Inquiry?   189
    Imprisoning Prisoner 'Truths'   194
    Prisoner Allegations and the Matter of Dixon-Jenkins   199
    The Autopsy and Consideration of Forensic Evidence   201
    Use of Expert Forensic Opinions   203
    Role of Forensic Experts in Post-Death Investigations   206
    'The 3.55pm Cell Visit'   207
    Further Internal and External Inquiries   209
    1990 Murray Inquiry   211

Chapter Seven
    Official Responses to the Jika Fire   215
    Events Preceding the October Fire   221
    Official Images of the Jika Five   228
    Official Discrediting of Prisoner Evidence   234
    Re-defining the Coroner's Powers   239
    Hallenstein's Findings   245
    Investigating the Inquest   250

Epilogue   258
Bibliography   266
Index   279

Acronyms

ACI - Australian Correctional Investments Inc.
CPO - Chief Prison Officer
DCC - Divisional Classification Committee
FOI - Freedom of Information
LOP - Loss of Privileges
MFB - Metropolitan Fire Brigade
NSWDCS - New South Wales Department of Corrective Services
OOC - Victorian Office of Corrections
PAG - Prisoners Action Group
PIC - Prison Industrial Complex
PRG - Prison Reform Group
PMSO – Prison Medical Support Officer
R&A - Review and Assessment Committee
RCIADIC - Royal Commission into Aboriginal Deaths in Custody
SPO - Senior Prison Officer
VDICWC - Victorian Deaths in Custody Watch Committee

Illustrations

Page x: Attorney-General Jim Kennan inspecting the aftermath of the fire at Jika Jika October 1987.

Page 70: Plan of Jika Jika High-Security Unit.

Page 71: Aerial shot of Pentridge Prison & Jika Jika High-Security Complex 1980.

Page 72: Interior of prisoner cell 1980.

Insert:

David McGauley, Robert Wright, Arthur Gallagher and James Loughnan (undated photograph taken in Jika Jika). Inset Richard Morris.

Interior of prisoner accommodation unit 1980.

1987 bronze-up campaign.

Jika Jika interior of spine leading to Unit 2 taken during the aftermath of Sean Downie's death.

Staff control area and entry to Unit 2 taken during the aftermath of Downie's death.

Grille in Sean Downie's cell.

Scene in Unit 2 cell five where Downie was alleged to have taken his life.

Door of Unit 2 cell five where Downie allegedly lit a fire taken during the aftermath of the emergency response.

Unit 2 corridor leading to prisoner cells taken during the aftermath of Downie's death.

Unit 4 corridor taken during the aftermath of the October protest fire and emergency response.

Interior prisoner day room area taken during the aftermath of the October protest fire and emergency response.

Interior of Unit 4 prisoner accommodation area taken during the aftermath of the October protest fire and emergency response.

ACKNOWLEDGEMENTS

There are many people who provided generous support throughout the difficult journey of researching, writing and publishing this work. Mark Peel, Jude McCulloch, Charandev Singh and Vicki Peel gave ongoing encouragement, inspiration, practical support and generous assistance. Thanks to Jude for her friendship and for being there in dark times and Mark for his infectious optimism and relentless faith in my abilities. I extend my sincere gratitude to Charandev for his endless assistance, friendship and support. Phil Scraton has provided ongoing mentoring, comradeship, inspiration and encouragement to publish this story. Rob White also contributed much valued assurance and support.

Many thanks go to Craig Minogue for his words of wisdom and ongoing generosity. Peter Reed and Bernie Matthews generously contributed time to talk and trusted me with their stories. Cheryle Morris has given invaluable moral support and I thank her for her friendship. Jeff Lapidos gave advice and practical assistance with transcripts. My sincerest thanks go to Catherine Gow and the Victorian Deaths in Custody Watch Committee, all the folk at Justice Action in Sydney and particularly Brett Collins.

Malcolm Feiner from the Victorian Department of Justice Resource Centre provided generous and helpful practical assistance in the early stages of research. Rick Robinson and Katrina Beesley at the State Coroner's Office helped with locating stray inquest files. Thanks to all staff at the Public Records Office Victoria, the Coburg Historical Society and the Coburg Library. Thanks to the Age and Lucas Carter in particular for his generous help in tracking down and providing digitised versions of early photographs of Jika Jika. The Public Records Office also arranged the reproduction of archival photographs for the book. Simon Eyland, John Partridge and all the staff from the New South Wales Corrective Services research division provided assistance with New South Wales documents. Tony Vinson also contributed support and advice.

Mark Findlay, Chris Cunneen, Duncan Chappell, Julie Stubbs, Nina Ralph, Dawn Koester and all at the Sydney Institute of Criminology made the publication of this work possible. Special thanks go to Dawn for her tireless efforts and support during the production stages. Many thanks also to Karen Gillen for the index and Daniel Bryan for the cover art. Thanks to the two anonymous reviewers who provided invaluable commentary and feedback. The Monash University School of Political and Social Inquiry provided the funding to get the publishing project up and running. This book could never been possible without the support of the Monash School of Historical Studies and the ongoing mentoring and encouragement from my colleagues in Criminology, Dean Wilson and Sharon Pickering.

It would be impossible to name the many people who have contributed in big and small ways to the end product and supported with information, proofreading, advice, discussion, and those who have given encouragement and their unconditional emotional and practical support – you know who you are. Notable thanks go to Jane Connors, Shelley Burchfield, Amanda George, Julian Knight, Richard Light, Peter Norden, Helen Neville, Alisoun Neville, Marion Macgregor, Vicki Sentas, Marie Segrave, Jessica Raschke, Marijana Bosnjak, Melissa Meager and 3CR Community Radio.

I'm indebted to my beloved partner Daniel Bryan who has cooked many meals, washed many dishes, made many cups of tea, provided much reassurance, given many cuddles and who above all has remained consistently supportive and understanding. Nick Drake maintained my sanity, while Sharki, Belle, Klaws and Mr Moo provided much comfort and company. The Bryans have provided much love and cheer. My mum, Chae Paterson listened to frequent crises in confidence, provided much love, laughter, support and reminders to believe in myself. Many thanks go to Sharon Carlton and my dad Ray Carlton for all their support. Finally, I extend much love and gratitude to my lost brother Geordie Robert Carlton for opening my eyes to the darkness and in turn, to humanity.

FOREWORD

by Phil Scraton

In the mid 1980s at Scotland's Peterhead jail a series of increasingly violent protests by long-term prisoners dominated media reports and political debate. In late September 1987 they climaxed in a second roof-top protest during which a prison officer was taken hostage. While the media railed against the 'savagery' and 'evil' of the hostage takers little coverage was given to the context in which the protest took place. Almost a year earlier prisoners had held another prison officer hostage, occupying the prison roof for over 90 hours. The obvious question was why prisoners, with nowhere to run and no way of hiding their identities, would take a prison officer hostage and initiate a public protest knowing that eventually they would retreat, most probably to be beaten by guards and given further, substantial prison sentences. It was even more remarkable that having witnessed the fate of the previous protesters, other prisoners decided to restage the event. The explanation was written on white sheets draped on the prison roof: 'Brutality: We Need Help'; 'Living Death Must End'; 'Long Term Mental Torture'; 'We Are All Hostages'; 'They Treat Us All Like Animals'. The protests were not only about appalling conditions of incarceration, they were a response to endemic violence and brutality.

Peterhead Prison was built by convict labour and opened in August 1888. Situated on the north-east coast of Scotland it is a long and difficult journey from the southern lowland band where the majority of the Scottish population lives. For most visiting families access was restricted by poor public transport. Regarding prison accommodation and regime, conditions for prisoners were harsh and regularly threatening. Within the Scottish Prison Service Peterhead had developed a fierce reputation for independence in operational policies and practices. While prison officers moved

The

postings within the Service those at Peterhead tended to stay, retaining a discernible pride in their reputation for containing Scotland's 'most dangerous prisoners'. Jimmy Boyle, held at Peterhead prior to his move to the progressive lifers' unit at Barlinnie confirmed Peterhead as a prison 'infamous for its institutional brutality ... the Scottish equivalent of its American cousin, Alcatraz'.

Following a series of public meetings held in Edinburgh in 1986 I was commissioned with Joe Sim, now Professor of Criminology at Liverpool John Moores University, to research the historical background and contemporary circumstances of the Peterhead protests that eventually extended to other Scottish jails. At the time my research was concerned primarily with deaths in custody. We were completing the final report as the second roof-top protest occurred (Scraton et al 1987). What followed was massive disruption across Scottish prisons, particularly focusing on the regimes under which long-term and life-sentenced prisoners were held. We were denied direct research access to the prison by the Scottish Prison Service but were permitted to issue questionnaires to any prisoners whose name and prison number was in our possession. Despite being aware that their extensive written responses were closely monitored, the picture that emerged from prisoners' accounts was one of brutality, corruption and neglectful health provision.

The research revealed a draconian regime underpinned by violence in which 86 per cent of prisoners felt unsafe, with nearly three-quarters experiencing constant fear. Bullying and predatory exploitation by other prisoners was reported consistently. The use of the 'silent cell' within solitary confinement and the 'unlawful and unreasonable use of force by prison staff' constituted the most serious elements of 'the violent institution' (Scraton et al 1991). While some prisoners externalised their violence others turned in on themselves. Clearly evident was institutional failure in the state's duty of care coupled with prisoners' subjection to inhuman and degrading treatment. Our report made 17 major recommendations including the closure of the prison. Yet 20 years on Peterhead remains part of the prison estate used primarily as a prison holding those convicted of sex offences.

At the time we were conducting our research a predatory culture of male violence was consolidating in an Australian prison that also housed prisoners considered a serious management problem. As eventually happened in Scotland, with the opening of Shotts Prison, the State of Victoria had established a high-security unit, Jika Jika, at Pentridge Prison. Jika Jika, like its supermax counterparts in the United States and the United Kingdom, was designed and built as a prison within a prison. Based on highly restrictive regimes, minimum social interaction and severe punishment such regimes epitomise ultimate polarisation between staff and prisoners. In addition to academic research, numerous autobiographical accounts reveal the institutionalisation of masculinity within male jails whose currency is threat and intimidation invariably leading to alienation and escalating violence. Deteriorating regimes are characterised by hostile relations between staff and prisoners, longer hours of lockdown, lack of constructive activities and the constant spectre of pain and death. The all-pervasive climate within punishment blocks or special units such as Jika Jika is that of mutual loathing and hatred.

Within prisons, power rests directly with guards and only indirectly with managers. High walls and electrified fences not only serve to confine prisoners, they also present a more than symbolic barrier to those seeking access. The prison as an island and prisons as an archipelago are well-used yet accurate metaphors. Independent monitoring or visiting committees, inspectorates and ombudspersons, rarely glimpse the excesses of violent staff who exploit their immense discretion to victimise some prisoners while manipulating others. Within high-security units the cloak of secrecy that renders daily life invisible to the outside world also casts a long shadow over transparency. This leads guards to believe, not without reason, that with their power comes impunity. Given the vilification of those within their charge there are few people external to the prison prepared to question, let alone challenge, the professional competence and integrity of prison managers or their staff. There are no votes won, and few newspapers sold, defending the rights of those perceived to be the 'worst of the worst'.

In the United Kingdom during the 1980s a number of prisoners died in police or prison custody. Invariably the deaths occurred at the hands of their captors and often as a consequence of the application of control and restraint by groups of police or prison officers. Others, particularly women and children, took their own lives while enduring harsh, intimidatory and negligent regimes. Much has also been written on the deaths of Aboriginal people in similar circumstances in Australia. Even those cases where clear evidence of institutional brutality and/or negligence existed, where coroners recorded unlawful killing verdicts, there were few prosecutions. When prosecutions occurred convictions were rare. At the time, our research demonstrated how negative imagery and deeply institutionalised ideologies provided 'the ready justification for the marginalisation of identifiable groups', thus deflecting responsibility from state institutions (Scraton & Chadwick 1987: 220). The political management of identity transformed into 'a process of categorisation which suggests that the "violent", the "dangerous", the "political extremist", the "alien", the "inadequate", the "mentally ill", contribute to their own deaths either by their pathological condition or their personal choice' (Scraton & Chadwick 1987: 233). It was a process consistent with the institutional response to prison protest.

During such a protest in Jika Jika in October 1987, Arthur Gallagher, James Loughnan, David McGauley, Richard Morris and Robert Wright died in a fire. Two months previous to the protest fire prisoners Sean Downie and John Williams died in contested circumstances. The regime was in crisis. Whatever the ascribed or 'achieved' status of those who died, it was assumed that Victoria's Office of Corrections would conduct a full inquiry into their guards, their custom and practice, their acts or omissions. Following the fire, the coroner criticised the Office of Corrections for its contribution to the deaths of the five men. Subsequently, the Attorney General referred to Jika Jika as an 'electronic zoo'. A public inquiry was expected as a decade earlier there had been an inquiry into allegations of brutality at Pentridge Prison's H Division maximum-security unit, Jika Jika's predecesor. The Jenkinson Inquiry condoned the violence used by guards as a response to that used by prisoners. Thus the tragic events at Jika Jika did not occur in a vacuum. They were the consequence of H Division's legacy and Jika Jika's regime, each a site of physical violence and psychological intimidation. No staff or managers were held responsible for the circumstances surrounding the 1987 deaths, thus providing a clear illustration of institutional abuse of power with impunity.

In this meticulously researched book Bree Carlton revisits the history of H Division at Pentridge as the precursor to Jika Jika. She examines the development of prisoners' resistance and protest in the 1970s and questions the impartiality and efficacy of the Jenkinson Inquiry and the Victorian Ombudsman investigations that followed in 1978. In the late 1970s the authorities became increasingly concerned at the level of violent conflict and confrontation in H Division, and were also embarrassed by publicised allegations that prisoners were subjected to a regime of brutality. However, rather than accepting the warning signs evident in the conflict at H Division, the authorities pressed on with the construction of a hi-tech facility that imposed even greater restrictions on prisoners, less visibility and harsher containment. With guards vindicated by Jenkinson, the spiral of polarisation and violence continued unabated through the 1980s. Prisoners, desperate about their conditions, reacted with all forms of violent protest including hunger strikes, barricades, assaults and cell fires. Bree Carlton unpacks and closely interrogates the official discourse around the deaths at Jika Jika. She demonstrates perfectly how, read through a critical lens, official accounts combine diversion and denial. Her documentary research reveals serious flaws in the processes of official investigation and coronial inquiry, demonstrating how state institutions have the capacity to use privileged access to ensure that their policies and officials will not be held to account.

Whatever the reputations of those who died, whatever the crimes for which they were convicted, in accordance with international conventions and standards as prisoners they had rights. Of primary significance is the right to life including the state's obligation to protect those in their care. This is closely followed by the right to be protected from inhuman or degrading treatment. Given the violent history of H Division and the institutionalised abuses of Jika Jika, the guards, the prison authorities and the state had serious questions to answer concerning the abuse of these foundational rights. They were never asked. This book courageously and accessibly engages the key questions. It is published 20 years after the deaths at Jika Jika yet the story of Pentridge and the persistence of the supermax mentality within prison services internationally remain as relevant today as it was then.

In discussing the endemic abuse of prisoners within the United States prison-industrial complex, long-term prisoner Michael Santos states that imprisonment conditions prisoners to fail and that the proposition that 'correctional officers actually correct' is but a 'delusion'. He continues:

> In reality, life in prison is punitive, repressive, and degrading. If preparing people to live as contributing citizens were an actual goal, the use of incentives would replace the threat of punishment. The system is built for corruption, a scheme with an exquisite design to self-perpetuate. Prisons remove hope. They create resentment. They thwart family relationships, degrade each individual's sense of self, separate offenders *in every way* from society. The system fosters unnatural us-versus-them, Orwellian worlds. (Santos 2006: 290)

The prison-industrial complex in the United States, the United Kingdom and Australia has expanded beyond all projections over the last 20 years and its corrosive operation is promoted and exported globally through giant corporations and the privatisation of jails. In these circumstances it is essential that critical analysis of what happens inside jails, particularly those special units hidden by extra layers of security, exposes the inhumanity, danger and rights abuses that have become institutionalised in advanced democratic states. Bree Carlton's work reveals the contradictions implicit in the notion of 'corrections' through demonstrating the potentially lethal consequences of incarcerating prisoners labelled as 'dangerous', 'unmanageable' or 'subversive' in conditions that maximise punishment, diminish humanity and encourage violence. Not only does her excellent scholarship challenge the 'view from above', but it contributes to a deeper understanding of the institutionalised violence central to the seemingly inexorable growth of supermax jails.

References:

Santos, Michael 2006 *Inside: Life Behind Bars in America* St Martin's Press New York

Scraton, Phil and Kathryn Chadwick 1987 'Speaking Ill of the Dead: Institutional Responses to Deaths in Custody' in P Scraton (ed) *Law, Order and the Authoritarian State: Readings in Critical Criminology* The Open University Press Milton Keynes

Scraton, Phil, Joe Sim and Paula Skidmore 1987 *The Roof Comes Off: The Report of the Independent Committee of Inquiry into the Protests at Peterhead Prison* Gateway Exchange Edinburgh

Scraton, Phil, Joe Sim and Paula Skidmore 1991 *Prisons under protest* The Open University Press Milton Keynes

Attorney-General Jim Kennan inspects the aftermath of the fire at Jika Jika during a press tour in October 1987. Photographer Sebastian Costanzo/Courtesy of *The Age*.

PROLOGUE

29 October 1987, Jika Jika High-Security Unit, H.M. Pentridge Prison, Coburg, Victoria, Australia[1]:

On 29 October 1987, 10 prisoners in Unit 4 of the Jika Jika High-Security Unit executed a joint protest action they had planned collectively for over eight weeks. Each Jika Unit was physically divided into two separate prisoner living quarters or Sides, but prisoners were able to maintain communication through the bulletproof glass that divided them by using sign language. At approximately 3.25pm Side 1 prisoner Robert Wright gave Side 2 prisoner Craig Minogue 'the nod', that both sides should commence putting the plan into action. Prisoners on both sides then commenced barricading the Unit doors. In Unit 4 the doors were opaque bulletproof glass, fortified by steel bars facing the interior of the prisoner quarters. Side 1 prisoners used a wire table tennis net to tie their doors, while Side 2 tied chairs onto the bars with sheets to prevent prison officer access. Side 1 prisoners used the table tennis top as an additional barrier and then started stacking flammables such as books, newspapers, magazines and foam ripped from the chairs. Other larger items such as foam mattresses were then heaped on top. In order to obscure their activities from the duty prison officers in the control room or 'fish bowl', Side 2 prisoners smashed surveillance cameras and began plastering newspaper sheets across the bulletproof glass windows. It was alleged that while prisoners were barricading, certain prison

---

[1] The following italicised account is based on the unpublished transcript of proceedings at the Coroner's investigation into the deaths of James Richard Loughnan, David McGauley, Arthur Bernard Gallagher, Robert Lindsay Wright and Richard John Morris, 1988-89, Public Records Office Victoria, file number 1989/680 (hereafter 'Inquest 1988-89a'), pp 1074-1260.

1

officers goaded them, telling them to 'take their time' and one officer allegedly yelled, 'you're gonna be flogged for this'. Other prison officers allegedly sat writing conduct reports about what was happening while Chief Prison Officers (CPO) Mackie and Thorp reportedly made attempts to diffuse the situation and negotiate with Wright.[2] These attempts were unsuccessful and Wright set fire to the barricade on Side 1 at approximately 4.05pm (Hallenstein 1989: 36). Prisoner Richard Light reported that the power was turned off immediately and all went quiet as smoke began to billow into Side 2.

After the fire was lit, Unit 4 filled rapidly with acrid, toxic smoke produced by the burning foam mattresses and electrical goods. In Jika, security stipulations dictated that there be no natural ventilation, no opening windows and no sprinkler systems in the Units. It was therefore Wright's plan that prisoners would empty the water from the S-bend of their toilets and cover their heads with wet blankets in order to breathe fresh air while waiting to be rescued. However Side 1 prisoners soon discovered the plan was flawed when smoke came up through the toilets. At this point, panic set in.

Minogue reported that prisoners shouted to one another to keep calm. Eventually Wright shouted to Minogue, 'Slim, we're fucked mate ... we can breathe nowhere'. He then told Minogue to break a window and get out. Minogue heard further incomprehensible yelling. He shouted, 'Are you there Bob?' but Side 1 was all quiet. In a state of alarm, Minogue screamed out to the officers, 'Will you let us out?' but there was no answer. Minogue, Light and prisoner Michael King alleged they could hear the voices of prison officers shouting, 'die you bastards' and 'hope you choke'. Light was asthmatic and collapsed in his cell. Minogue, King and prisoner Dimitrovski attempted to smash the bulletproof glass windows

---

[2] State Coroner Hal R Hallenstein, *Finding of Inquisition upon the Bodies of James Loughman, David McGauley, Arthur Gallagher, Robert Wright and Richard Morris*, 28/7/89, Victorian Department of Justice Resource Centre (hereafter 'Hallenstein 1989'), pp 30-1.

using chairs and a toilet Minogue ripped out of a cell but such attempts proved fruitless as the objects bounced straight off. Minogue then urged King and Dimitrovski to smash property and make noise to let the officers know they were still alive. The prisoners then tore apart the barricade in a flurry.

Evidence presented at the fire inquest indicated that the emergency response by prison staff was a disordered shambles. Reports suggested there was a range of activities and rescue attempts taking place and it was unclear who was in charge. The fire alarms in Jika were not directly linked to the Metropolitan Fire Brigade (MFB) and officers had to get a free telephone line out of the prison to notify the MFB of the emergency. All pneumatic doors within the Jika Jika High-Security Unit were opened and closed by an hydraulic, electronic, remote control system. After the fire was lit the doors malfunctioned and officers were faced with the task of breaching these doors, which were doubly obstructed by prisoner barricades. While it was alleged that Governor Penter had initially ordered officers not to damage the costly doors in the process of breaching them, equipment such as axes, oxy-acetylene blowtorches and angle grinders were eventually used as the situation became more desperate. At first CPO Thorp managed to force open the spine door that led to the barricaded doors, using an override key. However, he immediately became trapped in the spine and as the small area filled with smoke, officers concentrated their efforts on rescuing him.

When the MFB finally attended the scene, the numerous doors situated throughout Jika posed further problems in that they kept closing, thus cutting out the water supply. Meanwhile, Governor Penter was alleged to be instructing officers with a video camera what to take pictures of, while many other prison officers attending the emergency situation milled about the foyer providing little assistance and wasting the limited breathing apparatuses available. Coroner Hallenstein (1989: 53) later described the scene as chaotic:

> In the heart of this scene of apparent chaos, was Thorp trapped in the spine, and the six prison officers trying to open the spine doors and free him. There was a lot of yelling. Nothing was

being done to open Sides 1 and 2 corridor doors, and the foyer was becoming crowded with the many prison officers who were arriving.

Certain officers were reported to have selflessly exposed themselves to the toxic fumes in their courageous efforts to breach the doors and get the prisoners out. Some of these officers did not use breathing apparatuses, to avoid wasting time. Unit 4 Prisoner Dietrich witnessed the emergency operations from a distance as he was on a visit during the protest. He acknowledged the bravery of certain officers but also alleged that he witnessed other officers roughly dragging smoke-affected prisoners out of the Unit. He also alleged that some prisoners were beaten with batons. Disturbingly, he further claimed that when half-conscious Side 1 prisoner Arthur Gallagher was brought out the officers stood around arguing about who would administer mouth to mouth. Gallagher subsequently died.

When the Side 2 doors were finally breached, Minogue alleged prisoners were told to 'unbarricade' and come out with their hands up, to which he replied, 'wake up to yourself, we're dying in here'. Minogue was carrying Light who was suffering from an asthma attack. He stated that he asked for assistance but was refused. When he collapsed, Minogue alleged he had his arms twisted behind his back and was run up to Unit 7, smashed against a wall where he was told, 'we're going to get you, you cunt'. Light alleged that he was dragged out of the Unit so that he suffered painful grazes to his back. He stated that he was shaken when he saw the body bags, 'I knew what had happened and I just went into shock'. The emergency operation was unsuccessful and while Side 2 prisoners narrowly escaped death, all Side 1 prisoners, Arthur Gallagher, James Loughnan, David McGauley, Richard Morris and Robert Wright, died of asphyxiation as a result of smoke inhalation.

The deaths of the five prisoners in the October fire sparked the immediate closure of the Jika Jika High-Security Unit, by Attorney General Jim Kennan, in November 1987. A frenzy of controversy ensued as lengthy inquest investigations led by State Coroner Hallenstein commenced. Amid the focus upon emergency operations, staff training and questions of institutional and departmental accountability, the wall of secrecy protecting the Jika Jika regime was momentarily disturbed. However, as the inquest progressed it became increasingly clear that an acute sense of institutional crisis bubbled deep below the surface of the immediate events surrounding the fire and had been steadily building since the opening of the division seven years earlier.

Jika Jika opened in 1980. Built of concrete and steel, the hi-tech prison complex was designed to secure the Victorian prison system's most violent, dangerous, high-risk and troublesome long-term prisoners. At the time of its conception the multi-million dollar complex was celebrated as an impressive technological first. As an 'escape-proof', 'anti-terrorist' and humanely modern facility for high-risk prisoners, Jika was geared towards total containment and security. From the outside, the complex resembled a spider-like futuristic space station. Groups of 12 prisoners were housed in detached 'Units' and segregated into 'Sides' in groups of six. The complex was completely sealed, providing no openings for fresh air. The Units were connected via corridor spines that led to a central administration area and the entire facility was suspended on stilts. Prison officers and prisoners were physically divided by bulletproof glass to enable supervision, and prisoners were subjected to constant video camera surveillance. Electronic consoles allowed prison officers to remotely control power, heating and prisoner access through the pneumatic steel doors within each Unit, thus limiting the need for physical contact with prisoners. Outside, prisoner recreation took place within the exercise yards enclosed by angular 'escape-proof' cages and the perimeter of the complex was protected by advanced microwave technology and alarm systems.

Despite the emphasis on security, technology and efficiency, the supposedly modern and 'humane' Jika[3] complex was plagued

---

[3] 'Jika' is a shortened name for the Jika Jika High-Security Unit. The name 'Jika Jika' is an appropriated local Indigenous term. Jika Jika was renamed 'K Division' by the authorities in 1984 (see Chapter Two). This name change was purported to address local Indigenous concerns. However it was also a strategy to counter the increasing negative stigma publicly associated with the prison. Despite this, prisoners who experienced Jika Jika have continued

with violent incidents and fraught with entrenched management problems from the time that it opened. The complex initially provided garden areas, programs, and limited freedoms for prisoners, to compensate for the apparent harshness of the high-security environment. However, each of these small freedoms was gradually eroded as a variety of incidents and security breaches occurred, thus vindicating calls for increased security and disciplinary crackdowns. Between 1980 and 1987 there were multiple escapes, escape attempts, assaults, murders, prisoner campaigns, protest actions, barricades, fires, hunger strikes, acts of self harm, attempted suicides and prisoner allegations of misconduct and brutality by prison staff (Prison Reform Group (PRG) 1988; see also Inquest 1988-89a: Units 68-79).[4] Above all, the impact of the harsh high-security atmosphere and environment on both staff and prisoners produced polarised relationships and contributed to the escalation of tension. The pressure and strain that stemmed from such conditions exacerbated an intense sense of fear and paranoia, while giving rise to a predatory culture of physical and psychological violence between prisoners and between staff and prisoners.

Matters escalated during 1987 and in January of that year emerging accounts of mismanagement and incidents of abuse and violence prompted a public statement by Attorney General Jim Kennan, who branded the complex a 'dehumanising electronic zoo' (*Herald* 30/10/87 p 1). During this time, Prisoners Action Group (PAG) spokesperson Jeff Lapidos publicly revealed he had obtained statistics through Freedom of Information from the Office of Corrections documenting 2500 incidents that had occurred in Jika between 1985 and 1987 that were serious enough to report to the Attorney General (*Herald* 30/1/87 p 8). However, it was not until the deaths of prisoners John Williams and Sean Downie in late

---

to remember the institution as 'Jika'. Thus, throughout this book I have chosen not to adhere to the official renaming to 'K Division' and will use both the names 'Jika Jika' and 'Jika' interchangeably.

[4]   See also, Unpublished transcript of proceedings at Coroner's investigation into the death of Sean Fitzgerald Downie, 1988-89, Public Records Office Victoria file number 1989/664 (hereafter 'Inquest 1988-89b'), Units 64-67.

August 1987 that matters truly began to deteriorate. Williams died on 22 August in Unit 5 and Downie died two days later in the punishment section of Unit 2. While the deaths occurred in what were essentially unrelated circumstances, allegations of staff mismanagement and prison officer misconduct were later raised at both inquest investigations. The very fact that two deaths in custody occurred within two days of one another illustrates the acute urgency of the problems experienced in Jika during this time. The failure of the authorities to adequately address the allegations and concerns arising from these deaths and the lack of official action in response to the polarised culture and harsh conditions within Jika, all contributed to a further descent into crisis that led ultimately to the cataclysmic events surrounding the October 1987 fire and the deaths of the five men.

State Coroner Hal Hallenstein investigated the five deaths in 1989 and found that while the prisoners played a hand in their own deaths, the Victorian Office of Corrections (OOC) also contributed to the deaths through staff incompetence, lack of emergency training and mismanagement. Despite the criticisms and prisoner allegations of misconduct, violence and abuse, there was no restitution or justice either for the families of the deceased or any official validation of the personal experiences and impacts on prisoners who endured Jika. Subsequent public inquiries appointed to investigate allegations considered outside the ambits of the Jika fire and Sean Downie inquests were neatly dismissed, thus exonerating and legitimising the OOC in the eyes of the public.

The idea to write this book surfaced in 1999. It corresponded with the decommissioning and closure of Pentridge Prison and the subsequent 'selling off' of the site by the Victorian State Government to make way for the multi-million dollar housing estate and commercial development 'Pentridge Village' (*Moreland Courier* 7/2/2000 p 8). While this process was accompanied by much community debate at the time about heritage significance and preservation (Allom Lovell & Assoc 1996: 241), those who were touched in some way by the violence and deaths that occurred in Jika Jika wondered if the physical eradication of the site would serve to further 'disappear' and bury such experiences beneath the incongruity of a 'Pentridge Village' housing estate.

Landscapes provide a critical context for locating and reconstructing violent and traumatic histories and mapping relations between the powerful and the marginalised (Cresswell 1996). Having had their immediate context physically eradicated, sanitised landscapes are further neutralised by processes of official rationalisation, denial and whitewash. Mona Oikawa (2000: 41) characterises these processes as deliberate, systematic 'hegemonic ideologies of forgetting'. In Australia, there is a long tradition of historical selectivity, collective amnesia and 'forgetting' about sites and landscapes steeped in the unsettling and indelible residue of racism, dispossession, dispersal, violence and incarceration (Gibson 2002; Perera 2002). Yet these violent histories cannot be forgotten as they underpin the very origins, experience and administration of criminal justice in contemporary Australia (Cunneen & Davis 2000; see also Cunneen 2001). This book is therefore motivated by a desire to resurrect and reconstruct the Jika experience in order to recognise past injustices and circumvent the continuing proliferation of harm and violence producing prison regimes in the present.

Above all the objective of this book is exposure; to unveil officially obfuscated and unresolved accounts of power from within the controversial Jika Jika complex. It intends to reconstruct, describe and mediate human experiences of life and death in high-security, an institution traditionally sealed from public view. There is very little analysis of Jika Jika or documentation available outside official reports, inquiries and inquest investigations. With one exception, ex-Jika prisoner and prison officer interviews were not used, due to the anticipated complexity of departmental ethics procedures and difficulties associated with locating ex-Jika prisoners, many of whom are scattered throughout various sections of the Victorian prison system. There was also an anticipated probability that formal applications to interview would be met by official antipathy in response to the potential resurrection of a controversial and shameful past.

This work is based on official documents available on public access. I found that official inquiries, reports and inquest investigations surrounding the Jika deaths and 1987 October fire provide a rare window into the hidden workings of Victoria's first hi-tech high-security institution. This has involved a subversive process of excavation, to draw out unauthorised accounts of Jika Jika and provide a critical examination of the actions of the Victorian Office of Corrections officials who managed, during 1980 and 1987, to divert scrutiny and accountability in the face of institutional culpability, complicity and crisis. The interrogation of official discourse and officially constructed 'truths' is integral to this analysis. Overall this book performs the political task of reading and writing 'against the grain' (Nancy Scheper-Hughes cited in Sim 2003: 245) with respect to the available primary empirical data.

This book addresses the specific experiences of a particular group of men prisoners in Jika during the 1980s. The prisoners attracted considerable official attention in response to their concerns about prisoner rights and their continual involvement in protests. This focus stems primarily from the fact that their stories were detailed throughout the extensive inquest transcripts and files that form the basis of this research. While these accounts provide the focus of this book, it is acknowledged Jika Jika held other groups of prisoners with distinct experiences. One such group is women, who were in the early 1980s, confined in Jika as punishment for non-compliance in other sections of the Victorian prison system. In the post-1987 and fire era of Jika, the complex was also used to house women with special needs such as those with HIV and drug addiction.

While there is limited official documentation surrounding the treatment of women in Jika, their conditions were reported as neglectful, brutal and damaging (P Reed Interview 14/5/03). Most important is the under-acknowledged and painful legacy of post-release deaths of women prisoners held in Jika Jika and other high-security facilities in Victoria, Australia and in other western states. Women's accounts of life and death in high-security more generally, encompass gendered experiences of institutional power, violence and resistance that are distinct from the men and should be recognised accordingly (George 2002; Kilroy & Warner 2002; Shaylor 1998; O'Melveny 1992; see also Corcoran 2006). This fact, along with limitations of time and space led to the decision not to detail such experiences in this book.

The process of researching and reconstructing the Jika experience has presented an inherently political and emotional research task. It must be considered in the context of transformative research agendas dedicated to the exposure of injustice, systems of domination and gross violations of human rights associated with powerful state bodies and agents (Green & Ward 2004; see also Tombs & Whyte 2003; Ross 2003).

It is well established that the expert gaze and the construction of professional discourses not only subdue people's lived experiences but also 'drive a wedge between subjective experience and objective knowledge' (Pickering 2001: 485). Such a wedge effectively displaces the subjective and often emotional experience of research in the interests of maintaining neutrality and balanced scientific objectivity. However, as Alison Liebling (2001: 474) argues, the capacity to 'feel, relate and become "involved" is a key part of the overall research task'. Furthermore, it is crucial to recognise that the practical experience of academic research requires the researcher to draw upon subjective bodies of knowledge situated 'beyond the orbit of traditional academic discourse' (Farrell & Hamm cited in Liebling 2001: 474). The values of neutrality and objectivity within traditional academic discourse are increasingly undermined by the practice of researching highly emotive and subjective experiences associated with power relations, institutional injustices and human rights abuses. It is my experience that it would be impracticable and indeed unethical to disassociate the processes of research and writing from the emotionality associated with the experiences and struggles subject to examination. This belief accords with Sharon Pickering's (2001: 486) assertion that:

> The researcher is obliged to do "emotion work," to understand the ways emotion assumes importance and to disrupt the taboo status of emotion in the research process. To reveal emotionality about one's self, is not only to reject the neutral observer and

knowledge maker role, it is also to take responsibility for the power relations inherent in the research process.

My experience of researching and writing this book has involved the examination of a host of reported misconduct and violent practices, some of which were alleged to have resulted in death. Writing about these traumatic episodes was often a difficult and painful experience. Contrary to the work of many ethnographic prison researchers and criminologists conducting fieldwork in live prisons, much of my research or 'fieldwork' was spent in isolation, piecing together the jigsaw puzzle of Jika through official documents and archives. The isolation, and the language of official discourse, brought about polar experiences of extreme detachment or desensitisation and intense distress. Often the material placed me in a position where my desire to expose injustices and institutional violence conflicted with my ability to produce a measured analysis.

The practice of researching violence raises a powerful potential for academic research and writing as a 'site of resistance', as a means to write 'against' violence and terror rather than merely writing 'about' it (Nancy Scheper-Hughes cited in Sim 2003: 244-6). Some may take the view that it is the role of researchers, not to expose, but to analyse and understand. However, there is a profound danger that an emphasis on 'objectivity' and 'value-free' research mutes the potential transformative role critical research can play in the illumination of injustice. Moreover, to engage in 'rational' discussions about the political and social meanings of traumatic events can only serve to overshadow, trivialise and compound the struggles, harms and suffering experienced by victims of injustice (Davis 2005). The effect is to further marginalise victims and their families while reproducing the cycle of violence, trauma and injustice.

The intention of this book is to open up debate about the conditions in which we imprison those written off as beyond rehabilitation and redemption. Discourses of dangerousness and identities constructed around social inadequacy, criminality and violence too frequently cloud such debates and are often actively deployed by officials to justify and shield institutional practices of neglect, abuse and violence from scrutiny and criticism. It is my hope that this book will open up broader dimensions to debates surrounding these issues, injecting reason and humanity, and most importantly, calling attention to the human costs of high-security.

INTRODUCTION

This book is titled *Imprisoning Resistance* because it is concerned with how high-security prisons were intended and devised as an official solution to managing the growing problem of prisoner non-compliance and resistance in the 1960s and 1970s. Central to this focus is the manner in which such prisons have been subject to ongoing challenge by prisoners from within. Officials hoped that through the use of hi-tech security devices, sophisticated architectural design, and complex managerial and disciplinary strategies they could increase physical and psychological control over prisoners. However, as the Jika experience demonstrates, in practice such regimes have worked only to exacerbate the very violence, disorder and resistance they were supposed to prevent. In high-security pre-existing tension, conflict and cultures of violence are often magnified by the psychological effects and pressures associated with extended periods of lockdown, social isolation, sensory deprivation and unaccountable power structures integral to the operation of the institution. In focusing on official imperatives and the drive to manage resistance, this book also focuses on the challenges posed by prisoner resistance within high-security and how these have been officially represented in the context of institutional shortcomings and failings, to justify the intensification and escalation of security. In this respect it is paradoxical that 'security', the prevailing official response to problems in prison, in practice only serves to intensify institutional polarisation and disorder and can lead to acute crises and harm.

Jika Jika presents a traumatic and markedly violent institutional history that the authorities, during the 1980s and 1990s, strategically attempted to bury. Therefore a critical analysis of the adequacy of official responses to discreditable episodes, including

13

prisoner allegations about conditions and treatment, prisoner protests and deaths in custody, comprises an additional focus.

This book does not present a study of a 'live' prison, nor does it provide an extensive and generalised comparative assessment of the origins, functions and efficiencies/deficiencies of high-security. Instead an historical account is provided and the Jika experience itself is used as a vehicle to shed light on broader contemporary issues associated with the politics of high-security confinement in Australia and internationally.

There is a sense of exigency surrounding the resurfacing of the Jika experience in present times, as many of the themes resonate with pressing national and international issues. These include the ongoing and widespread arbitrary use of high-security and supermax prisons and their association with exertions of unaccountable state power and human rights violations; links between the increasing use of such prisons and the expansion of the prison industrial complex in western states; demands for increased levels of scrutiny and accountability for state agencies; the administrative detention of asylum seekers in Australia and internationally; and the controversial use of torture and indefinite detention taking place under the banner of the United States-led 'war on terror'.

Of principal concern in this book is the increasing overuse and normalisation of high-security and the human costs associated with such regimes. During 1987, the seven deaths that occurred in Jika represented 38.8 per cent of the total number of deaths in the Victorian prison system during that year.[5] This is an excessive figure for a prison that on average represented 1.4 per cent of the entire Victorian prison population.[6] While some may argue Jika

---

[5]   From 1987 to 1988 there was a total of 18 deaths in custody occurring within the Victorian prison system as a whole (OOC *Annual Report* 1987-1988). There is a dearth of research focused on any relationship that may exist between high-security and segregation regimes and deaths in custody (see Brown 1988a: 56).

[6]   The total daily average prison population in Victoria from 1987 to 1988 was 2017. The daily average for Jika Jika during this time was 28. It should be

represents an isolated, exceptional case, there is a growing body of research, particularly relevant to the United States experience, which confirms the physical and psychological harms associated with solitary confinement in combination with sensory deprivation and extended periods spent in high-security or supermax prisons (see e.g. Funnell 2006: 70-4; Rhodes 2004; Haney 2003; Fellner & Mariner 1997; Haney & Lynch 1997). This research also documents the relationship between such regimes and exertions of abusive and unaccountable power, the use of dehumanising and brutalising disciplinary practices, polarisation between managerial staff and prisoners, violent cultures, crisis and death. In this respect the Jika experience is conceived as more than merely a 'bad' chapter in Victorian prison management. Rather, it is situated within a continuum of proliferating high-security prison regimes and their associated harms in Australia and other western states.

Modern High-Security in Australia: The Proliferation of a 'New Generation' in Imprisonment

Modern high-security prisons combine hi-tech security devices and sophisticated spatial and managerial strategies with the time-honoured punishment of solitary confinement. Also known as control units and in the United States supermax, such prisons have been characterised by Cassandra Shaylor (1998: 387) as the 'penultimate synthesis of technology and space in the service of social control and dehumanisation within the prison'. These 'new generation' prisons came to prominence in the 1970s and 1980s and were designed to 'isolate, regulate and surveil more effectively than anything that has preceded them' (Davis 2003: 50). High-security blueprints were based on new and experimental pseudo-scientific American principles of 'behavioural modification' and 'adjustment' that came about through an era of behavioural and psychological experimentation conducted on prisoners (Fitzgerald 1977: 68; 1975; Ryan 1992; McCoy 2006; see also Gordon 2006; Physicians for

---

noted that from July to October in 1987, Jika averages fluctuated between 39 and 42 total prisoners (OOC *Annual Report* 1987-1988).

Human Rights 2005; for commentary on this issue relevant to Australia see also Lucas 1976).

Once transferred to high-security, prisoners experience a repressive intensification of disciplinary control and coercion through the application of new technologies and psychologically geared management strategies. These include prolonged periods of isolation, limited social interaction and periods spent outside cells and the use of restraints and shackles when prisoners are transported (Haney 2003). Heightened institutional security and secrecy, physical separation of prisoners and guards, hi-tech monitoring equipment, constant surveillance, electronic controls, pastel colours, bulletproof glass, a sealed interior environment, sensory deprivation and overload, limited prisoner 'privileges', constant cell searches by specialist security squads and open-ended sentences are additional hallmarks. In high-security, technologies and psychological strategies are mutually reinforcing, giving new meaning to the expression 'total confinement'. Marion Federal Penitentiary, Illinois (Dunne 1992), Pelican Bay SHU California (Haney & Lynch 1997) and the Lexington Control Unit Kentucky (O'Melveny 1992) in the United States; the Wakefield Control Unit in the United Kingdom (Fitzgerald 1977); Kent Maximum-Security Unit, Canada (Jackson 1983); the Katingal Special Security Unit (Matthews 2006: 167-99) and Jika Jika High-Security Unit in Australia all represent pioneering examples of modern high-security regimes developed by western prison authorities.

The rise to prominence of modern high-security blueprints in Australia cannot be considered without reference to critical case studies such as Jika Jika and Katingal. The windowless Katingal preceded Jika as Australia's first anti-terrorist and escape-proof high-security prison comprising regimes of social isolation and sensory deprivation (*National Times* 3-8/5/76 p 12; see also Lucas 1976). Katingal was officially reserved for the system's most violent criminals and terrorists. However, prisoners alleged many were transferred for internal prison offences and some for involvement and concern with prisoner rights (Matthews 1978). Prisoners and staff found the Katingal system disorientating and inhumane. In practice it failed to prevent non-compliance and violence between staff and prisoners as it was intended to (Vaux 1978). In the three years it was open there were attempted suicides, self-harm, prisoner outbursts and violence, protest fires, sit-ins, security breaches, including an escape and a break-in; not to mention the use of official brutality, including the deployment of chemical gases to quell a peaceful prisoner disturbance in 1978 (Vaux 1978; see also Matthews 2006: 167-99). Justice Nagle conducted investigations into the unit as part of the 1978 Royal Commission into New South Wales Prisons. He referred to it as an 'electronic zoo', and recommended its closure (Nagle Report 1978: 122, see also 34). Nagle's recommendation in conjunction with increasing internal disorder and community campaigning prompted the ultimate closure of Katingal just three years after it opened (Zdenkowski & Brown 1982: 86-90; see also Zdenkowski 1979: 220-1; Matthews 2006: 167-99). In contrast to Jika Jika, Katingal has been the subject of substantial attention (see Lucas 1976; Zdenkowski & Brown 1982; see also Vinson 1982; Findlay 1982). This discrepancy can be directly attributed to a combination of cohesive community opposition to the inhumane nature of Katingal and the level of exposure the institution received during the Nagle Royal Commission (see chapter on Katingal in Nagle Report 1978: 121-34). Despite the demonstrated willingness to document and critique the uses and functions of Katingal within the New South Wales prison system, similar contributions in regard to Jika Jika are absent. This book for the first time establishes the case study of Jika Jika firmly within critical and contemporary histories of punishment in Victoria and Australia.

In Australia as elsewhere, the human costs of high-security are yet to be acknowledged through the implementation of prison policy and practice. Human rights advocate Charandev Singh recently stated:

> The reproduction of what's called high-security or special handling units has always been linked in Australian colonised history to very high rates of deaths and killings and very severe human rights violations ... What the research has indicated is that it causes people to separate themselves from the capacity to be human, the capacity to empathise, the capacity to understand what is real and what is imagined; it constitutes a form of severe

human suffering and control ... The lesson that's taught in these institutions is that violence, the use of unaccountable power and abuse is the norm. (Radio interview 9/5/06)

There is an official unwillingness to acknowledge or account for such considerations and a string of high-security units proliferate post-Katingal and Jika Jika. The Barwon Prison Acacia Unit, Victoria (see Derkely 1995),[7] Risdon Prison, Tasmania (Prison Action and Reform (PAR) 1999, 2005), Woodford Correctional Centre Maximum-Security Unit, Queensland (Fletcher 1999), and Casuarina High-Security Unit, Western Australia (*Age* 18/11/00; Office of the Inspector of Custodial Services 2001; see also Carter 2000) comprise a continuum of Australian high-security regimes associated with reported human rights abuses, institutional disorder, violence, crisis and death.

In New South Wales, the Goulburn High-Risk Management Unit has recently attracted much public attention and criticism (Funnell 2006). Opened in 2001, Goulburn was designated by officials to house 'psychopaths, the career criminals, the violent standover men, the paranoid inmates and gang leaders' (*Australian* 16/7/05). However, contrary to this official posturing, Goulburn has served to house a variety of prisoners, at the discretion of the New South Wales corrective services Commissioner, including those on remand and the mentally ill (Funnell 2006; see also *Australian* 16/7/05). Within three years of its opening, Goulburn prisoners sent out an 'offer of hope', stating, 'in this place where we are kept there is no sunlight, no fresh air, nothing but grey concrete, self mutilation, desperation, hunger strikes, sensory deprivation and psychological damage' (Justice Action 2003).

High-security units are repeatedly officially deployed to house new breeds of 'high-risk' criminals and prisoners. Such threats are reinvented and repackaged each time a new facility is on the agenda. Presently the focus rests with terrorism and high-security

---

[7] For recent concerns regarding prisoners held on remand in Acacia for terrorist offences see, 'Submission to UN High Commissioner for Human Rights Regarding conditions of detention of unconvicted remand prisoners in Victoria, Australia', Human Rights Law Resource Centre, Melbourne, 3/8/06.

units have been advanced domestically and internationally to house the 'worst' terrorists and terror suspects as part of the 'war on terror' (Davis 2005; see also Gordon 2006). Currently, in Victoria the development of a new multi-million dollar 'super prison', the 'most secure' of its kind in Australia, awaits construction in the already maximum-security Barwon Prison (Holding Media Statement 11/9/06). The 27-man block, according to officials, is needed due to the 'dramatic increase' in 'high-risk' prisoners, which can largely be attributed to the arrests of individuals for 'gangland and terrorism related offences' (Holding Media Statement 30/5/06; see also *Herald-Sun* 31/5/06; 12/9/06). Officials justify the need for this new facility despite the fact a group of unconvicted men on remand for terrorist related offences are already isolated and shackled in the restrictive Barwon Prison Acacia Unit in Victoria (Human Rights Law Resource Centre 2006: 12-3).

Imprisoning Resistance: the Politics of Modern High-Security

The historical organisation of collective and individual resistance against authority is integral to understanding the political and volatile dynamics of imprisonment (Bosworth & Carrabine 2001: 501). Rather than experiencing incarceration passively, prisoners have always been concerned with rights and conditions. They have resisted and attempted to transgress their restrictive circumstances through numerous inventive and diverse acts. These include prisoner refusal and non-compliance, unauthorised communication with other prisoners, hunger strikes, 'no-wash' protests, industrial action, letter writing, campaigning, undergoing official complaints processes, legal action, barricades, fires, riots and escaping. Mark Finanne (1997) recognises that any attempt to trace the historical origins of punishment and reform in Australian prisons requires a consideration of the transformative impacts of resistance from below upon disciplinary regimes and institutional structures. For prisoners, resistance has served as a logical avenue for challenging and negotiating power in prison. It is an effective vehicle for voicing grievances to the 'outside' (Carter 2000: 365) and perhaps most importantly, as Cohen and Talyor (1972) have argued, resistance serves as an avenue for survival, particularly for long-term prisoners.

The scale and violence associated with prisoner disturbances during the 1970s in the United States, the United Kingdom and Australia revealed the potential for collective prisoner resistance in prison. The extent of prisoner resistance during this time created the fundamental basis for retributive changes in penal policy and more specifically resulted in the use of high-security, supermax or control unit models. During the 1970s, prisoner militancy resulted in siege situations, the destruction of prison property and buildings and in some cases entire prisons being burned to the ground. Events such as the 1970 Attica siege in the United States (Wicker 1975), the 1972 widespread rooftop protests and 'no-wash' protests throughout British prisons (Fitzgerald 1977), and the explosive 1974 Bathurst Gaol riots in New South Wales Australia (Zdenkowski & Brown 1982), present examples of a movement that gave rise to an acute sense of anxiety among prison authorities regarding the maintenance of prisoner discipline. Much to the distaste of officials, these disturbances and campaigns had the additional impact of drawing critical public attention to prisoner accounts of archaic and brutal conditions in antiquated prisons.

Throughout the 1970s in Victoria, Australia the various divisions of Pentridge Prison, including the existing maximum-security H Division, saw hunger strikes, ongoing campaigns of prisoner non-compliance, escapes, riots, the destruction of entire divisions, strikes and rooftop protests. In 1979 the Victorian authorities publicly presented the design and construction of the Jika Jika High-Security Unit as a solution for the secure and humane confinement of high-risk and long-term prisoners that accorded with international trends in penal policy (Swan 1977-78; see also Department of Community Welfare Services (DCWS) 1980). It was also argued that the 'decriminalisation of some minor offences and the use of parole resulted in the prison population being dominated by some intractable long-term career criminals', and that Jika would serve the security and management requirements for such prisoners (Armstrong & Lynn 1996: 157). Despite these justifications, it is argued that the construction of the new high-security facility stemmed from official concerns about the risks posed by prisoner disorder.

Joe Sim (2004: 128) argues that discourses and concerns about 'risk' are disproportionately focused on the powerless and have been central to the legitimisation of state power and the implementation of authoritarian policies and clampdowns in criminal justice. In this respect, concerns about prisoner dangerousness and risk are frequently deployed as official explanations for violence and disorder in prison. Such discourses represent powerful justificatory drivers for the implementation of draconian policies and practices in prison, while serving as a perennial vindication for tighter management and security. Violence in prison is officially attributed to the 'risk' posed by individuals and in particular the prison system's 'worst of the worst'. Moreover, in the case where excessive use of official force is reported to take place, it is not uncommon for the state to cast itself as victim, justifying forceful action as retaliation and self-defence in the wake of threatening and violent behaviour of individual prisoners (Sim 2004: 128).

Discourses and concerns about risk are central to understanding the problems associated with high-security and particularly the documented prevalence of institutional dysfunction and violence. Such disorder must be considered within the context of the origins and official objectives informing the development of such regimes and their associated practices. In particular, real and imagined threats of prisoner violence, dangerousness and non-compliance provide significant concerns within official justifications for the development of high-security and associated practices (Rodriguez 2006: 145-84). Dylan Rodriguez (2003: 184) notes that 'state power enunciates domination over (and ownership of) human bodies as the measure of peace, security and social order'. It is in this context, he argues, that terror becomes the moral of the story, that prisoners 'ought to live in fear, in return for the fear they have wrought (as retroactive threats to a presumably civilised order) and continue to extract (as caged, violent quasi-people always on the cusp of returning to freedom or overtaking the facility)' (Rodriquez 2003: 186). In this manner, discourses of 'risk', dangerousness and threats of rebellion are central to the very operation of power in high-security, serving to justify a range of coercive measures as necessary to maintain control. In light of the disturbances taking place in the 1970s, strategies associated with high-security were also intended to silence and destroy those concerned with their rights (Ryan 1992). The Jika Jika High-Security Unit must be considered in this context, as a system devised to ensure total surveillance, control and discipline over long-term prisoners identified and cast by the authorities as unruly and dangerous; the 'worst of the worst' intractable prisoners. However, as this book will demonstrate, rather than quelling the threat and event of prisoner resistance, these disciplinary strategies merely intensified prisoner responses, opening up new possibilities for resistance within the extremities of a high-security prison.

Disciplinary Power, Resistance and High-Security

As stated above, the escalation of institutional security, disciplinary power and control exacerbates resistance and disorder in high-security. In this respect, the oppositional forces of disciplinary power and resistance comprise a fierce institutional dynamic of struggle further heightened by the physical and psychological pressures of the oppressive regime and environment. Central to Foucault's work is the notion that power is not static but determined by a complex flow of varying sets of relations and structures that change with circumstances and time (Danaher et al 2000: xiv; see also Foucault 1991a, 1991b: 81). According to Foucault (1991a, 1991b: 81), power does not solely function for negative, repressive or coercive purposes. He argues it is productive in that it produces resistance to itself. In this sense, it logically follows that where there is power, there also exists the constant threat or occurrence of resistance.

While Foucault acknowledges the productive relationship between power and resistance, Michel de Certeau focuses exclusively on the constant threat of resistance and provides a deeper exploration of its potentialities and occurrence in practice. De Certeau (1984: xiv) characterises resistance as the 'obverse' of power. More specifically, he argues resistance comprises the 'tactics' and corresponding weapons of the dominated or powerless. Resistance in a high-security prison like Jika requires the subversion and use by prisoners of already existing disciplinary strategies or topographies of power to achieve their ends. As De Certeau observes, 'the weapons of the weak are those which already exist as strategies of the strong ... the powerful in any given context can tabulate, build, and create spaces and places, while the relatively powerless can only use, manipulate and divert these spaces' (cited in Cresswell 1996: 164). The dynamic of power and resistance in prison can be thus characterised as a productive and reactive relationship wherein the 'strategies' of the powerful comprise direct responses to the 'tactics' of the powerless and vice versa.

The study of resistance in various contexts reveals that discipline and power do not in any way comprise an unchallengeable or unchanging system of control and domination (Scott 1985). As William Bogard (cited in Rhodes 1998: 286) contends, 'discipline always creates gaps, spaces of free play which embody new possibilities for struggle'. Moreover, an escalation or intensification of discipline and control often results in the emergence of correspondingly extreme forms of resistance (Rhodes 1998: 286). Such a correlation is pertinent to the hidden dynamics of high-security or management units for intractable prisoners. Lorna Rhodes (1998: 288) observes in her studies of high-security that, 'although they suppress, disciplinary spaces also invite and magnify disorder'.

Despite the challenges and possibilities posed by resistance, domination and subordination remain the defining forces at work within the institutional structures of prison. Both Foucault (1991a) and Ignatieff (1978) have addressed the historical shift away from public spectacles of punishment centred on the body towards privatised and institutionalised punishments directed at the mind. The prison emerged as a dominant form of punishment in the eighteenth and nineteenth centuries and while it was intended by reformers to create a more humane system of punishment, its ultimate impact on those sentenced to life imprisonment, was to emulate the result of death (Dayan 2002: 13).[8] Such an experience is tantamount to civil death. In place of physical mistreatment, torture or death, a newly sentenced prisoner's civil status in organised society is subject to total destruction (Dayan 2002: 13). In this way, prisoners are remoulded and defined by the institution that asserts and maintains ownership of their incarcerated identities and bodies.

Erving Goffman (1961) argues that while factors such as civil death, loss of self-determination, the stripping of identity, and constant invasions of privacy prompt initial resistance, inmates ultimately submit and adapt to the institution. Like Goffman, Scraton, Sim and Skidmore (1991: 5) have recognised the symbolic implications of this process whereby the denial of liberty becomes the 'confiscation of citizenship'. This is essentially a process of institutionalisation and disempowerment; a symbolic exertion of state power that moves beyond the physical confines and realities of imprisonment. Such a process inevitably renders the prisoner invisible to the outside world and fosters the maintenance of institutional secrecy. Joseph Pugliese (2002: 2) has referred to the exertion of such power with respect to asylum seekers presently incarcerated in Australian detention centres:

> The penal exercise of state power must be seen to produce a body that does not simply and self-identically belong to the individual subject. The incarcerated body's range of significations is shaped and invested by the very forces that detain and imprison it and, simultaneously, by the government and media discourses that represent it. The state overtly exercises a bio-political power over the body of the imprisoned refugee.

Of course the racialised punishment and political imprisonment of asylum seekers constitutes a profoundly separate experience to that

---

8 The origins of the prison are strongly associated with the birth of industrial capitalism; liberalist ideologies and the idea of individual rights; the American Revolution, and resistance to English and European colonial power in Asia and African regions. Early reformers intended the prison to impose an institutional regime of religious self-reflection and reform, while others such as Jeremy Bentham advocated it as a system of total surveillance to internalise productive labour habits (Davis 2003).

of Jika prisoners, some of whom were convicted of violent and terrible crimes. Nonetheless, Pugliese's comments provide insightful parallels to the institutional experience of high-security confinement. Pugliese (2002: 2-3) argues that because of the nature of detention, asylum seekers are sentenced to 'a temporal open-endedness that knows no limits … this is surely the "locus" of the madness and despair that leads to resistance'. Here parallels can be drawn with respect to those Jika prisoners classified as 'violent', 'dangerous' or who because of their political activities or beliefs were considered by the authorities to pose a security threat within the mainstream system and were therefore indefinitely classified as 'high-security'. As this book will demonstrate, a key objective for the new modern high-security prisons and control units was to keep prisoners in high-security for longer and in many cases indefinite periods. The experience of Jika illustrates that an open-ended period in extreme conditions of confinement served to magnify prisoner experiences of disempowerment and hopelessness, which in turn contributed to violent expressions of resistance.

Cultures of Violence and High-Security

In Jika the harshness of conditions were often mirrored by prisoner responses including violent attacks and assaults on staff or other prisoners, destructive outbursts and acts of self-harm (PRG 1988). It is therefore recognised that not all violence can be unproblematically or unambiguously characterised as resistance and in many ways, 'protection rackets, dealing, settling scores and victimisation', are features of an institutional culture of violence that permeates all prisons (Scraton et al 1991: 66).

Prison violence is predominately understood and explained through an official lens focused on the violent and threatening behaviour and identities of individual prisoners. Within this context prison officers are cast as frequently 'at risk' and 'perennial victims' of prisoner brutality. As Sim (2004: 127) argues, 'dangerous situations inside are conceptualised as events that are faced by, and done to state servants rather than as processes which are also engaged in by them'. In rare instances where misconduct or violence by prison officers is confirmed, there is a tendency to attribute such abuses to aberrant individual officers or 'bad apples' (Sim 2003). Such discourses, promulgated through official discourse and popularly accepted, prevent any real understanding of how institutional visibility and power structures shape prison culture and might give rise to injustice, abuse and violence.

Phillip Zimbardo's Stanford Prison Experiment in the 1970s demonstrated how power structures and a lack of public visibility within draconian institutional regimes can foster polarised relationships and abusive cultures (Haney & Zimbardo 1998). However, there are few comprehensive criminological studies seeking to extend upon such a finding and develop complex explanations for the systemic nature of violence and the role institutions and state might play in the generation of violent cultures. This is surprising given there is an ongoing preoccupation among criminologists and sociologists with the detrimental effects or 'pains of imprisonment' and when violence, irrespective of its form, is widely accepted as a taken-for-granted aspect of prison life (Liebling & Maruna 2005). Accounts of violence in prison and particularly the spectre of official abuse have predominantly emanated from prisoner voices, which are often marginalised and discredited, constituting a form of 'subjugated knowledge' (Sim 2004: 115). Other studies have focused disproportionately on prisoner on prisoner violence (e.g. Kimmett et al 2003). In short there are few studies that provide a comprehensive, complex understanding of institutional violence that move beyond explanations focused on individual 'badness'. While this book does not claim to fill such a gap it must be acknowledged that there is a dearth of research dedicated to violence in prison and the manner in which institutional and occupational cultures are implicated in and shaped by such violence.

In Australia Richard Edney (1997) provides a rare attempt to understand official violence in prison and its relationship to prison officer occupational cultures, which are defined by moral justifications surrounding the use of violence and force. Edney (1997: 290) argues violence by prison officers takes place and is rationalised in defence of 'security and good order' or more abstractly the 'good' of the institution. According to Edney (1997: 291), such violence is more likely to occur in management or segregation units where prisoners are outnumbered and officers have a 'working philosophy' that prisoners deemed 'worst of the worst' are 'doubly deserving of any violence'. Edney (1997: 292) connects such violence to institutional secrecy and concealment, and the influence of a prison culture, which he argues is so omnipresent and powerful that it short circuits or destroys the ability of law to protect prisoners.

Scholars such as Sim and Scraton highlight the way in which power structures, hierarchies and cultures of masculinity permeate all relationships and aspects of life in prison, underpinning the workings of what they term the 'violent institution' (Scraton et al 1991; Sim 1994, 1990; for key contributions on the issue of masculinity and violence in the United States see Sabo et al 2001). Sim's work draws attention to the influence and impacts of broader social paradigms, specifically gendered cultures of masculinity in combination with penal power in producing conditions for violence in prison. Using Bob Connell's (1987) conceptual framework for a gendered analysis of state institutions and specifically his concept of 'hegemonic masculinity', Sim argues that social norms, power structures and specifically the goals of male supremacy are embedded within the institutional objectives of prison. In prison, violence and force are a legitimated part of the taken-for-granted; they are normalised vehicles for expression to preserve hierarchies and defend individual dominance and supremacy. Sim demonstrates how such a system suits the disciplinary goals and objectives of the institution and is therefore promulgated by prisoners, staff and officials alike. He (1994: 103) argues:

> The institution sustains, reproduces and intensifies this most negative aspect of masculinity, moulding and remoulding identities and behavioural patterns whose destructive manifestations are not left behind the walls when the prisoner is released but often become part of his taken-for-granted world on the outside.

Prisoner on prisoner rape in male prisons is a common example and expression of masculine violence designed to feminise other prisoners and reinforce individual dominance. Prison rape is an act protected by prison codes of secrecy 'not to lag' and official complicity. Christian Parenti (2000: 188) argues with respect to prison rape that 'in the big house, layers of collective, individual and institutional violence act in concert to culturally manufacture the prison's "second-sex" and thus reproduce the binary gendered world of the outside'. In this context, violence can be seen to not only mimic broader gender inequities of the outside world but also serve as a pervasive instrument of control.

Official Discourse and Official Responses to Disorder, Death and Institutional Crisis

The ideological and political functions of official responses, and more specifically how modes of official discourse prioritise official accounts of prisoner disorder and deaths in custody, are central to the examination of power and resistance within the Jika Jika High-Security Unit. In assessing the adequacy of inquest investigations and departmental and public inquiries following the Jika fire and deaths, powerful strategies of official discourse, and processes of 'obstructive secrecy' (Scraton et al 1991: 5) that featured in such 'official' modes of inquiry, will be identified and analysed in so far as they have prioritised the interests of the Victorian Office of Corrections (OOC). Moreover, this book will demonstrate that such strategies have functioned to protect, legitimise and exonerate the OOC in three ways. First, by claiming privilege to confidentiality and secrecy, the authorities were able to protect the inner workings of the disciplinary system from outside scrutiny and accountability. The maintenance of institutional concealment also served to preserve the broader social control mechanisms of prison in the outside world. As Paul Wright (2000: 16) has argued, 'the intimidation and deterrence factor of prison is served by keeping it distant, remote and unknown, but at the same time, nearby, an immediate threat of unimaginable evil'.

Second, official discourses prevalent in the administration of the numerous official inquiries sought to represent instances of prisoner disturbances as individual disciplinary issues that could be attributed to the extreme views of a minority of troublemaking prisoners. By downplaying prisoner disturbances as stemming from individual management and security issues, the authorities were able to divert the focus away from systemic or material concerns back onto the individual management problems posed by prisoners. As Scraton, Sim and Skidmore (1991: 45) have demonstrated with respect to Scottish case studies during the 1980s, such 'reductionist' official explanations have too often 'ignored the centrality and influence of the material context in which disturbances occur'. By focusing on individual pathologies, management and security issues, the authorities were able to continue to justify the need for institutions such as Jika, while fortifying proposals for tighter security and more stringent prisoner discipline measures.

The final function is the process wherein prisoner allegations and accounts are marginalised and discredited as 'untruth', while official accounts are privileged as 'truth'. Prisoner accounts of prison life rest at the bottom of Becker's (1967: 241) 'hierarchies of credibility', where those with the most power 'have the power to define how things really are'. Becker's 'hierarchy of credibility' draws attention to the fact that the right to define reality or 'truth' is not equally distributed and the powerful or the 'primary definers' in this context, the prison authorities, departmental officials and custodial staff, hold a monopoly over what constitutes 'the facts'. As Hogg and Brown (1998: 19) have acknowledged, far from encapsulating a conspiracy or broader structure of dominance, the authoritative status of officials as 'primary definers' 'derives from differences in power and status within particular institutional settings'. In the context of prison, prisoner criminal records, prison conduct records and individual pathologies are often used as vehicles to discredit unfavourable prisoner accounts that allege misconduct or challenge the legitimacy of the institution. Such legitimising processes effectively divert attention away from the issue of official responsibility by focusing on the unreliability of prisoner representations, thus hindering scrutiny and public accountability for state agencies. While in a Foucauldian sense

29

prisoner accounts thus constitute a form of 'subjugated knowledge' (Danaher et al 2000: xv), it is also recognised that this hegemonic dominance and marginalisation does not remain static or unchallenged. Rather, as Hogg and Brown (1998: 19) argue, 'it is always, to one degree or another, being resisted or contested by subordinate groups'.

Book Overview

This book charts the strategies of disciplinary power and reactive responses of prisoner resistance within the Jika Jika High-Security Unit between 1980 and 1987. It provides a critical examination of the internal disciplinary regimes and how the institutional dynamics produced polarised relationships between prison staff and prisoners, which led to violence, crisis and ultimately death. This book also critically considers and analyses the adequacy of official responses to prisoner disorder and particularly deaths in custody. It is argued that such responses were geared towards protecting the interests and defending the legitimacy of the Victorian Office of Corrections rather than providing independent scrutiny, appraisal, public accountability, truth and justice.

The book is divided into Parts One and Two. Part One, 'Power and Resistance', provides an examination of Jika's predecessor the Pentridge maximum-security section H Division and the political conditions, objectives and official rationale leading to the development of Jika. The gulf between official theory and practice in the conceptual design and managerial operation of Jika are also critically considered. Overall, this section establishes that while Jika set out to maximise order and security, pressures created by the high-security environment and the prevailing institutional dynamics of disciplinary power and prisoner resistance compounded to create a culture of polarisation and violent disorder within Jika.

Chapter One examines the institutional workings of H Division during the 1970s. More specifically, the rise of prisoner disorder and the official uses of H Division as a coercive deterrent for non-compliance are considered. Official responses to prisoner allegations of ill-treatment and systematic brutalisation within H Division are presented and assessed in terms of their adequacy. This chapter contends that official anxieties about the rise in prisoner unrest throughout Pentridge played a key factor in the perceived need for a new high-security facility in Victoria.

Chapter Two presents an official developmental history of Jika Jika and examines the immediate context and factors that informed the conceptual design and intended uses for Jika. This chapter is also concerned with the early institutional problems experienced from 1980 to 1984. It highlights the apparent gulf between official ideals and objectives in the design process and the practical functioning of Jika Jika as an institution.

Chapter Three unveils institutional accounts of life in Jika. This chapter departs from dominant official representations, foregrounding prisoner accounts and allegations. In examining institutional experiences, this chapter contends that high-security conditions and an abusive culture only served to exacerbate frustrations, prisoner violent resistance, conflict and disorder.

Chapter Four is primarily concerned with prisoner resistance, transgression and survival within Jika. It describes and analyses forms of resistance deployed by prisoners and considers how such resistance intensified cultures of retribution and violence which built to crisis point in Jika Jika with the fire and deaths.

Part Two, 'Concealing Crisis', provides a critical analysis and assessment of official responses to institutional crisis and deaths in Jika. The circumstances surrounding the deaths of prisoners John Williams and Sean Downie, and the deaths that stemmed from the fire, Arthur Gallagher, James Loughnan, David McGauley, Richard Morris and Robert Wright, are addressed. Chapter Five focuses on the deaths of John Williams and Sean Downie and reconstructs the events surrounding the deaths, which occurred in highly contested circumstances. Competing accounts of these events are compared and contrasted.

Chapter Six provides an extensive assessment and critical analysis of OOC responses to Sean Downie's death. It considers the obstructive and deflective strategies inherent within official responses to deaths in custody and how these are geared toward the diversion of scrutiny away from official responsibility and liability. More particularly this chapter assesses the adequacy of coronial inquests in providing independent appraisal and public accountability mechanisms when deaths in custody occur in controversial and contested circumstances. Specific questions are posed in relation to the effectiveness of the coroner's powers to investigate and make findings with respect to deaths in custody and the *Coroner's Act* 1985 (Vic).

Chapter Seven brings the book full circle in considering the aftermath of the 1987 fire. Using the frameworks established in Chapter Five, this chapter considers the various strategies employed by the OOC and Victorian Government to avoid scrutiny and organisational accountability in the face of ensuing liability stemming from the Jika protest fire and deaths.

As this book is concerned with challenging official discourses of concealment and denial surrounding Jika, each chapter (with the exception of the introduction) has been prefaced with significant moments, descriptive reconstructions or personal accounts that highlight the internal and often hidden experiences of institutional power, resistance and struggle in high-security. They form the basis for the contested accounts that constitute the officially unacknowledged and unauthorised experiences of H Division and later Jika Jika. These italicised flashpoints are distinguished from the analysis and placed at the beginning of each chapter in order to symbolically recognise the ongoing prioritisation and dominance of rationalised official perspectives and representations with respect to these histories.

CHAPTER ONE

Polarisation, Power and Prisoner Resistance in Australian Maximum-Security During the Explosive 1970s[9]

On 13 January 1972, Governor Ian Grindlay of Pentridge Prison attended H Division for an inspection. As he approached from outside he could hear prisoners banging and shouting from a number of cells. When he entered the prison Governor Grindlay alleged that the noise from the cells ceased, with the exception of a solitary cell on the top tier where 24-year-old prisoner Dennis Kane was held. Grindlay walked to the door of the cell and allegedly warned Kane, 'Behave yourself and pull your head in or you will be in trouble'. Kane, who had been transferred to H Division as punishment for his role as political agitator in another Pentridge Division, was reported by prison officer Daniels to shout, 'all you men in H Division. We have come to get you out. This is 1972. There is no more breaking rocks. There is no 'I' Division – This is the end of the line! What can they do to us?' Kane was again warned by prison officer Daniels to keep quiet, yet Kane continued his appeal to other H Division prisoners, 'If we all stick together they can't do a thing. We will help pull it down if they like!' Because of his efforts to generate unrest, Kane was charged with making unnecessary noise. The Visiting Justice found Kane's charges proven and consequently he was to be isolated and set to rock breaking as punishment for his offence.

---

[9] The following italicised account is based on *Herald*, 'Show H Division lawful', 15/2/72.

However, this was not enough to dampen Kane's spirits. Since 1948 prisoners had been legally entitled to appeal any charges affecting the length or nature of their sentence in an open court, and Kane took advantage of this as part of an ongoing campaign by H Division prisoners to publicly expose the prison and 'bring it down' by forcing an independent and open inquiry into its regime. County Court Judge Rapke, who heard the case, stated he could find no regulation within the Divisional standing orders to justify the charges against Kane. Furthermore, he agreed with Kane's argument that it seemed ridiculous to be charged with making unnecessary noise when the noise he was making was in fact completely necessary as he was deliberately communicating with his fellow prisoners (Rinaldi 1977: 96). In a move that would further embarrass the authorities and inflame an already tenuous and hostile state of affairs inside Pentridge, Judge Rapke went on to question the 'lawfulness' of H Division: 'we have conceded for many years that H Division is a necessary jail within a jail but, if it comes to a showdown – and this case may be that showdown – the crown must show that it is lawful'. The department appealed Rapke's decision in the Supreme Court where they successfully reversed the finding in favour of prisoner Kane and limited the scope of 'necessary noise' to such noise as is required to achieve objects approved of by the prison authorities (Rinaldi 1977: 96). However, prisoner Kane's victory lay not in the winning of his appeal, but in the exposure and publicity generated by his case. As in many such instances of resistance, it laid bare – at least in part and for a brief moment – the inner workings of H Division.

Introducing Power and Resistance in H Division

Like respectably ancient myths, the H Division myth was compounded of truth and falsehood, and it was understood in different senses by different people ... To the prison officers it was not a matter of great concern how much or how little truth there was in the myth, provided that it remained an efficacious disciplinary influence.

Kenneth Joseph Jenkinson (Jenkinson Report 1973-74: 82-3)

The bluestone walls of H Division enclosed an archaic and punitive regime established in 1958 to deal with the system's 'worst' prisoners. Aside from its interior functions, the Division served as an effective disciplinary tool in other divisions and prisons in the Victorian prison system. In this context, the secrecy, rumour and sense of fear surrounding H Division as 'the last stop' for 'difficult' and 'troublemaker' prisoners was built up by the authorities and officers so that it would prevent prisoner disobedience in other divisions and prisons. During the 1970s prisoner campaigns fostered the emergence of prisoner allegations suggesting that for 12 years prisoners had been subjected to an organised regime of terror. Prisoner allegations of systematic brutality, abusive power and neglect by prison officers comprised subversive accounts of life in H Division vehemently denied by the authorities.

The rise of prisoner resistance in H Division during the 1970s must be seen in the broader context of a generalised movement of prisoner dissent throughout Pentridge. Efforts by the authorities to quell such a movement were challenged by the influx of educated political activists imprisoned as conscientious objectors to the Vietnam War or for other political offences during the 1970s (*Sunday Review* 3/9/71). This fostered a significant radicalisation of prisoners about their rights, while giving rise to collective protests, riots and general prisoner unrest. This unrest exacerbated the corresponding politicisation of H Division as it was increasingly used by the authorities as a punishment section for prisoners identified as politically active in prison protests. Segregating 'political' prisoners as a means of restoring order and curbing rebellion was a classic strategy used by the authorities during this time (Zdenkowski & Brown 1982: 148). However, during 1972 prisoners ran an internal campaign to discredit and undermine the H Division regime. Central to this campaign was the exposure of the physically and psychologically brutalising practices deployed to instil fear and compliance within prisoners. Prisoner Kane's protest marked a significant moment in the breakdown of discipline and rise in rebellion in H Division, which directly challenged the shroud of secrecy and legitimacy of H Division.

This chapter documents competing accounts of the H Division regime by officials and prisoners. The purpose of such an examination is to illuminate the internal dynamics of disciplinary power and resistance integral to the experience of H Division. Ultimately, official responses to prisoner resistance provide a vital context for the later design, construction and uses of the Jika Jika High-Security Unit as a modern, resistance-proof 'prison within a prison'.

This chapter focuses on the adequacy of official responses, namely official inquiries and investigations, into disturbances and prisoner allegations about conditions and treatment in Pentridge and H Division in the 1970s. Of central concern is the 1973-1974 Jenkinson Inquiry, commissioned by the government to inquire into prisoner allegations of brutality and ill treatment. A critical examination of the ways that official discourse functions within inquiries to privilege official accounts over prisoner allegations is a principal focus. Ultimately it is argued that the Jenkinson Inquiry was ineffective in that it was more concerned with protecting and servicing the interests of the authorities than providing public scrutiny and accountability. Overall the intended effect of Jenkinson was the exoneration of H Division officers, the renewal of institutional legitimacy and the foreclosure of adequate public accountability. The establishment of the *Ombudsman Act* 1973 (Vic) and its effectiveness as the primary avenue for prisoner complaints is also briefly assessed, with particular reference to the Report by Ombudsman Dillon into the 1978 H Division riots. Again in this case, it is argued that rather than providing adequate and independent recourse for prisoner complaints and grievances, the Ombudsman privileged official accounts and interests over that of prisoners.

Because during the 1970s official discourse dominated public representations of prison life, the discussion begins with a focus on the counter-discourse posed by prisoner accounts. The very act of such writing is considered briefly as a form of resistance.

'Unauthorised Accounts': Prisoner Representations of Violence and Resistance in H Division

Ex-prisoner and escapee Gregory David Roberts released a book in 2003 about his escape from H Division during the late 1970s. Roberts discloses he had been so badly beaten by H Division officers that he was taken to St Vincent's hospital with broken ribs, a smashed cheekbone, broken nose and multiple cuts and bruises. He refused to report the officers responsible and instead approached one of them, pleading not to be hurt again. The officer allegedly laughed, boasting he had broken him. Roberts states his subsequent escape stemmed from his fear that he might be killed or crippled if he was again transferred to H Division (*Age Good Weekend Magazine* 9/8/03 p 27). He reflects in his autobiography:

> No beatings I'd ever suffered were as savage as those inflicted by the uniformed men who were paid to keep the peace, the prison guards ... That was the memory: being held down by three or four officers in the punishment units while two or three others worked me over with fists, batons and boots ... it's the whole system, the whole world, that's breaking your bones. And then there was the screaming. The other men, other prisoners, screaming. Every night. (Roberts 2003: 143-4)

Prisoner accounts of abuse in H Division were prior to the Jenkinson Inquiry largely mediated in the interests of maintaining institutional legitimacy. These strategies comprise a defensive official discourse of truth making and denial consolidated through performances such as the official inquiry, as objective and authoritative. Having said this, official discourse is by no means immune from independent or outside challenges. The powerful, in this case the prison authorities, are often forced to acknowledge the potential power and potency of unauthorised prisoner accounts of institutional violence, which are represented outside the realm of the official inquiry (Morgan 1999: 329). The power of such accounts lay in their ability to challenge official representations, by utilising the apparent power of subjectivity, or as Foucault would see it, the 'insurrection of subjugated knowledge' (Foucault cited in Morgan 1999).

The potential power of the unauthorised account is perhaps best illustrated through ex-H Division prisoner Ray Mooney's controversial play *Everynight! Everynight!* (1978). In this work, Mooney describes in graphic detail the alleged brutality of the H Division regime and how, through the building up of solidarity, prisoners 'resigned' from the system in order to expose their treatment and force an inquiry into conditions. Like Roberts, Mooney's account moves beyond sanitised official representations and provides a subjective window into the world of H Division.

Ray Mooney's play revolves around a fictitious headstrong 18-year-old remand prisoner called 'Dale' who, when accused of assaulting a prison officer, is sent to H Division. Dale is naïve, hot headed and eager to impress the more experienced prisoners who cultivated the belief that doing time in H Division was 'a piece of cake ... you weren't a fair dinkum crim unless you'd done time in the slot' (Mooney 1978: 1). When Dale is received in H Division he is surrounded by officers and brutally assaulted for each breach he commits against the strict Divisional standing orders: a set of rules with which he is unfamiliar. The lengthy ritual reduces Dale to a state of semi-consciousness. Prior to placing him in his cell, the officers use a baton to rape him.

According to Mooney's prisoner characters, in prison no matter what division a prisoner is in, there is a universal code that to be an informer is to be a 'dog': 'you don't give anybody up. Not even a screw' (1978: 18). This unofficial rule was actively reinforced by the prison officers who were quick to publicise the identity of any prisoner responsible for any breach of the code, thus resulting in ostracism, victimisation and the marring of his reputation for the remainder of his sentence. In complying with this code, Dale refuses to report the incident. However, the beatings continued, 'It just went on and on. People don't believe you when you tell 'em what they did. They think you've got a chip on yer shoulder, trying to make the screws out cunts' (1978: 27).

The prisoners in Mooney's play eventually defy the officers and their disciplinary regime to 'resign' collectively from the system. The act of 'resigning' in *Everynight! Everynight!* involves prisoners taking control of their situation by refusing to comply with the basic rules and regulations of H Division. Prisoners also make a pact that they will support each other in making official complaints about their treatment. Mooney's depiction, though based on fictional characters, is reminiscent of prisoner Kane's case heard in the County Court for making unnecessary noise along with the other bang-ups and riots in H Division during the 1970s.

Mooney was transferred to H Division in the 1970s after his role as spokesperson during a riot in another division (Davison 1996: 56). While inside, he was politically active and worked towards the completion of his Social Science degree. After Mooney's classification to H Division he believed that he had reached a turning point where he had a choice. He was well aware that he could finish up, as most H Division prisoners did, with an extra seven to eight years tacked on to his original sentence for minor disciplinary infractions committed within the Division:

> I could see, ultimately, that if I was going to survive H Division and get through it without ending up like a raving ratbag or ending up a deadset crim, that I would have to find a way of getting them back for what they had done. Because that's the way it is inside. It's part of the culture. (Davison 1996: 56)

Steve Morgan (1999: 329) argues that a major problem presented to prisoners writing personal accounts is the task of confronting a potentially hostile dominant 'public textual discourse' that functions through an agenda of condemnation and a stigma associated with criminality. In this way, when *Everynight! Everynight!* was first performed as a play, Mooney was confronted with public anger and disbelief. He was accused of not presenting 'all sides of the story' and for being polemical. While characterising his writing as a means of survival and to an extent a form of revenge, Mooney defended his account of H Division as unbiased and in his own words, 'more unbiased than a lot of the propaganda that masquerades as being objective. I try and draw out the truth so that somebody can assess it and then come away and make up their own mind' (Davison 1996: 57). With regards to including the prison officers' point of view, Mooney stated:

> If they had written Everynight – then the brutality wouldn't have existed. It would have been a figment of the imagination of the prisoners, which is exactly what they said when they went to the Jenkinson Inquiry. Now I lived through it, so I don't see any

> value in writing a play which pretends that it was anything
> other than it was. (Davison 1996: 57)

It is evident through the controversy generated by Mooney's work that it also served to expose the role and extent of public denial and resistance to the process of naming the unnameable, or in other words naming something determined by officials not to exist. The stigma surrounding H Division was aided by the existence of an unauthorised account of prisoner abuse. In many ways the process of prisoners openly publicising and writing their experience as 'it was', as Mooney did, constitutes a powerful challenge to the culture of denial that exists both inside and outside prison. Stanley Cohen (cited in Scraton 2002: 114-5) observes that the unwillingness of democratic societies 'to confront disturbing or anomalous information' is the direct product of a 'complex discourse of denial'. Prisoner accounts are easily dismissible due to their stark content, apparent subjectivity and the power of the institutions by which they are surrounded and defined. For this reason, it is useful in the context of uncovering the unauthorised accounts of H Division to subject the available official inquiries and investigations to the same process of questioning and interrogation levelled at prisoner accounts. This process involves the excavation of official documents in order to reveal their weaknesses while also drawing out marginalised accounts of the H Division disciplinary regime.[10] In this context, the 1972 Jenkinson Inquiry is used to flesh out competing accounts, revealing a more comprehensive picture of the disciplinary regime and its challenges.

The Jenkinson Inquiry and the Politics of Maximum-Security Classification

On 15 May 1972, Kenneth Jenkinson was appointed to head a board of inquiry established to investigate allegations of brutality and ill treatment at Pentridge. At this time Pentridge Prison was fraught with prisoner complaints, unrest, allegations, industrial strife by the prison officers and what seemed to be a state of deepening

---

[10] For a brief discussion on the complexity of using official sources to interrogate official versions of events see introduction to McCulloch 2001.

polarisation between staff and prisoners. There was growing public concern that the Victorian prison system was, through lack of funding, experiencing a state of crisis (ANZJC 1972: 67-9). There were criticisms that Pentridge was obsolete, overcrowded, understaffed and ill equipped (ANZJC 1972: 67-9). State Chief Secretary Hamer commissioned the Jenkinson Inquiry after allegations of a baton charge by officers against 14 prisoners in D Division was leaked to the public. The announcement also comprised a response to months of prisoner protests against conditions in the form of sit-ins, fires and protests throughout Pentridge. The Victorian prisoner riots and resistance in Pentridge during the 1970s were part of an international trend in western prisons also witnessed in the United Kingdom, the United States, Europe and New Zealand (see Zdenkowski & Brown 1982; see also Fitzgerald 1977; Churchill & Vanderwall 1992). Prisoner militancy in response to overcrowding, antiquated prison structures, conditions, not to mention the unaccountable use of brutalisation and terror by prison staff to maximise disciplinary control, prompted official action during this time (see Fitzgerald 1977).[11]

The Jenkinson Inquiry was allocated limited investigatory powers and was criticised for its lack of openness and narrow terms of reference (*Herald* 17/5/72). The terms of reference allowed the Board powers to inquire and make findings into a) whether since 22 May 1970 Pentridge prisoners were subjected to brutality or ill treatment; b) should provisions be made within the *Social Welfare Act* 1970 (Vic) for any changes relating to the maintenance of discipline in prison; if officers or prisoners should be allowed legal representation at the hearing of charges in prison; should changes be made in regards to the punishment of prisoners for offences committed in prison; and finally c) whether further provisions should be made for remissions as a reward or incentive for good behaviour for prisoners with minimum sentences (Jenkinson Report 1973-74: 5). The Jenkinson Inquiry heard evidence from prison officers, officials and prisoners.

---

[11] For a vivid Scottish account of beatings used as a form of disciplinary control, see Boyle 1979.

While the inquiry was allocated scope to investigate Pentridge as a whole, over half of the investigations and findings focused on H Division, as this was where the broad majority of prisoner complaints and allegations originated. Complaints by H Division prisoners were concerned with allegations of prison officer brutality, the strict standing orders and disciplinary regime that resulted in harsh punishments and lengthy periods spent in H Division. Most of all, prisoners rejected official classification stipulations and procedures used to justify transfers to H Division on the basis of their arbitrariness.

H Division accommodated up to 39 prisoners. According to the 1972 Jenkinson Inquiry, there were three categories under which a prisoner could be classified to H Division:

> Those thought to be in danger of serious ill treatment by other prisoners; those who are undergoing, or who face the immediate prospect of, disciplinary punishment for misconduct in prison (including escapers from all Victorian prisons); and those against whose anticipated misconduct or escape confinement in H Division is thought to be the appropriate safeguard. (Jenkinson Report 1973-74: 44)

The application of the third official category of classification, 'anticipated misconduct or escape' was used subject to the discretion of the authorities. In practice, such discretion was used to justify the transfer of prisoners who were vocal about their rights, involved in prisoner campaigns or suspected of potential participation or organisation of protests in other divisions of the prison (Rinaldi 1977: 93-4). In response to escalating prisoner rights campaigns in Pentridge during the 1970s, H Division was used as a disciplinary measure to punish 'troublemaker' prisoners known to officials for their involvement in rebellion (Rinaldi 1977:93-4; see individual cases outlined in the Jenkinson Report 1973-74).

While historically officials have advocated the necessity of maximum-security prisons to contain the system's 'worst' prisoners, such institutions have also served to segregate and punish prisoners engaged in resistance and concerned with their rights (Fitzgerald 1977; see also Churchill & Vanderwall 1992). The arbitrary nature of official classification procedures comprised a major grievance for H Division prisoners which, it was argued, could often result in long or indefinite periods spent in maximum-security for political involvement or relatively minor offences. Many prisoners reported they had been classified to H Division without adequate explanation and that after their reception they were given no indication of how long they would remain there. One documented incident in February 1972 saw a Pentridge prisoner charged with refusing to get dressed and consequently sentenced to time in H Division (Rinaldi 1977: 93-4).

A further concern was once prisoners were classified to H Division it was very difficult to get transferred out due to the nature of the disciplinary system. H Division had extremely strict standing orders and rules. Any breach of those regulations – even a minor breach such as a dirty cell, failure to salute or dress correctly – could result in a charge. These charges were heard in a closed prison court before a visiting magistrate and this would result in more time spent in H Division and possibly a longer prison sentence overall (Jenkinson Report 1973-74: 44-7, see also 89-90). Prisoners complained that on reception to H Division the standing orders were not made available to them. Consequently, they would then receive numerous charges during their initial stay in the Division until they eventually cottoned on to the rules. It was also argued that some rules and regulations were unwritten and subject to change and officer discretion. Fiori Rinaldi (1977: 83-5) discusses this as a widespread problem in Victorian prisons during this time. He states that attempts to maintain a list or keep track of standing orders were impossible due to the fact that they were often contradictory, continually subject to change, and scattered across departmental gazettes and amendments.

'H for Hell'[12]: Two Versions of the H Division Regime

When received in H Division prisoners were taken to the reception area, stripped and searched. They were given a military style

---

[12] Quote from Kevin Childs, 'H for Hell: a chilling look at a prisoner's life in Pentridge Prison's feared H Division', *Sunday Press*, 30/9/73 (Courtesy CHS Local History Collection).

uniform and inducted to the practice of saluting and military marching (Jenkinson Report 1973-74: 46). Prisoners were required to stand to attention on white crosses painted on the concrete floors throughout the Division and were required to memorise a detailed series of strict standing orders (Jenkinson Report 1973-74: 47).

Each day prisoner cells were subject to rigorous inspection. Failure to meet the requirements resulted in disciplinary charges and longer sentences in H Division. Jenkinson reported in 1971, 36 out of the 120 disciplinary proceedings that came before the Governor of H Division were based upon charges that the prisoner's cell was dirty, while several others related to the incorrect placement of bedding (Jenkinson Report 1973-74: 45). Regulations were exacting, as Jenkinson reported:

> The bedding must be folded in a particular way and with the exactitude popularly associated with the barracks of a guard's regiment. The aluminium ablutionary bowl must present a mirror surface and the floorboards shine. No speck of dust escapes the probing finger or censorious eye of the locker. (p 47)

Most newly received prisoners were assigned to the task of rock breaking in the labour yards (p 47). While working, prisoners were supervised by armed officers stationed in watchtowers. During work hours labour yard prisoners were required to urinate and defecate in a bucket under the full scrutiny of officers. While prisoners worked, officers conducted further cell searches leaving prisoner bedding and belongings in a state of disarray.

Work ceased at 3.30pm and prisoners filed in for the evening meal, security checks and lockdown. The evening was spent preparing cells for morning inspections. Some prisoners who had progressed beyond the initial labour yard status had access to books and magazines from the library or perhaps a radio until 8.30pm 'lights out'. Others engaged in light industry work. Labour yard prisoners were not allowed to converse with other prisoners and were kept in isolation. In contrast, industry yard prisoners were entitled to converse while working and permitted to socialise in the exercise yards on weekends (p 46).

The official version of the H Division regime reported to Jenkinson by the Department of Social Welfare, contrasts with prisoner accounts. H Division was notoriously feared by prisoners and referred to as 'the slot' or 'the bottom', where one spent an indefinite and torturous period under the harshness of military discipline, solitary confinement and hard labour (p 82). Above all, first-time prisoner fears stemmed from rumours that beatings were a cornerstone of disciplinary control in H Division.

Prisoners alleged they were habitually subjected to unlawful physical violence, torture and abuse up until January 1972. They claimed a cessation in the frequency and severity of violence correlated with the public commissioning of the Jenkinson Inquiry. However, prior to this period it was sardonically suggested the 'daily carnival of violence' produced a greater incentive to behave and get reclassified out of H Division than the strict standing orders and regulations (p 48).

Jenkinson's narrow terms of reference limited the inquiry's focus to complaints and allegations received during 22 May 1971 and 23 May 1972. This created a situation where it was impossible to ascertain whether the violence was systemic and ongoing as complaints were dealt with as isolated, individual matters. During the period of investigation, 82 out of the 282 prisoners complained that they had witnessed or experienced a multiplicity of violent assaults by officers. Only 40 of the 82 complaints were heard during the inquiry because the other 42 occurred before the prescribed dates covered by the terms of reference (p 48).

One case revolved around 14 prisoners classified to H Division in May 1970 for their involvement in protests in Pentridge's A Division. Each prisoner alleged they both experienced and witnessed reprisal beatings on reception to H Division (pp 48-59). Such accounts mirrored those put forward by other prisoners. Prisoner Garry Mayne told Jenkinson that he had heard the rumours about the beatings from other prisoners, but did not believe such treatment was possible in a country like Australia:

> When I first went down there, the first three weeks were the worst. That is when I got all the beatings, and after three weeks they started to lay off me ... I didn't know when I got down there, I was that muddled up. I was getting roared at, and at the time I was getting smacked ... Every time I got struck they said it was for something. (p 66)

Prisoners also drew attention to the prevalence of prisoner self-mutilation in H Division, arguing it was a phenomenon closely associated with the official regime of brutality and harsh conditions. It was reported prisoners regularly self-harmed to escape the pressures of the regime. One case referred to a prisoner who had been physically brutalised and bullied by a group of officers into accepting responsibility for a series of rapes that had occurred in another section of Pentridge. The prisoner maintained his innocence but eventually broke, confessing to the rapes in order to stop the beatings. The prisoner reported he was in a state of fear: 'I didn't know what was going on, I was just a cabbage then, I could feel myself falling apart. I got a cup that night ... I cut myself'. Officers denied the allegations and on that basis, the Governor and the authorities did not believe it necessary to investigate the matter further (p 48). Because the prisoner refused to name the officers involved for fear of reprisals, Jenkinson declined to further investigate or make findings about the incident (p 62).

Prisoners also voiced allegations of maltreatment and psychological abuse by staff. In one case a prisoner had the 'urinous and faecal' contents of his urine bucket poured over his head while breaking rocks. He was thereafter not permitted to wash prior to evening lockdown. That night, it was reported by neighbouring prisoners that the prisoner hanged himself (p 71). Officials denied the incident was brought about by ill-treatment arguing that if officers knew about the prisoner's intentions they would have taken swift preventative action. Jenkinson raised his own reservations about whether the preceding events took place:

> If [the prisoner] had been befouled by excrement, the Board is convinced that he would have been showered and re-clothed before the Division closed for the night, for the standard of cleanliness is high in H Division. (p 71)

The general response by prison officers to allegations by prisoners was consistent denial of any participation in or knowledge of unlawful violence (p 48). Most officers did concede that on some occasions it was necessary to use 'lawful force' in the case of threatening and non-compliant prisoners (p 48, see also pp 50-5). One officer argued the objective of H Division was to enforce a military style regime upon people who as a body, resented it, and in many cases an officer might raise his voice or use some 'psychology' to achieve a desired end. He further stated those refusing to conform were necessarily shuffled and dragged along as in extreme cases 'only a clout behind the backside will get the desired result' (p 55). In addressing prisoner allegations overall prison officers submitted violence was not practised:

> [Prisoners] were isolated from their fellows and, in isolation, they were bullied into brisk obedience by harsh and loud command and by the menacing presence of several officers whenever they moved about the Division. On release from H Division they magnified their own hardiness – and reputations – by telling tall tales about the rigours of H Division and the brutality of its more celebrated warders, and by boasting of their capacity to withstand the physical punishment they falsely claimed to have suffered. (p 53)

Officers felt the circulation of such 'tall tales' served Divisional discipline well, as fearful first-time H Division prisoners were quick to obey the standing orders and regulations. In this way officers characterised discipline to function on the basis of 'bluff' (p 53). The Governor of Pentridge Ian Grindlay maintained that in his time as Governor he had never seen signs of brutality in H Division., He characterised force used by officers as acceptable and necessary to maintain prison discipline and order, 'I have heard from prisoners and from other people that any provocation was greeted with perhaps a slap to the tail with a baton, perhaps a backhander, or an open hand' (p 58).

Official denials emerged despite the escalating polarisation, violence and crisis in H Division. The course of the Jenkinson Inquiry correlated with increased prisoner unrest and militancy in both Pentridge and H Division, along with industrial action by prison staff. Prison staff, furious about the 'blackening' of prison officer reputations, struggled to maintain disciplinary control and secure the legitimacy of the institution. In contrast, prisoners campaigned to publicise allegations and lobby for increased accountability and reform. Prisoner militancy peaked in 1972 with a series of riots and protests in Pentridge and H Division and the authorities responded with heavy handed tactics (*Truth* 24/4/76 pp 14-5; see also *Sun* 4/10/72 pp 1-2; *Age* 3/10/72 p 5). As Jenkinson's findings emerged, H Division prisoners were highly critical, arguing Jenkinson did not go far enough in naming the systemic nature of the beatings that were central to the regime since 1958. They argued there was dire need for a comprehensive inquiry or Royal Commission into prison conditions in Victoria.

Investigating H Division: The Jenkinson Inquiry and the Power of 'Official Truth-Making'

Out of the 82 allegations and instances of violence reported to the Jenkinson Inquiry, it was found that individual prisoners had been subjected to beatings in H Division. Overall, Jenkinson's findings listed the names of five prisoners with regards to 'proved' allegations of ill treatment and brutality. These included, Raymond Chanter, Michael Godfrey, Garry Mayne and Colin O'Toole. Other officers, including CPO Carrolan and SPO Lindgren were named as responsible for ill treatment through their failure to interrupt or report to the Governor ongoing ill treatment they were found to have witnessed during 1970, 1971 and 1972 (Jenkinson Report 1973-74: 89). No H Division prison officers were charged as a result of the Jenkinson Inquiry.

In addition to the H Division findings, two officers serving in D Division of Pentridge were found to have used unlawful violence when they led a baton charge against prisoners on 28 June 1972 (Jenkinson Report 1973-74: 90). The two officers were charged with assault but later acquitted due to 'lack of evidence' in 1973 (*Sun* 31/8/73).

Jenkinson stated that despite the baton charge in D Division, allegations of ill treatment were mostly confined to H Division. Additionally, he commented:

> All but a small number of the men who have served as prison officers at Pentridge ... have abstained from subjecting prisoners to ill treatment and most of them have maintained in their dealings with prisoners an equanimity which is not easily preserved in the circumstances under which they have served. (p 90)

In conclusion, Jenkinson presented a somewhat contradictory and ambiguous admission that throughout the inquiry allegations of ill treatment were found to have occurred under circumstances 'too varied and complex to state summarily' (p 90). The problem can again be traced back to the limited terms of reference, which allowed Jenkinson scope to investigate individual prisoner allegations only. The terms of reference did not allow for broader inquiry into the official objectives and management of H Division as a maximum-security institution.

Regardless of their gross limitations, Jenkinson's investigations and findings prompted much discussion within the public and political arena about penal reform (*Age* 20/7/73; *Age* 26/9/73a; *Age* 26/9/73b; *Sunday Press* 30/9/73; *Age* 23/11/73). Jenkinson made recommendations that prisoners classified to H Division should be given official reasons for their transfer within days of their reception. In conjunction, he stated that prisoner disciplinary charges should be heard in an open court and the closed Visiting Justice system abandoned (*Sunday Press* 30/9/73). Yet while the Jenkinson Inquiry led to some reforms, overall it was structured to individualise prisoner reports of abuse in order to dispel allegations of systematic brutality and ill treatment and reinforce the legitimacy of H Division.

The Jenkinson Inquiry was not intended to provide an open investigation of events in H Division. On the contrary Jenkinson subjected H Division to a short-term, limited and very temporary gaze in order to reclaim institutional legitimacy and ultimately seal its doors from public scrutiny completely. As Phil Scraton (2002: 112) observes, far from seeking to provide independent appraisal and accountability, official inquiries represent self-interested legitimising strategies aimed at reaffirming public confidence in a flawed and much criticised criminal justice system.

Jenkinson can be characterised as an official performance used to secure the institutional legitimacy of H Division through a series of strategies aimed at discrediting accounts that pose institutional challenges. These strategies function in all forms of official discourse, as processes of 'official truth-making' (Scraton 1999). Prisoner accounts were relegated to the bottom of Becker's 'hierarchies of credibility' and were interrogated and discredited as 'political' or 'unreliable' (Becker 1967: 242-3).

Throughout the Jenkinson Inquiry official evidence was privileged as 'truth' over prisoner evidence. A large number of prisoner allegations were dismissed on the basis that they were unreliable or they did not accord with the corroborated testimony of the Governors, H Division officers or the 'official' divisional record books. In contrast many officers were found to be convincing in their denials due to their reputation and generosity in offering their assistance throughout the inquiry. To give an example, H Division officer Norman Banner, who had lent his assistance to the Board throughout the course of the inquiry, was accused of striking a prisoner on the 'rump'. Banner admitted to the charge and stated that the prisoner had refused to straighten up while marching. Jenkinson was convinced that Banner's use of force was lawful. Banner was an impressive character; he was helpful throughout the inquiry and appeared as Jenkinson stated, 'intelligent, of good appearance and pleasing demeanour' (Jenkinson Report 1973-74: 65). Incidentally, Banner's role in Jenkinson earned him a step up in his career and in 1987 he rose to the position of the Deputy Director of Prisons.

Scraton and Chadwick (1987: 213-14) have argued that state agencies and officials strategically divert scrutiny from their own actions by questioning the reliability of prisoner accounts. This is achieved through the strategic construction of 'reputations' and the use of imagery associated with violence, criminality and social inadequacy to disqualify and discredit prisoner accounts as 'untruth'. Such strategies were well illustrated throughout the proceedings of the Jenkinson Inquiry as each individual prisoner allegation was prefaced with a summary of the criminal and institutional background of the witness and the actual records were formally tended as evidence. The result was that each prisoner's reliability was questioned on the basis of his criminal and prison records and to what extent that he had demonstrated 'violent tendencies', psychiatric instability, dishonesty or a disregard for authority.

To offer some examples, Jenkinson (1973-74: 63) reported, with reference to Colin O'Toole, who was a free citizen during the proceedings of the inquiry, 'from his fifteenth to his twenty-first year he had repeatedly committed offences connected in one way or another to motor cars ... [and was seen to be] a defiant prisoner who used to talk back'. With respect to Michael Godfrey, he was, according to Jenkinson, exactly 10 years older than O'Toole, and his 'criminal record, and consequently his experience of institutional life' were similar to O'Toole's with his involvement in criminal activity extending to his 30th year. With regards to Stanley Taylor, Jenkinson stated, 'now aged 35, Taylor's career of crime began when he was thirteen. Twelve of his many convictions were for robbery' (p 70). Prisoner Richard Scullin, who served as a witness to alleged reception beatings was, according to Jenkinson's findings, 'a man of many convictions in his early forties. Little reliance could be placed on his uncorroborated testimony, for his demeanour gave as little assurance of truthfulness as his criminal record' (p 61). Prisoner Neil Allen, also a witness, was deemed an unreliable witness due to the fact that 'his demeanour in the witness box and his history of mental disorder precluded reliance on his evidence' (p 64).

During the inquiry, prisoner evidence was treated with additional scepticism due to the fact that officers claimed many of the prisoner allegations were part of a campaign to blacken the reputations of officers and bring H Division down. Prisoner Joseph Tognolini gave evidence in accordance with other H Division prisoners that 'physical ill-treatment by prison officers declined substantially in frequency and in severity after the first weeks of a prisoners' confinement in the Division'. Jenkinson conceded Tognolini's allegations were complemented by unanimous evidence by other prisoners and he did on the surface appear as a 'persuasive witness'. However, Jenkinson found that 'his long dedication to crime and his family connection with a prisoner who was prominent in the rebellion against H Division discipline has deterred the Board from relying on his evidence in support of a finding adverse to the interest of a prison officer' (p 58).

On the one hand, Jenkinson expressed his surprise at the intelligibility of certain prisoner witnesses who, during their evidence to the Board, spoke frankly and articulately about their views on prison issues, therefore demonstrating an almost philosophical or 'scholarly interest' in penology. However, by the same token, Jenkinson believed these witnesses used their notorious identities to advance their own political objectives while demonstrating a rather distasteful and calculated 'histrionic talent'. Coupled with his own impressions, Jenkinson found credence within prison officer evidence that each of these prisoners had on occasions 'exhibited a savagery which chilled the blood ... each of them is a dangerous, violent, mature criminal, enjoying among prisoners a reputation and respect commensurate with his criminal record' (pp 69-70).

Jenkinson recognised that officers throughout the inquiry had been subjected to unprecedented psychological pressures and the threat posed to the personal safety of officers and their families by prisoners had intensified this pressure (*Age* 26/9/73b). Throughout this period, Jenkinson reported that the disobedience of H Division prisoners was 'pregnant with the threat of violence' and fears among officers that such indiscipline could spread to other Pentridge divisions and that their safety was threatened may have led prison officers to act 'irrationally' in these intense circumstances (*Age* 26/9/73b). Such comments stood as an appeal for public support, and functioned in a manner that insidiously redirected the scrutinising eye of the public toward the criminality and dangerousness associated with prisoners, and away from the alleged violent misconduct of H Division prison officers.

Despite its momentary disturbance during the Jenkinson Inquiry, the protective shroud of secrecy surrounding H Division remained intact. Ultimately, Jenkinson's findings served to protect the legitimacy of H Division. They provided little public accountability or hope for reform and as prisoner accounts continued to reveal up until the division's closure, the violence did not cease.

The 1978 Prisoner Rebellion and The Ombudsman's Report into H Division

In April 1978 H Division prisoners rioted (*Sun* 17/4/78 p 1). Once again prisoners were protesting against conditions, which they argued remained unchanged since Jenkinson handed down his findings in 1974. The rebellion accelerated after prisoners read reports in the newspapers in early April about the outcomes of the landmark New South Wales Royal Commission into Prisons led by Justice Nagle (*Sun* 17/4/78 p 1). One of Nagle's many recommendations, that the electronic Katingal Special Security Unit be closed, particularly stirred H Division prisoners. Most significantly, Nagle also recommended that New South Wales's equivalent of H Division, the Grafton Intractables Unit, should also be closed. Nagle found that since the 1940s Grafton officers had run a violent regime of terror where prisoners were subjected to a 'reception biff' and thereafter terrorised by regular beatings by officers in what Nagle referred to as 'one of the most sordid and shameful episodes in New South Wales penal history' (Nagle Report 1978: 108). While Nagle publicly recognised the systematic brutalisation of prisoners and recommended Grafton's closure, no officer was charged or disciplined in any way due to the fact that they were seen to be carrying out their duties with respect to what was essentially departmental policy. Despite these shortcomings, prisoners were angered that H Division had not been subjected to the same level of scrutiny and accountability.

One of the reforms to increase the accountability of the prison authorities after the Jenkinson Inquiry was the *Ombudsman Act* 1973 (Vic). The Act allowed for the appointment of an independent representative who was allocated broad powers 'to investigate complaints from aggrieved persons against Government administration' (Ombudsman Victoria 2004). Under the Act prisoners were able to make confidential complaints to the Ombudsman who would then use his powers to investigate and resolve them. The ongoing role and effectiveness of the Ombudsman has been questioned by legal professionals and prisoners, who argue it is a time consuming process that more often than not functions in the interests of state agencies and does not provide adequate scrutiny and accountability (Minogue 2002: 202-3). The Ombudsman has broad and extensive powers to investigate but it is rare that these powers are used when investigating complaints. This is partly due, as Craig Minogue (2002: 202-3) has argued, to informal procedures of investigation where the Ombudsman is more likely to seek and rely upon information provided by state agencies subject to complaint. While the ongoing functions of the Ombudsman are outside the focus of this study, it is an area requiring further research in Victoria. A brief examination of the 1978 Ombudsman report into H Division signifies the limitations of the Ombudsman as a satisfactory mechanism for accountability.

In April 1978, Victoria's first Ombudsman Mr JV Dillon was requested by the authorities to investigate conditions and complaints leading to the H Division riots. Prisoner complaints were not dissimilar from those submitted to Jenkinson and included grievances associated with classification procedures, allegations of prison officer brutality and the arbitrary imposition of solitary confinement and prisoner loss of privileges (LOP) (Dillon Report 1978).

Throughout his report Dillon reiterated his disbelief at prisoner complaints in light of what he perceived to be a series of reformative changes to the H Division regime implemented since Jenkinson. He stated 'in view of the relaxed conditions approved by the Director-General, I found it difficult to understand why the inmates of H Division should have reacted the way they did during the week-end of 15/16 April, 1978' (p 14). Key changes, according to officials, included the abolition of rock breaking and new rules allowing prisoners to earn 75 cents per day for industry. Dillon reported that, prior to the 1978 riots, he had raised concerns on behalf of prisoners about the arbitrary imposition of LOP in already 'oppressive' conditions of 'separate confinement'. Accordingly the authorities had alleviated these concerns with the assurance that new provisions necessitated a formal hearing before the Superintendent 'or a delegated officer' pursuant to s 131 of the *Social Welfare Act* before the imposition of punishments such as LOP (p 9).

Dillon prefaced his report with extensive official documentation detailing the reforms in H Division. It was not until page 14 that he commenced his investigation into prisoner complaints. The ultimate effect was that from the outset, prisoner complaints and protests were invariably questioned and discredited against official representations that suggested conditions in H Division had been significantly 'relaxed'.

Dillon's subsequent findings, based on written complaints by H Division prisoners and interviews conducted in person, did not reflect adequate investigations or accountability in response to allegations of misconduct and assault raised by prisoners. During the interview process Dillon reported that a number of prisoners made allegations that they had experienced or witnessed assaults by prison officers in H Division (pp 8-19). However, Dillon raised his concern that these prisoners were unable to provide further details or evidence. He subsequently informed prisoners he could only take formal action if they were able to provide supporting evidence (p 20). After his visit, Dillon received two written complaints alleging assaults and one alleging the deliberate provocation of prisoners by officers. He reported that of these three complaints, one was 'not proved' and the other two 'were withdrawn'. Dillon did not document any details of his investigations beyond his assertion that the allegations were disproved.

Overall, not one of Dillon's findings found in favour of any prisoner complaint. In his concluding comments he again noted the irony that prisoner riots should coincide with directions from the Director-General to 'relax conditions'. He further concluded that existing conditions in H Division could not be described as:

> inhumane, harsh or unjust. The environment and atmosphere of H Division will, however, always be such that prisoners would prefer to be accommodated elsewhere and they will continue to ask "how long will I be here?" (p 23)

Dillon stated that it was beyond his powers to overturn classification decisions that were ultimately subject to the exercise of discretion by the authorities. This was also the case for prisoners concerned about the indeterminate length of their sentence in H

Division as such cases were also regarded by Dillon as subject to discretion by the authorities. In response to allegations that the authorities used H Division as a punishment section, Dillon refuted the claim, stating that such assertions conflicted with the department's assurances that H Division existed only for the purposes of providing security.

Dillon did not report on allegations by some prisoners that they were unlawfully subjected to periods in solitary confinement due to the fact that these cases were during this time subject to further investigation. Overall he commented that classification appeared the most prominent issue concerning prisoners at the time of the 1978 riots. He dismissed other complaints as largely frivolous, stating:

> Alternatively, if they are to remain there [in H Division] they want the amenities and the more relaxed conditions of other Divisions and they ask, "Where is the pool?" "Where can I run?" "Where is the T.V.?" These are questions to be answered by the administration. (p 27)

The 1978 Ombudsman's Report reflected little accountability in response to prisoner allegations and demonstrated a lack of thorough investigation or consideration of evidence beyond official assurances that conditions in H Division were considerably better. This was the case despite the broad powers to investigate afforded to the Ombudsman under the Act. While many of the concerns raised by prisoners were reminiscent of those during Jenkinson's investigations, they were dismissed as largely groundless. As with Jenkinson, the 1978 Ombudsman's report demonstrated the legitimising power of official discourse and suggested that the establishment of the Ombudsman served the interests of the authorities, not accountability.

The Legacy of H Division

While prisoner accounts have over the years been marginalised and dismissed as 'tall tales', they have continued to emerge as a form of powerful 'resistance-writing' long after the closure of H Division. Craig Minogue spent time in H Division during the 1980s and also in the Jika Jika High-Security Unit up until the 1987 fire, which led to his transfer back to H Division. For Minogue the act of writing continues to serve as a fundamental means of survival in prison. Writing powerfully about his experience in H Division, he states:

> I am only a few cells down from where I remember laying on the concrete floor, my naked body shaking from the bitter cold and isolation that ran through me like an alternating current. With the sound of dried blood crackling on my beard and toilet paper wrapped around my hands and feet, I wondered what I had left as a human being ... I am a prisoner in a 140-year-old bluestone cell in a first world and otherwise modern city. We know this place simply as 'H'. It has other names: Pentridge Prisons' H Division, The High-Security Unit, the Punch Factory, The Go Slow, Hell Division and the Slot. (Minogue 1994: 23)

Allegations of prison officer brutality did not cease during the 1970s. Prisoners throughout the 1970s and 1980s and a 1988 report by the Uniting Church all reported ongoing prison officer violence in H Division (PRG 1989; Austin 1988: 21). In particular it was alleged by prisoners that in response to the protests of the 1980s and particularly after the fire and closure of Jika, H Division provided a platform for violent reprisals.

Though it was not officially acknowledged, H Division also comprised a site for the infliction of racialised violence and terror since its inception in 1958. Such violence was momentarily exposed in the 1980s, when a photograph of duty prison officers wearing Ku Klux Klan hoods was leaked to the media. It was subsequently alleged that prison officers donned the hoods, terrorising Aboriginal and Maori prisoners with cross burnings and night-time visits to cells. It was reported that some of these attacks involved beatings, the stripping down and placement of prisoners of colour in observation cells (Cunneen 1997: 145-7). As Chris Cunneen (1997: 145-7) notes, at the time the authorities were forced to act due to the existence of photographic evidence and some of the officers were charged with misconduct. Officials denied the existence of an ongoing regime of racialised harassment, arguing the officers merely used the hoods as a way of relieving tension and boredom while on the job (Cunneen 1997: 146). As Cunneen (1996) has established, the infliction of racist violence and terror by state agents via criminal justice processes and institutions is intimately linked to the historical experience of colonialism and dispossession in Australia. In their localised context such incidents also underpin the ongoing use of H Division as an instrument of terror and oppression.

In order to comprehend the complex dynamics of power, politics and resistance within H Division it is critical to recognise how official investigations such as the Jenkinson Inquiry and the 1978 Ombudsman investigation catered to and were constructed around the maintenance of institutional legitimacy, while preserving official cultures of concealment and denial. Such cultures and processes, grounded in official discourse and self-interest, have fostered cultures of concealment when it comes to investigating unlawful brutal practices in maximum-security.

Thus it is paradoxical yet not unsurprising that the authorities' solution to H Division, the new Jika Jika High-Security Unit, led to the transfer of unresolved problems, tensions and legacies into new institutional settings. As the authorities contemplated new hi-tech and security-based blueprints and solutions to maximise prisoner control in the late 1970s, it became increasingly clear that the ground on which the struggle between the authorities and prisoners was played out would be radically transformed.

CHAPTER TWO

Managing a Resistance Proof Panopticon: The Official Beginnings of the Jika Jika High-Security Unit

When completed in 1979, the $7 million Jika Jika Security Unit resembled the stark and ominous landscape of a hi-tech, futuristic panopticon prison within a prison. The eerie modular, symmetrical structures were surrounded by modestly landscaped gardens and high fences lined with menacing layers of keen razor wire. Inside, maxi-maxi security prevailed, with the systematic placement of closed circuit television cameras, multiple electronic alarm systems, fish-eye lenses, bar grilles and 32mm thick bullet resistant glass throughout the accommodation units. Declared 'escape-proof' and benefiting from the highest security in Australia, Jika Jika was protected by the latest 'microwave technology', and a 'stellar screen energy field' erected in priority security areas (Swan 1977-78: 4). When floodlit at night, Jika Jika mirrored popular science fiction images of a futuristic space station. Its spectral central observation tower comprised the focal point from which descended four 'pod like' units, linked by 'tubular' corridors raised on stilts (Allom Lovell & Assoc 1996: 280). These tubular corridors consisted of 15cm thick prefabricated concrete walls (Sun 22/8/79). In order to walk through the lengthy 'corridor links', it was necessary to progress through a series of remote controlled, pneumatic and bulletproof steel doors or 'security locks' that would open one at a time only (Department Social Welfare & Public Works Department (DSW/PWD) 1978). Throughout Jika Jika there were approximately 128 of these monitored security locks, all functioning in response to remote control computer command (Australian 17/2/87; Age 25/7/80).

Prisoners were segregated into groups of six in units with individual windowed cells and a communal day room. All door access for prisoners was controlled by prison officers, who supervised the unit from a control room protected by bulletproof glass and grilles. The entire facility was air-conditioned due to the absence of natural circulating air. The exercise yards extending beyond the prisoner quarters were secured by an escape-proof 'space frame' or steel cage roof that enclosed a concrete base court. The unique angular zigzag shape of the overhead caging prevented any potential helicopter landings on the roof of the prison, while allowing 'maximum sunlight and fresh air penetration' (Swan 1977-78: 15). In addition, 'passive recreation areas' with garden plots were provided with the intention of allowing prisoners a reprieve from the security-driven environment.

The Jika Jika Security Unit was designed for the secure confinement of long-term and high-risk prisoners and so the prevention of escape, fire and sabotage were primary considerations in the design process (DSW/PWD 1978).

In December 1976, Victorian Premier Mr Hamer publicly announced proposals to develop a multi-million dollar 54-man high-security unit within Pentridge (Swan 1977-78: 4). It was subsequently announced that a series of factors necessitated significant upgrades to the high-security section of Pentridge. Featuring prominently amongst these were concerns about prison order and public safety. Above all, the authorities raised serious misgivings that the overcrowded and antiquated 100-year-old H Division was adequately equipped or secure enough to hold the increasing population of high-risk and potentially dangerous prisoners. However, despite the highly charged rhetoric regarding public safety, 1977 internal planning briefs cited concerns about the breakdown of prison discipline and the frequency of prisoner protests and riots in the 1970s as weighty driving factors behind calls for the new security unit (Inquest 1988-89a 'Security Planning Committee Minutes and Brief' 16/8/77).

The Jika Jika High-Security Unit comprised an initiative by the Victorian prison authorities to deal with prisoner non-compliance through the use of new psychologically geared disciplinary strategies and methods of control. The growing radicalisation of prisoners and problems posed by the rise of prisoner campaigns during the 1970s constituted a chief driving force behind the perceived need for hi-tech and modernised approaches to segregating the system's high-risk and 'worst' prisoners (Zdenkowski & Brown 1982: 148). As demonstrated by the use of the Katingal Special Security Unit by the New South Wales prison authorities, these new strategies manifested in the experimental use of high-security units built on behavioural modification principles, high levels of sensory deprivation and social isolation (for a prisoner account of life in Katingal see Matthews 2006). Blueprints for Jika mirrored international trends led by the United States and the United Kingdom towards the implementation and use of controversial draconian measures to maintain control (see Fitzgerald 1977; see also Churchill & Vanderwall 1992).

The public face of official plans for Jika Jika stressed 'humane containment' for difficult prisoners, the impacts of total security and constant surveillance offset by generous provisions of space, light, gardens, meaningful work and rehabilitative programs (DSW/PWD 1978). In this respect, on the surface Jika Jika presented a seemingly workable response to containing those designated 'difficult' or 'high-risk'. However, the early years revealed a series of problems and the institution itself presented unresolvable contradictions. First, a 'humane' system of confinement is not compatible with high-security confinement, and moreover, a system of 'total' confinement is perhaps least of all compatible or synonymous with institutional order.

In Jika's early years it became readily clear that restrictive conditions, the separation of prisoners and staff, the dehumanising application of security technologies and the prevalence of unaccountable managerial structures all combined to impact negatively on institutional relationships. Such pressures created the context for future crisis from early on. In this respect the Jika complex reproduced the very disorder officials purported it would contain. Such conditions and impacts have been experienced in many high-security institutions (see Matthews 2006; see also

61

Rhodes 2004; Churchill & Vanderwall 1992; Fellner & Mariner 1997), and may be referred to as the self-fulfilling prophecy of security. Such a prophecy, which results in the escalation of security based measures and harsher regimes in response to systemic shortcomings and failures, including prisoner indiscipline is, according to Rodriguez, a fully intended feature of such regimes. He argues:

> [The state] thrives on its own endemic insufficiency and structured institutional failure to evaporate or fully neutralise dissent, resistance, and incorrigibility among its captive subjects – in fact, the prison regime requires and produces such institutional crisis as a premise for its constant revision and reinvention of technologies of domination. (Rodriguez 2006: 146)

Within this context, ensuing disorder and crisis prompts further stringent disciplinary strategies and security 'crackdowns', which in turn exacerbate disorder, and the cycle goes on. Therefore the very blueprints and objectives behind Jika Jika presented an unsustainable system. By enforcing a system of inflexible disciplinary control, the authorities would ultimately induce prisoner frustrations and dissent, which would in turn create tension and polarisation. The fatal crisis that unfolded in Jika throughout the 1980s must be firmly situated in this context.

This chapter highlights the gulf between the publicly advocated developmental objectives and rhetorical ideals by officials and the practical operation of Jika as an institution. It provides an 'official' history of Jika Jika and begins with an examination of the official objectives that informed the design and construction of the high-security unit. Such developments are situated in the broader historical and political context of the coercive uses of hi-tech and security based models of confinement by western states. This chapter focuses on the problems experienced after Jika's official opening and how these prompted the department to commission an internal independent report by criminologist Dennis Challinger (Challinger Report 1982). Challinger's report and findings are examined in so far as they revealed a series of criticisms and recommendations. Overall this chapter demonstrates that serious operational and management issues were brought to the attention of the authorities soon after Jika opened. It is argued that the lack of decisive official action in response to these early concerns contributed greatly to the deterioration of conditions and institutional relationships that reached crisis point during the late 1980s.

Psychological Control and Coercion: A Hi-tech Fortress as 'Modernised' Response to Prisoner Non-compliance

Above all official calls for a new high-security unit in Pentridge comprised a response to the breakdown in prisoner discipline and the deterioration of relations between staff and prisoners, particularly in H Division. However, the authorities publicly argued they were faced with a 'new breed' of criminal, although such assertions were generalised and unsupported by empirical evidence.

Concerns about the increased risk and dangerousness of prisoners are a recurrent feature in official campaigns for more repressive prison regimes (Findlay 1982: 51). Yet, as Mark Findlay (1982: 51) has noted, while such notions are so often used by prison authorities and prison officers to justify prison administration decisions and operations, 'dangerousness' constitutes a category of behaviour that has no clear or operable legislative or clinical definition. Craig Haney (2003: 129) concurs, arguing there is little evidence to suggest that prisoners designated 'worst of the worst' are any worse than those adequately managed by less drastic measures. He further observes in prison there is an official tendency to individualise or demonise problematic behaviour while ignoring systemic or contextual forces that produce it. Joe Sim (1994: 106) argues that in this way debates about prison violence are constructed on 'the narrow terrain of psychopathic personalities while the everyday normality of domination, control, humiliation and violence is continually reproduced'. In this respect, the construction of Jika Jika was premised as a security based solution to housing problematic and high-risk prisoners. This presented a task that was perhaps easier to sell to the public than providing a critical investigation into the institutional conditions and contexts that gave rise to the violence, confrontation and rebellion in H Division.

Internal planning proposals for the development of a new security unit date back to 1972. Such proposals reflected official concerns that the profile or 'type' of criminal had changed, and that the prison system had to cater for a younger and more violent group of offenders serving indefinite sentences (Inquest 1988-89a 'Security Planning Committee Minutes and Brief' 16/8/77). The department publicly contended that they faced significant management and security issues stemming from an increasingly high-risk, long-term prison population with corresponding higher demands for segregation and protection from other prisoners (Swan 1977-78: 25; see also Department of Community Welfare Services (DCWS) 1980; for public statements by the Minister for the Department of Social Welfare see also *Age* 25/7/80). These prisoners, it was argued, were characterised as 'anti-authority'; some of them belonged to exclusive cliques and many played 'power games' with staff and other prisoners (Inquest 1988-89a: 443). Furthermore, it was perceived by the authorities that they posed a threat to other prisoners and themselves, not to mention to prison officers and the overall security and good order of the prison. The 'Overcoat Gang' constituted one particular clique operating in H Division during the 1970s. They engaged in retributive clashes fought out between prominent criminal personalities such as Mark 'Chopper' Read and other prison gangs like the 'Dockies' (Inquest 1988-89a: 444; see also Read 1991: 63-70). Such clashes resulted in ongoing violent assaults and attacks stemming from a range of petty criminal vendettas (Read 1991: 63-70).

A further official concern was the perceived rise in international terrorist activity, particularly in the late 1970s and in the wake of the Hilton bombing in Sydney 1978 (Inquest 1988-89a: 444). The prospect that fanatical terrorist groups might be absorbed into the Australian prison system helped fortify justifications for the use of costly hi-tech security devices enabling the prevention of elaborate escape plans and the 'springing' of prisoners perceived to be political (Inquest 1988-89a: 445).

The subsequent development of a sophisticated high-security prison was represented as urgent on these grounds alone. Confidential planning briefs specified that the new facility be designed 'to prevent escapes, outside penetration and to protect the lives of prisoners' (Inquest 1988-89a 'Security Planning Committee Minutes' 29/12/76). Early suggestions included the use of air-conditioning and the replacement of bars with glass. It was also felt that in the interests of security, prisoners should not leave the division to undertake employment in other divisions. Rather, the prisoner accommodation areas would be spaciously designed to cater for light industry, leisure, dining and personal laundry facilities. The authorities also hoped that utilising the latest security devices such as 'microwave curtaining' would benefit the new prison with the highest security in the state. Before any work was commenced on formal designs, officials inspected Australia's first high-security facility Katingal, which was operational at the time (Inquest 1988-89a 'Security Planning Committee Minutes' 29/12/76). Despite later attempts by the department to distinguish Jika Jika from the controversial windowless Katingal, internal planning briefs suggest Katingal was an influential model for high-security designs in Victoria.

The authorities advocated that new management strategies were required within the new facility to maintain discipline and order. During the late 1970s the authorities identified a number of 'troublemaker' prisoners who frequently posed management and security problems. They had built up numerous disciplinary charges on their records and had reputations for assaulting prison officers and other prisoners. It was anticipated that if a system could be developed whereby these prisoners could be physically segregated, while at the same time subjected to constant surveillance, the risk they posed could be substantially diminished. Segregation would also limit opportunities for collective organisation and, it was hoped, curb prisoner militancy. Lastly, Pentridge officials believed that if staff and prisoners were separated 'prisoners wouldn't have the opportunity to complain that they had been manhandled by prison officers' (Inquest 1988-89a: 446-7).

Early research conducted by the authorities focused on current international standards and trends in prison design and management, namely in the United States and the United Kingdom which were at the forefront in the design and use of high-security segregation and control units (Inquest 1988-89a: 445). Most pertinent to these overseas trends was the increasing use of segregation and classification systems to separate 'high-risk' prisoners from the majority. While segregation had been utlised in H Division, the early planning briefs for Jika Jika made reference to British penal policy and the use of high-security units as a major influence in design and management.

A notable overseas expert referred to was Lord Mountbatten, known for his 1966 report into security within British prisons (Mountbatten 1966). Authorities commissioned the report following a series of sensational and politically embarrassing escapes by prominent British high-security prisoners (Fitzgerald 1977: 49). Most significant was Mountbatten's recommendation that a centralised classification system determine the security risk of all prisoners from highest to lowest, and prisoners classified high-security be centrally contained in 'Alcatraz-type' segregation units (Fitzgerald 1977: 51-2). Mike Fitzgerald (1977: 50) argues that the Mountbatten report signified a repressive shift from 'treatment' and 'rehabilitation' within penal policy back to 'control' and 'security'. This is particularly evident when contrasting such approaches with alternatives such as the Scottish Barlinnie Special Unit, a small-scale rehabilitative unit established in the late 1970s to house the system's most difficult prisoners.

At a time when hi-tech security devices and 'control units' were increasingly embraced as a solution for housing violent and difficult prisoners, Barlinnie operated on therapeutic principles of collective responsibility and self-government where staff and prisoners worked together in the overall management of the unit (Donnison 1978: 80-1). Prisoners wore their own clothes and jewellery, decorated their cells as they liked, all staff wore plain clothes, prisoners had open visits with friends and family and the operation of the unit depended on mutual cooperation, consultation and respect. In Barlinnie prison officers and prisoners responded to one another 'not through physical violence and psychological intimidation but through the "community meeting" where each man was encouraged to examine and articulate his feelings about himself, his life inside and his actions outside the walls' (Sim 1994: 114). Sim (1994: 117) notes that this was a particularly challenging and painful experience for prisoners as 'they had never been encouraged to shine the searchlight of scrutiny on themselves as individuals ... nor had they been encouraged to take personal responsibility for their actions'. While Barlinnie was widely criticised as a 'sugar coated' option for men who had committed terrible and violent crimes, proclamation and praise for its achievements were well-publicised through the autobiographical writings of Scottish prisoner at the time Jimmy Boyle (1979). Barlinnie was closed in the mid-1990s, despite its proven achievements, vision for reform and therapy-based approaches to rehabilitating rather than punishing offenders. Conversely, high-security prisons came to proliferate as the key solution for housing difficult prisoners.

The increasing implementation of segregation principles, based on Mountbatten's report, in the 1960s and 1970s, was criticised as fostering the widespread controversial use of high-security and control units as 'prisons within prisons' (Fitzgerald 1977: 49). In Australia the use of punitive segregation and development of high-security units developed as a retributive response by officials to the growing movement of prisoner rights and specific events such as the 1974 Bathurst riots in NSW and widespread unrest and rioting in Pentridge Prison Victoria (Zdenkowski & Brown 1982).

In addition to measures focused on segregation and classification, the development of modern high-security formed an institutional basis for the application of principles and practices designed for behavioural 'adjustment' and control. These strategies rose to prominence through the cold war era of psychological experimentation and strategies designed for the purposes of counter-insurgency, interrogation and political imprisonment (McCoy 2006; see also Gordon 2006; Physicians for Human Rights 2005; Lucas 1976).

During this time research in the fields of psychology and particularly cognitive science revealed powerful potentials derived in the manipulation of human behaviour (McCoy 2006). In the 1950s and 1960s studies uncovered the devastating impacts of sensory deprivation and prolonged isolation on the human psyche (McCoy 2006; see also Physicians for Human Rights 2005). Other research highlighted the benefits of sleep deprivation, the administration of psychotropic drug and electroshock treatments and 'special' behavioural adjustment incentive programs and social isolation (McCoy 2006; see also Ryan 1992; Fitzgerald 1975). Much of this research and 'expertise', gleaned from the imprisonment and the interrogation of political dissidents in Northern Ireland, South Africa, Russia, East Germany and Korea, was applied in western domestic prison systems in the 1960s and 1970s to deal with the increasing problem of prisoner politicisation, subversion and non-compliance (McCoy 2006).

Domestic prisons came to serve as a laboratory for the experimental application of a range of behavioural controls described above. A primary example is the controversial deployment of the Special Training and Rehabilitative Training (START) behavioural programs in Marion Penitentiary, Illinois and the administration of painful drug aversion therapies in Vacaville, California (Ryan 1992). The phrase 'behavioural modification' fails to capture the extent of physical and psychic pain experienced through enforced social isolation, sensory deprivation, use of shackles and forced administration of drugs amongst a raft of other controversial 'treatments'.

The development of high-security and Jika Jika more specifically must be situated firmly within this historical context. Primarily high-security or control units were developed on principles of sensory deprivation, solitary confinement and constant surveillance in conjunction with various behavioural adjustment and incentive schemes to exact prisoner control. Such methods of disciplinary control are officially neutralised as painless psychological methods to achieve prisoner control. They are bound up in neutralising professional terminology and discourses associated with security, punishment and incarceration (Rodriguez

2006: 148-9). However, as argued by Lucas (1976: 156), whether the methods used are overtly structural, physical or psychological, 'the intent is to apply stress to the individual in such a way that normal psychological functioning and defence mechanisms break down and the victim becomes amenable to behaviour manipulation'. In this sense so-called 'psychological' methods are designed to curb independent thinking, 'break' and 'remould' difficult prisoners into a state of conformity and compliance (Rodriguez 2006; see also Ryan 1992).

The Jika Jika High-Security Complex: Philosophy, Design, Structure

The final blueprints for Jika Jika specified that the new Security Unit would be built to house as many as 54 prisoners. Prisoners would be segregated into four 12-man units with accommodation areas divided in half to house six men on each side and an additional smaller solitary confinement section to hold six men with three on each side. The design briefs thus stipulated 'that prisoners should be housed in modern single cell accommodation with an emphasis on current trends to segregate prisoners into smaller groups to enable greater control and better supervision' (*Architecture Australia* 1982: 74). The Minister for Social Welfare at the time, Brian Dixon, made public representations in attempt to reinforce that prisoner rehabilitation was also an official concern:

> The complex includes the latest in physical security tempered with facilities and comprehensive programs necessary to assist a prisoner with his social re-adjustment … We are endeavouring to change the concept of "men serving time," to that of "time serving men". (DSW/PWD 1978)

In spite of this, security remained a dominating principle in Jika's design. The Public Works Department's then confidential planning brief dated 1977-78, stated the need to 'provide security processes that would encourage confidence within prison staff without building up a threatening process for prisoners' (Swan 1977-78: 8). The underlying cornerstone of Jika's operation was the separation of prison officers and prisoners in the interests of better security: 'all access to services and security locks, will be operated either from

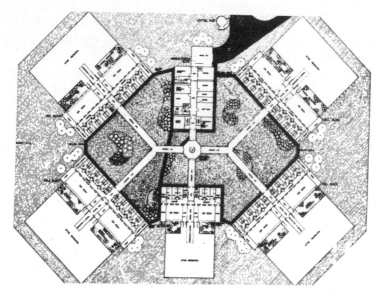

Plan of the Jika Jika High-Security Unit (DCWS 1980 Exhibit 23). Courtesy
Public Records Office of Victoria.

the master control room or from control points within security
areas'. The brief recommended the use of closed circuit television
surveillance over all 'traffic' and recreational areas as well as 'patrol
and direct visual supervision'. Hi-tech electronic alarm systems
placed throughout the entire complex, the provision of a 'stellar
screen energy field' and microwave technology, would present
additional security safeguards (Swan 1977-78: 8). The brief also
stipulated the complex required 'careful material selection and
detailing' in the interests of security (Department of Public Works
(DPW) 1979). It was therefore decided that the use of pre-cast
concrete would satisfy:

> security, fire resistance and water-proofing requirements, and
> with careful consideration of the exposed surface could provide
> a light, sensitive approach to the exterior of the complex; an
> approach in keeping with the enlightened Architectural design
> philosophy. (DPW 1979)

Aerial shot of Pentridge Prison and the Jika Jika High-Security Complex, 1980. Photographer John Lamb/Courtesy of *The Age*.

The centrepiece of Jika Jika's physical layout was the central observation tower. It was intended to serve as the administrative control nerve centre and comprise a post to observe all movement within the internal area of the facility while illuminating the landscape at night (DPW 1979: 11).[13] It was anticipated that through the maximum use of electronic and visual technologies, 'total surveillance' could be maintained (DPW 1979: 13). Each self-contained accommodation unit was connected to the central observation tower by a tubular corridor containing a series of electronic, pneumatic bulletproof steel doors referred to as 'security

---

[13] Ex-Jika prisoners maintain the tower was never actively used as the authorities had hoped. This was due to the fact that it had a secondary power plant underneath, which provided power and hot water to Unit 2 (other units were powered and supplied with hot water from the main power plant situated underneath Unit 1). The power plant raised the temperature inside the observation tower to an unbearable level, making it impossible for officers to man it. Personal prisoner correspondence 28/5/05; 21/1/07.

Interior of prisoner cell taken prior to opening during a press tour in July 1980. The Age Archives/Courtesy of *The Age*.

locks'. The layout and placement of units in this way was intended by the designers to ensure isolation from other accommodation units and impose restrictive access to units. Manned security towers would be placed to survey the outer perimeter and fences of the facility. The administration unit would provide monitored visiting facilities and a contact visiting area, as well as a designated area for medical services. Prisoner meals would be prepared elsewhere in Pentridge and reheated in the administration unit before being taken on trolleys for distribution to prisoners (DPW 1979: 13).

The blueprints for Jika provided a system of 'total' surveillance, 'unceasing' management and control. In order to fully convey the extent and impact of security within Jika it is useful to describe the pathway taken by prisoners during their reception. Prisoners were received into Jika Jika via the central administration unit. After being strip-searched and donning the Jika prison greens, they were escorted by officers through security locks leading into the lengthy tubular corridor links on the way to their allocated accommodation unit. Progression through the numerous security locks one by one was a time consuming process. The corridors were sealed from outside air or sound and this, paired with the slow movement through the security locks, created the sensation that one was progressing deeper into an underground location. When prisoners finally reached the end of the spines they passed through a series of security locks leading to the prison officer control station within their allocated unit. They then progressed through additional security locks leading into the accommodation unit corridor where they finally reached their cell.

Each and every accommodation unit included autonomous prison officer 'control areas' designed to 'enable total supervision' of prisoner daytime activities in recreation yards, day rooms and 'ablution areas' (DSW/PWD 1978). These areas were central to the electronic control of prisoner access in each unit and ensured minimal contact between prison officers and prisoners. All windows in each of the units, including those which separated prison officers from prisoners, were made of 32mm bulletproof glass 'capable of stopping high powered shots' (Swan 1977-78: 17).

Prisoner accommodation areas included a communal day room and shower, a store and servery areas. Cells measured five by two and a half metres. This was considered 'large' by comparison to a standard Pentridge cell, which measured three by two metres (DCWS 1980). A Public Works manual commented that a major feature of the overall design was the liberal use of space in order to overcome the effects of sensory deprivation and long-term imprisonment. Prisoner cells were air-conditioned with suicide-proof air vents. They were fitted with a double power point, a television outlet, two lights and a call button. Prisoner cells included a stainless steel toilet bowl and hand basin with hot and cold water. To prevent any potential tampering all plumbing was concealed in a duct and located outside cells. Cells were furnished with a pre-cast concrete bed base and workbench. All doors to cells were sliding and remotely operated. The walls were painted with light colours, 'to give the cells a light and airy appearance'; a decision arrived at through consultation with psychiatrists and psychologists (Swan 1977-78: 17). In case of power failure, the electronic doors throughout Jika Jika were fitted with an emergency manual system.

Each unit had a windowed day room measuring approximately 14 by 7 metres. It served as a communal area, intended for light industry during the day and recreation at night (Swan 1977-78: 17). One exercise yard, measuring 36 by 24 metres, was allocated to every unit. Each was fully enclosed within a wire cage or 'space frame' designed to allow 'maximum sunshine and ventilation' (DCWS 1980). The areas would be equipped for sports such as tennis, basketball and volleyball. Prisoners would be supervised from the control room, which extended through the units into the yard. From the exercise yard the control room resembled a concrete bus situated between the entry points to the yard. An additional smaller 'passive recreation' area would be provided for 'more relaxed recreation' with benches to sit on within a garden setting (DCWS 1980).

It was announced that there would be two fully staffed shifts run each day, enabling prisoners to spend up to 15 hours out of their cells as opposed to the present eight and a half hours for most other Pentridge prisoners (DCWS 1980). The staff to prisoner ratio was envisaged as 82 officers to 54 prisoners. The first shift would run from 6.30am to 2.30pm and the second shift from 2.30pm to 10.30pm (Inquest 1988-89a: 450). With the exception of meal times, when they would be locked in their cells, prisoners were expected to spend these periods out of their cells undertaking useful work, hobbies and physical recreation.

Walter Jona publicly recognised that the experience of long-term imprisonment in Jika Jika could have 'adverse psychological and social effects if appropriate measures are not implemented' (DCWS 1980). Yet he assured such affects would be avoided through the provision of a diverse range of programs for prisoners. Maximum use would be made of the exercise yards, and sporting activities administered by an appointed officer. Moreover, there would be a range of evening activities such as hobbies, table tennis, the screening of films and the facilitation of discussion groups. Education programs would be made available to interested prisoners and books would be brought in on 'wheel away' trolleys.

Prisoners would also have access to a welfare officer and 'providing enough interest was shown' group therapy sessions involving a departmental psychologist would be arranged (DCWS 1980).

After their classification and transfer to the Jika Jika Security Unit, prisoners would regularly come before a Review and Assessment Committee (R&A) comprising both uniformed staff and independent representatives, who would make recommendations regarding the prisoner's progress and whether they should be reclassified.

The Official Opening

On 24 July 1980 the newly developed Jika Jika Security Unit opened to take prisoners. During this time, Jika was proudly opened for a press tour, in a symbolic move that contrasted with the attitude of the New South Wales Corrective Services Department with respect to the ill-fated Katingal Special Security Unit.

The Victorian authorities sought to avoid the publicity disasters experienced by the New South Wales Corrective Services Department as a result of the secrecy and lack of public accountability and consultation surrounding Katingal. When Jika Jika opened, steps were taken to assure the public that the authorities had undertaken extensive research and engaged in consultative processes with numerous professionals about the possible impact of Jika on prisoners. In this way, the department attempted to distance Jika from the failings of Katingal (Semple-Kerr 1988: 137). New South Wales Comptroller of Prisons in the 1970s Walter McGeechan exercised full control over the design processes for Katingal and shielded the developments from professional and public scrutiny. This lack of consultation and secrecy was the subject of much criticism by Justice Nagle during the Royal Commission into New South Wales prisons (Nagle Report 1978: 122-34). Symbolically, one of the first planning briefs for Jika illustrated a prisoner playing guitar in the passive recreation area (DSW/PWD 1978). The idea that musical instruments might be permitted in Jika presented a contrast to

McGeechan's publicised refusal to permit a particular prisoner's request for a guitar in Katingal (Semple-Kerr 1988: 137).

Despite attempts by the department to distance the new Jika Jika Security Unit from Katingal, there remained criticisms regarding the adverse effects of sensory deprivation and calls of 'security overkill'.[14] Minister for Social Welfare Walter Jona stated in response that the department was confronted with many:

> well-motivated, idealistic people in the community who think we can run a prison like a well-run boarding school ... but a very minute percentage of the people who tell us how to run it have the knowledge or the expertise or the appreciation of the problems involved. (*Age* 25/7/80)

Given the public controversy generated throughout the Jenkinson Inquiry and the prisoner militancy in H Division throughout the 1970s, it is perplexing that the Jika Jika Security Unit did not initially attract the same level of public opposition that Katingal did in New South Wales. Public opposition to Katingal arose from the moment it was announced (Zdenkowski & Brown 1982). Initial protests involved a series of green bans imposed by the Builders Labourers Federation on construction and early attempts to detonate the construction site with explosives (Matthews 2006: 186). In 1978, Katingal's opponents were further prompted into action by the initial refusal by the New South Wales Department of Corrections to adhere to Justice Nagle's recommendation that Katingal be closed. Community protests involved the establishment of a formalised 'Close Katingal Campaign' and a protest rally and camp set up on the grounds of the Long Bay Prison Complex (see Zdenkowski & Brown 1982). At the time Jika Jika opened in Victoria, its critics and the community were subdued in comparison to the vociferous campaigns surrounding Katingal in New South Wales. Nonetheless, Pentridge prisoners emphasised their concerns about the potential uses of the new security unit:

---

[14] While officials responded to 'criticisms' in newspaper reports, there is no specific detailing of such criticisms during the time that Jika was initially opened. However, some journalist reports did reflect a critical stance on 'security overkill' (*Age* 25/7/80). Criticisms by the Prisoners Action Group were later reported in 1989 after the closure of the complex (*Age* 1/8/89 p 5).

> Quite apart from the official rhetoric, these new "control centres" are a direct response to a decade of prisoner revolt: revolt meaning a demand to the end of the systematic brutalisation and dehumanisation of Victorian prisoners. (Victorian Prisoner Action Group, *Prisoner's Voice*, October 1979 cited in Zdenkowski & Brown 1982: 147)

Regardless of general criticisms and concerns raised by Victorian prisoner rights groups such as the Prisoners Action Group, departmental officials publicly insisted that Jika was not intended as a punishment unit. Jika was represented as the first in many stages of redevelopment planned for Victorian prisons. Furthermore, Minister Walter Jona stated in 1980 that one of the objectives behind the proposed construction program was to improve conditions across the Victorian prison system as a whole to meet United Nations standards (DCWS 1980). In particular, Jika was represented as a 'step up' from the antiquated H Division and this contrast served to support the decision to commission the new security division (*Age* 25/7/80). It is significant that while officials had gone to lengths during the 1970s to defend the legitimacy of H Division, during this time it was used as a symbol of an outmoded and harsh 19th-century punishment block, to be replaced by a modern, humane system of high-security confinement. A department official later commented that a driving force for the development of a new high-security block stemmed from the poor conditions, brutality and violence by both prison officers and prisoners inherent within the H Division regime (Inquest 1988-89a: 442). In championing the construction of the new Jika Jika Security Unit as a progressive step forward it became expedient for officials to acknowledge prisoner accounts of abuse in H Division.

Irrespective of criticisms over sensory deprivation and charges of 'security overkill', there remained a public fascination with the spectral appearance of the futuristic panopticon and its state of the art technological gadgetry. Reports covering Jika Jika's press tour focused not on the potential effects the facility might have on prisoners but the striking physical appearance (e.g. see *Sun* 22/8/79; *Age* 25/7/80; and later *Sun* 29/9/82). As Allom Lovell described in a later heritage assessment of Jika, the blueprints by architectural and engineering professionals focused on the use of:

technological solutions, and specific details such as the pneumatic sliding doors and the inward sloping walls and curved corners of the corridors, derive[d] from the fantasy imagery of science fiction space stations and from the architectural imagery of plug-in modular structures publicised by Archigram in the 1960s. (Allom Lovell & Assoc 1996: 241)

The fascination with Jika Jika as a 'space-age prison' was accompanied by a sense of wonderment at the fact that the unit was 'escape proof'. One journalist commented with respect to the numerous security devices that for a prisoner to escape he would need 'the speed of a bullet, the luck of a lotto winner, and the ingenuity of Houdini' (*Herald* 13/2/87). Another journalist, who attended Jika after it was operational, expressed his thrill at getting a 'glimpse' of 'this strange sealed world' (*Sun* 29/9/82). In contrast, however, one journalist expressed reservations and referred to his experience on the exclusive two-hour press tour as 'mentally chilling' (*Age* 25/7/80). Charges that the designers of Jika had created a disturbingly sterile environment for prisoners were addressed in an *Architecture Australia* review. It was conceded that:

> The appearance of the complex is functional and somewhat brutal. Every square millimetre of the enclosed space must be thought of as a place of weakness where either a prisoner can in time break through to 'escape' or where he can hide contraband or weaponry. (*Architecture Australia* 1982: 75)

It was further observed that any 'normal preconceptions' of what constitutes a sterile environment were not relevant to a 'micro-society' such as Jika, which housed the 'most distant outcasts of society' for whom security could not be compromised (*Architecture Australia* 1982: 75). Minister Jona reiterated this point in defence of Jika when he stated that the public must remember that the unit was built specifically to hold 'the roughest, toughest and most violent' prisoners in the system. Jona further argued, Jika would be dehumanising to anyone other than the 'type' of prisoner it was designed for, 'you wouldn't put a traffic offender or a petty thief in there ... for them it would be horribly dehumanising' (*Herald* 13/2/87).

Just weeks prior to the official opening Jona disclosed the categories of prisoners intended for Jika. They included:

(a) Security:

Serious escapees from Pentridge or other prisons who have been recaptured and returned to custody.

Potentially serious escapees, i.e., those prisoners considered to be an extreme risk to the community should they escape.

(b) Protection:

Those prisoners who require the highest degree of protection from other prisoners.

(c) Prisoners who must be contained in the most secure environment because they pose a very serious risk of physical violence to staff and/or other prisoners. (Challinger Report 1982: 3)

In spite of such stipulations there remained a degree of discretion within official classification procedures in defining who posed a security risk and which particular prisoners constituted 'potentially serious escapees'.

Jika Jika was criticised for its exorbitant financial cost to the community. For design and construction the unit was priced at $7 million, while after it opened it would cost $130,000 for each prisoner per day (*Age* 25/7/80). However, department officials at this time emphasised that after considerable overseas research and consultation with various international experts they were convinced that Jika Jika was a product of the 'best thinking available in the world', in providing 'maximum-security with maximum humanity' (*Herald* 13/2/87).

The architects and engineers behind Jika received professional and public acclaim. In 1979, Public Works architects and engineers won the Concrete Institute of Australia Award for Excellence in the effective use of concrete (DCWS 1980). In 1982, Jika also won the Architecture Institute Award for New Buildings. When interviewed about their successes, architects Dennis Payne and Alan Yorke commented that the complex was designed and developed with the 'maxim that there is some good in every person ... we tried to implement Christian principles' (*Sun* 29/9/82 p 8). Payne and Yorke highlighted aspects of Jika's environment designed to soften the impact of high-security. In particular they made reference to the gardened passive recreation areas where prisoners could relax outdoors or tend to plots of shrubbery and grass. They also pointed to the generous allocation of space within the accommodation units and the liberal use of windows.

Troubled Beginnings: Jika Jika and the Challinger Report

At the time designers Payne and Yorke were honoured with awards, Jika Jika was already experiencing significant problems. Within two years, several prisoners attempted suicide and there were incidents of self-mutilation. There were prisoner assaults on other prisoners and despite the system of 'total surveillance', prisoner Glen Davies was murdered by prisoner Edwin Eastwood in one of the passive recreation yards in April 1981.[15] The prevailing official response to these events was that reports of violence were considerably less than that in the maximum-security section of H Division (*Architecture Australia* 1982: 75). But these were not the only problems. The sliding doors malfunctioned often and prisoners were difficult to place in accommodation units due to various personality clashes and conflicting protection needs (Challinger Report 1982). The facility as a whole became too expensive to run and so staff were minimised, which meant that prisoners were confined to their cells for longer periods than initially anticipated. Due to these numerous problems, officials were confronted with the task of defending an expensive and seemingly malfunctioning institution they had sold to the community as a forward thinking solution.

When significant institutional problems and issues emerge, a typical response by state agencies is to commission an internal or external investigation, so that the public may be reassured that the problem is being 'scientifically tackled'. Cohen and Taylor (1972: 205) argue that this is the essential function of 'official' research:

---

[15] Unpublished transcript of proceedings at Coroner's investigation into the death of Glen Joseph Davies, 1982, State Coroner's Office (hereafter 'Inquest 1982'), 'Victoria Police Homicide Brief' 30/4/81.

The research itself may not say anything significant, relevant or even interesting. Its results indeed may never get published. This is relatively unimportant. The main thing is the research's window dressing potential.

Cohen and Taylor (1972: 205) argue that the characteristics of such research include it being well financed and generally comprehensible. Its aims must be presented in a simple and direct way while complex methodological and theoretical issues are put to the side and 'the results when they appear, should be ambiguous enough to reassure, while at the same time generating numerous statements of the '"more research is needed" variety'. As will be seen in the context of Jika Jika, initial research conducted to investigate 'teething problems' served as a type of 'insurance' that could potentially be called upon to mollify any future community concerns.

Accordingly, in 1982, the authorities commissioned criminologist Dennis Challinger to conduct an independent, informal review of Jika Jika. Challinger's report and findings attempted 'to appreciate the atmosphere, practices and functioning of Jika Jika', while raising a series of managerial and operational problems and corresponding recommendations for improvement. These were not well received by the authorities and not initially publicised. However, despite his criticisms, Challinger (1982: 59) believed there was a positive future role for Jika if its inadequacies were addressed.

The tone of Challinger's report was dry and detached, and it offered little detail with respect to prisoner impressions of Jika Jika. Its significance lay in drawing attention to serious institutional structural and operational flaws. Of significant concern were prisoner classification procedures; the adverse impact of the high-security environment on officers and prisoners; a marked lack of officer training, experience and communication; a lack of clearly defined and supported prisoner programs; and gross inadequacies in the grading and placement of prisoners (Challinger Report 1982: 59). While the authorities might not have intended it, Challinger's report sheds light on the obscured operational and management problems that beset Jika in its early years.

Challinger: Official Classification Procedures

Challinger (1982: 4) expressed concerns about the 'misuse' of Jika to classify prisoners who fell outside the specified groups of high-risk and protection cases. Of primary concern was the fact that Jika was used to house psychiatrically ill prisoners and remand prisoners. While departmental stipulations for Jika did not explicitly exclude such prisoners, the design and construction briefs documented concerns raised by prison staff that psychiatrically ill prisoners placed in Jika could self-harm and thus facilities such as a padded cell should be included in the design. The Director of Correctional Services stated that as there were facilities for psychiatric prisoners situated elsewhere in Pentridge, there would be no need to consider these in the designs for Jika because, 'the high-security unit is for prisoners considered as a major security risk – and not for the psychiatrically ill' (Challinger Report 1982: 4). However, as Challinger pointed out, it remained a problematic area, particularly given that those who posed a serious risk of violence 'may well be psychiatrically disturbed' (p 4). This was clearly also a point of confusion for the Director of Correctional Services who in 1982 characterised the Jika prisoner population as containing 'inmates with massive protection needs, disturbed and extremely anti-social inmates, psychopaths and major security risk prisoners' (p 16). Clearly, psychiatrically ill prisoners were being confined within Jika and this was cause for serious concern. The pressures arising from the sensory deprived environment and enforced social isolation could only serve to amplify their illnesses, rendering them increasingly vulnerable.

The case of remand prisoners being classified to Jika Jika posed an additional concern for Challinger. He stated the principle that 'unconvicted persons should be kept apart from convicted prisoners' was integral to United Nations Minimum Standard Rules for the Treatment of Prisoners (p 14). Despite the prison authorities stated commitment to adhere to UN Standards, a number of remand prisoners had been transferred in and out of Jika over the two-year period.

There was also a concern that prisoners were classified to Jika for 'conduct reasons' or because their behaviour constituted a management problem within other areas of the prison system (p 15). While Challinger was non-specific about the reasons for prisoner classification to Jika, the predominance of prisoner complaints that there was a lack of fairness, consistency and accountability in classification procedures suggest, there were problems (PRG 1988: 14-17). During this time female prisoners, who had been transferred to sections of Pentridge after the 1982 February protest fire at Fairlea Women's Prison, were classified to Jika for disciplinary infractions committed in Pentridge's B Annex (Russell 1998). Yet the transfer of prisoners for conduct reasons, and those loosely defined as constituting a 'management problem', directly undermined the official purpose of Jika as an institution for 'high-risk' prisoners. While the authorities maintained it was not the function of Jika to serve as a punishment section, it was becoming clear that the division was being used to contain difficult prisoners to maintain prison discipline..

The logistics behind official classification procedures and the functions of Jika's classificatory bodies are central to Challinger's concerns relating to the 'misuse' of Jika. They are also central to understanding later prisoner concerns regarding classification, a dominant grievance that led to the 1987 protest fire. The official classification procedures fell to two bodies that functioned in various divisions throughout the Victorian prison system. They were the Review and Assessment Committee (R&A) and the Divisional Classification Committee (DCC). It is noteworthy that these bodies were established in 1976, after numerous complaints by H Division prisoners about the arbitrary nature of classification decision-making procedures (Dillon Report 1978: 10). Official classification procedures and decisions were organised in the following manner.

The Jika R&A included the Governor of that Division, a Governor of the Metropolitan Prison, the Governor of Classification, the Assistant Supervisor of Classification, a psychologist, an educationalist, a welfare officer and 'sometimes' a Chief Prison Officer (CPO) (Inquest 1988-89b: 144). The R&A's essential role was to consider prisoner classification cases and make recommendations to the DCC regarding incoming prisoners as well as those considered for reclassification to the mainstream. Initially prisoners being considered for classification to Jika would be transferred to H Division pending further inquiry and assessment. If the incident in question was serious enough, the R&A would make a recommendation to send the prisoner to Jika. Once a prisoner was classified and transferred to Jika, the R&A would immediately review the prisoner's case on arrival. The Divisional Governor would then report to the R&A on how a prisoner was settling in. The standard practice in Jika was that all prisoner cases would come up for review on a quarterly basis. Remand prisoners were an exception to this rule and were reviewed on a weekly basis. Regular prisoners could 'apply' to see the R&A outside the quarterly review period if they were unhappy about their classification or wished to apply for further educational pursuits. The review process included an interview with the prisoner in question and a consideration of their case overall. Once the R&A made its assessment and recommendation, the case would go before the DCC.

The DCC was comprised of the Supervisor of Classification, the Associate Supervisor of Classification, a doctor, the Governor of Classification, an Aboriginal Welfare Officer, 'sometimes' a psychologist, and a Governor from a country prison (Inquest 1988-89b: 146). Taking into account the recommendations made by the R&A, the DCC would make a final assessment and recommendation. In order to make decisions to reclassify a prisoner both the R&A and DCC had to be sure that it was safe and appropriate to return prisoners to the mainstream. They needed to be satisfied that a prisoner no longer necessitated a high-security placement and ceased to pose 'a threat to security and the good order of the prison' (Inquest 1988-89a: 466). The R&A and DCC focused on a prisoner's conduct in Jika along with their overall prison history as essential considerations in the decision-making process of reclassification. They also referred to information prior to imprisonment 'if need be' and the primary offence for which prisoners were convicted (Inquest 1988-89a: 467). All records and minutes of R&A meetings were attached to a prisoner's file and retained for future consideration at the classification centre. It should be noted that regardless of R&A and DCC recommendations and decisions, the Governor of Jika had the power to authorise transfers and moves at his discretion. If a prisoner was considered by the authorities to be 'controversial' his case could be referred to the Director of Prisons for final approval (Inquest 1988-89a: 199). While it was not specified what exactly constituted a 'controversial' prisoner, it is assumed this included convicted violent offenders (particularly those who committed high-profile and especially violent crimes); prisoners who had been charged with violent offences while in prison; repeat escapees and those with records of bad behaviour and repeated failures to conform to the disciplinary regime; and prisoners known to be active in the pursuit of their legal rights or their involvement in protests while inside. 'Controversial' prisoners constituted a very large section of the Jika population.

The role, functions and fairness of classification in practice were subject to contest. The above overview based on official sources stands in stark contrast to prisoner complaints about R&A and the DCC. Classification procedures and prisoner grievances are subject to closer examination in Chapter Three.

The Physical Impact

While there had been much acclaim for Jika Jika's revolutionary electronic security solutions and space-age appearance, it was yet to be assessed how prison officers and prisoners would respond to the environmental constraints and conditions. In prefacing this aspect of his inquiry, Challinger praised some of the 'good' physical aspects of Jika. The windows allowed prisoners views from both the day room and cells. Challinger (1982: 17) further observed that the day room areas were characterised by generous space allocation and the concrete furniture, which had drawn some community criticism, was functional and economical. Perhaps the most praiseworthy aspect of Jika was the vegetated areas of the passive recreation yards, which allowed prisoners the opportunity to cultivate garden beds.

While Challinger recognised the architects had taken into account the negative aspects of Katingal in their designs, and the large windows did to an extent relieve the harsh conditions, he remained concerned that sensory deprivation was a dominating feature of the facility. This was confirmed by Challinger's reports that there was a general 'feeling of enclosure' in Jika and prisoners expressed they experienced the sensation of being 'buried in a tomb' or in 'some sort of submarine' (p 18). Prisoners complained that the electronically operated doors were dehumanising, and Challinger observed that the act of getting an officer's attention to open any particular door resulted in a damaging 'dependency' and 'loss of initiative' for prisoners.

Excessive noise comprised a source of frustration for prisoners. Due to the lack of soundproofing, the daily sounds of various activities and industries, televisions and radios permeated throughout the accommodation units making it difficult for prisoners to find silence. Furthermore, prisoners complained that any attempts to relax in their cells were thwarted by the grating 'four second hiss clunk' of the doors (p 18). Prisoners reported each door could be heard at all times and caused a major source of irritation.

Prisoners were highly critical of the exercise yards, which they referred to as 'the cage'. They felt that such a security measure was dehumanising and only necessary for housing 'terrorists' or 'prisoners of the future' (p 20). As Challinger commented:

> Some prisoners indicated that they often preferred to stay inside where they felt "sort of normal" rather than move into the strange world of the cage ... It is worth noting that neither the Special Security Block at Parkhust Prison or the segregation unit at Albany Prison in England have any protection from above in their exercise yards. And each of those houses most serious IRA terrorists. (p 20)

Aside from the controversial 'cage' like structure of the space frame, prisoners who enjoyed physical activities complained that the concrete floor of the exercise yards was inappropriate for activities such as running due to potential damage that could be done to leg joints when running on hard surfaces (p 20).

Prisoner Management, Placement and Privileges

Quality of meals was an additional grievance for prisoners. Having been prepared in the D Division kitchens in a trolley behind an electric truck, the meals had to be reheated within microwave ovens in the units and distributed to prisoners. It was reported that the several hunger strikes in Jika were a direct response to the poor quality of food. Prisoners informed Challinger that if they had not been given access to electric sandwich toasters along with provisions of bread, eggs, cheese and fruit, the food situation would have been intolerable (p 24).

Perhaps most difficult for prisoners was the fact that they were confined in the same unit with the same six men 24/7, their only escape to solitude being to stay in their cells. Prisoners often stated their preference for H Division because at the very least they could mix with a wider, more diverse group of prisoners. In Jika, even if prisoners got along, it was highly likely that general grievances and frustrations, compounded by the environment, would lead to conflict and in some cases violence. The situation was further exacerbated for protection prisoners who were housed within an entire unit devoted only to them.

When prisoners did develop stable groups these were often short-lived, as officers would need to somehow 'fit' another prisoner in. It was often the case that harmonious groups were disrupted or disbanded through the removal of one prisoner and the introduction of another (p 50). The arrival of a new personality disrupted activities and industry programs for other prisoners within the unit, straining prisoner relationships and intensifying frustration. Senior officers responsible for prisoner placement decisions often found it necessary, as a result of the above limitations, to confine incompatible prisoners together in Jika units until a better option arose. This inevitably led to the segregation of prisoners and the confinement of individual prisoners in their cells. Use of the day room had to be organised in shifts until more appropriate arrangements could be made. Sometimes entire units would be locked down completely as the risk of allowing such prisoners to mix far outweighed the benefits of communal activities held in the day room. Challinger noted that decisions about compatibility were critical as serious assaults using weapons such as homemade knives and scalding water, had been made by prisoners upon other prisoners (p 48).

The role of senior management staff and prison officers in the prevention of such incidents was critical to the smooth functioning of Jika. However, the apparent inexperience and lack of training among the 71 recruited officers resulted in the operation of Jika Jika by relatively 'junior staff' (p 6). This was remarkable considering the level of technology involved in running the facility. There were no procedures to assess how the new officers would cope and in a high-security unit such as Jika this was critical. The training programs specific to Jika were mostly 'security oriented', including riot control, the use of radios and batons, procedures in cell-searching and the operation of the enunciator, which was the electronic console in each unit from which the doors, power and all other facilities in the unit were operated by officers (p 6). Such training contributed to an acrimonious attitude among officers toward prisoners. As Challinger commented:

> This training undoubtedly gave Jika Jika officers, and "outside" officers certain expectations about the Division and its activities. In particular the totally security orientated nature of the training must have confirmed in many people's minds the notion that the Division was aimed at nothing more than rigorous containment. (p 6)

Lack of training and inexperience among officers also resulted in a number of security breaches and situations where doors were opened at the wrong time. For example, protection prisoners reported being placed in a situation where their cell door was opened at the same time as another cell or day room, leaving them in 'bodily fear' (p 6).

Within an institution that relied so heavily on the operation of remote-controlled doors, neither staff nor prisoners welcomed the event of malfunction. The Honeywell computer system operated as a 'fairly basic' device used to open and close doors in Jika. It also had a function that double-checked no two doors were ever open at the same time within any sections of Jika (p 21). However, the system had been known to malfunction before Jika was opened.

During simulated security tests, malfunctions occurred after the computer system went 'haywire' (*Australian* 17/2/87). Reportedly, a prison officer who participated in a simulation test posed as a prisoner and while he sat in a Jika cell thinking of ways to escape, the cell door burst open of its own accord (*Australian* 17/2/87). Challinger (1982: 21) also noted an occasion, in Unit 6, when doors everywhere began to open and close uncontrollably to the point where 19 doors were in alarm at once. Both prisoners and staff raised their reservations about such malfunctions occurring in units where prisoners were segregated for protection or in the event of emergencies such as fire. Disturbingly, there was limited technical support and no contingency plans in the event of serious malfunction. While there was a manual override key to be used if the system went down, it would take considerable time to manually open all doors in one unit, let alone the entirety of the Division. In addition, the software system was not tested regularly and there was no available duplicate package for reloading in the event of a system failure or collapse (p 22).

Aside from issues regarding the electronic doors, Challinger criticised the inadequacy of prison record keeping and the lack of communication between staff about prisoners (pp 44-5). He saw the maintenance of an intelligence network between officers and senior staff as critical in making prisoner placement decisions as well as keeping track of prisoner requests. On a fundamental level, such a flow of intelligence could prevent a suicide or a serious assault. As Challinger argued, a comprehensive record keeping system along with officer communication could equip staff to make informed decisions about prisoners throughout their daily duties.

A fight between prisoners Glen Davies and Edwin Eastwood in one of the passive recreation yards resulted in Davies' death in 1981. As the first death to occur in Jika Jika, the incident reinforced issues associated with the adequacy of prisoner officer training, communication and prisoner placement in Jika. Davies and Eastwood were confined together in Unit 5 in Jika despite the fact that an ongoing dispute between the two, originating from their time in H Division, was common knowledge among staff (Inquest 1982 'Victoria Police Homicide Brief' 30/4/81). Governor at the time Walter Tipping stated that while the two prisoners had initially been separated, both had provided assurances the feud was over. According to Tipping, Eastwood and Davies were known to him as particularly 'aggressive and troublesome prisoners' (Inquest 1982 'Statement Governor Walter Tipping' 30/4/81). Yet despite the risks senior staff made a placement decision that resulted in Davies' death.

The Davies incident signalled a period where problems began to accumulate and the optimism associated with the initial designs, construction and opening of the complex withered. Security was increased, resulting in the lockdown of units at 4.30pm (Inquest 1988-89a: 454). This was significant as the extended out of cell hours had been a feature of Jika's management program to counter the far-reaching effects of sensory deprivation. This was also partly the result of financial constraints and staff cuts (Inquest 1988-89a: 454). Behind closed doors during 1981 and 1982, department officials began quietly reconsidering whether a 'hands-free' approach to confining high-risk prisoners was having the desired effect (Inquest 1988-89a: 454). Part of the problem was a steady deterioration in prison officer and prisoner relationships. At the time of his report, Challinger (1982: 37) was understated in characterising the relationship between officers and prisoners as 'tolerant' rather than 'harmonious'. However, officials later acknowledged the extent of deterioration in relationships:

> Prisoner areas became what was known as "no go" areas. Prisoners existed on their side of the wall and officers worked on the other side and very seldom was there much association between the two groups. (Inquest 1988-89a: 455)

Overseas research suggests institutional separation of staff and prisoners teamed with the designation of prisoners as 'the worst' serves to dehumanise prisoners in the eyes of staff and give rise to negative attitudes, abuse and mistreatment (see Fellner & Mariner 1997: 47-59).[16] These conditions and tendencies are further

---

[16] This is further evidenced through the Stanford Prison Experiment, which demonstrated the potentially dehumanising and harmful consequences

magnified by the distinct lack of public scrutiny and exertions of unaccountable power associated with high-security regimes. In Jika Jika the physical separation between officers and prisoners contributed to an increasing sense of tension and polarisation. In one sense, prisoners were forced to cooperate with officers due to their ability to exert full control over prisoner movements throughout the unit. However, on another level the physical divides of the glass and doors made it easier for prisoners to refuse to comply with prison officer orders than if they were in H Division, where contact was face to face. Restrictive and harsh conditions further compounded frustration and resentment on both sides.

Challinger: The Absence of Adequate Programs and Useful Work for Prisoners

A philosophical cornerstone of the Jika Jika Security Unit was that prisoners be provided with constructive activities and useful work. Yet the inevitable prioritisation of security, teamed with the disciplinary objectives of senior staff, meant that these ideals did not necessarily translate into practice. The authorities appointed an activities officer who would devise and supervise a range of activities and 'diversions' for prisoners. However, from early on irreconcilable conflicts arose between the security and disciplinary objectives of Jika and prisoner rehabilitation. Officials prescribed that activities programs should 'ensure that prisoners do not deteriorate, but rather that their creative ability and skills may be fostered for the future', while also aiming to easier 'facilitate the task of managing and controlling prisoners' (Challinger Report 1982: 32). Clearly the activities officer was presented with a dilemma as he or she was expected to develop satisfying programs for prisoners to aid in their future rehabilitation, while at the same time prioritising prison security, discipline and order. The limitations inherent within such a balancing act and the restrictive security-driven environment were reflected in concerns raised by the activities officer. They reported blanket management policies

---

associated with institutional systems of control and unaccountable power structures (see Haney & Zimbardo 1998).

concerning prisoner compatibility and restrictions (for security reasons) on hobby equipment and materials were preventing the development of any ongoing hobby work, craft and industry. Endless difficulties and strains were placed on potential activities due to the Jika policy of 'absolute security'. Challinger also found that extended programs involving potential participation by outside community representatives were hindered by a combination of invasive security procedures and the lengthy time period it took to visit Jika (p 32).

The department argued numerous industries were made available for prisoners to do useful work: clothing manufacturing, brush-making, broom-making, boot-making, some hydroponics, screen-printing and some Braille work (Inquest 1988-89a: 453). Challinger pointed out however, that from the beginning there were issues associated with lack of work and a series of setbacks from which the Division's industries never recovered. Contrary to official representations Challinger reported that in the immediate period after Jika opened there was only work available for 12 out of 39 prisoners (Challinger Report 1982: 33).

Due to the inflexibility of the environment, cost cutting and the constraints stemming from security concerns, industry was made difficult and frustrating for prisoners. Officers on duty as overseers were rostered in small numbers and therefore stretched between the various units, making it difficult for them to assist prisoners. Industries such as shoe-making, tailoring and bookbinding were selected on the basis that equipment could be obtained for little cost, while prisoners would have to work individually on tasks. A further consideration was the portability of the equipment so that if a disturbance or emergency arose it could be quickly moved. However, even after the equipment was purchased many of the industries were short-lived. Bookbinding ceased due to security concerns stemming from the need to use chemicals and the manufacturing of seed boxes was also suspended due to prisoners using the hammers in attempts to damage windows (Challinger Report 1982: 34).

Prisoners became frustrated with these ongoing setbacks and limitations. In one instance, prisoners sabotaged shoemaking machinery resulting in the removal of the equipment. In another unit prisoners threatened to damage the brush-making machinery and refused to accept it with the accompanying noise and dust 'in a room with insufficient ventilation' (p 34). It was reported by overseers that prisoners appeared disinterested and refused to work while at the same time complaining about the lack of useful work. At the time of Challinger's inquiries, under half of Jika prisoners were engaged in work with laundry duties, the manufacturing of plastic pegs, clothes manufacturing, screen printing and Braille typing and the remainder of them were 'given whatever part-time scrap work can be found for them' (p 34). Throughout the 1980s, this work diminished. The department submitted that industry work in Jika was scaled down as a result of prisoner disinterest, sabotage and vandalism of equipment. The continual replacement of equipment was reported to have become a cost issue (Inquest 1988-89a: 456). Thus the anticipated fruitful industries, an essential component of Jika's successful functioning, were largely abandoned.

Challinger (1982: 33) stated given the 'type' of prisoners housed in Jika, enforced idleness could present future management problems not experienced in other sections of Pentridge. He noted prisoners reclassified to Jika were given the assurance before Jika opened that 'meaningful, productive full-time work would be made available to them' and such assurances were made in good faith. Challinger warned that:

> High standards of conduct and personal relationships will deteriorate quickly unless drastic action is taken to enable the proper employment of Jika Jika prisoners who were ... frustrated and making daily complaints about lack of work. (p 33)

From Jika Jika to K Division: Concealing Institutional Fractures

Between 1980 and 1982 counts of prisoner verbal abuse against officers in Jika far exceeded those in H Division. There was also a strong sense of prisoner distrust towards officers, based on their experience in H Division (Challinger Report 1982: 37). Prisoners felt that when they requested officers to open doors to go to their toilets or cells, they were ignored until officers chose to respond. They also reported officers listened in on prisoner conversations in the day room through a two-way intercom installed for officer/prisoner communication. There were also numerous allegations that prison officers read the private mail of prisoners when it was not their duty to do so.

Challinger (1982: 11) attributed malcontent among officers to 'tiredness' and a growing sense of 'boredom' with the 'monotony of unit work'. There was also frustration with the slow, painstaking security procedures associated with moving around. Low-ranking officers had to consult with senior staff about each and every issue arising, no matter how trivial, before making a decision. Jika officers were becoming increasingly detached from Pentridge, which led to views by other divisional staff that Jika Jika prison officers were elitist. According to Challinger, this was an additional factor contributing to the growing stigma surrounding Jika.

Dennis Challinger's report was not well received by officials. It was stated that while Challinger's ideals were 'good in theory', they were not as easy to implement due to a variety of 'practical concerns relating to the management of high-security prisoners' (Inquest 1988-89a: 457). Challinger's 1982 findings were not made public until the Victorian Prisoner's Action Group made a Freedom of Information request for the report in January 1987 (*Herald* 21/1/87). Many of the problems and concerns in Challinger's report foreshadowed the crisis to come.

In August 1984, Jika prisoner Barry Quinn was murdered when another prisoner doused him with craft glue and set him alight in the day room of Unit 2.[17] Quinn's murder attracted media attention and added to Jika Jika's mounting public image problem. As the second death to occur in Jika, the incident illustrated Challinger's concerns about the risks associated with fire in the electronic

---

[17] Unpublished transcript of proceedings at Coroner's investigation into the death of Barry Quinn, 1985, State Coroner's Office, Inquest Case No 1996/84 CR.

environment, and the ability of prison officers to respond promptly to Units in an emergency situation.

It was only a matter of weeks after Quinn's death that Minister for Community Welfare Services Pauline Toner announced that Jika Jika would be renamed K Division. Toner publicly stated that the name change was prompted by complaints from the local Indigenous community who had campaigned against the appropriated use of the tribal name for a prison (*Age* 17/8/84). While this may have been partly the case, this announcement also correlated with departmental attempts to counter the increasing public stigma associated with the name Jika Jika. The name change from Jika Jika to K Division signified a symbolic attempt to reintegrate Jika Jika with the remainder of Pentridge. Officials did not adequately deal with Challinger's report and recommendations openly nor did they address critical lessons arising from the deaths of Davies and Quinn. Officials changed the name of the institution, but Jika Jika in essence remained the same.

The so-called 'humane' aspects of Jika were inevitably and gradually eroded in the interests of 'tighter' security. In 1983 the authorities levelled the passive recreation yard gardens, covering them with concrete. This was a response to the successful escape by four prisoners and allegations that the garden beds were used to conceal contraband (Inquest 1988-89a: 448). Staff cuts, combined with increased security measures, translated into longer periods in cells for prisoners.

The Jika Jika High-Security Unit was devised as a direct official response to the breakdown in prisoner discipline during the 1970s. This breakdown in prisoner discipline was prevalent in both Australian and overseas prisons. Blueprints for Jika were based on overseas trends and new methods of psychological control including sensory deprivation, behavioural modification, social isolation, total surveillance and security. In spite of this and the early problems experienced, the authorities persevered in representing the institution as an efficient, secure, humane and above all necessary advancement in penal policy. Zdenkowski and Brown (1982: 148) point out that 'official practices and responses tend to be continually reproduced when administrations refuse to debate or challenge the objective features, which induce rebellion and then rely on such rebellion to invoke and justify a new draconian regime'. This vicious cycle points to the very contradiction embodied in Jika. As a result of the refusal to adequately address prisoner allegations of prison officer abuse and concerns about conditions during the 1970s, the authorities unwittingly created an even more oppressive and soul-destroying system than the antiquated H Division. Jika was a system devised to curb prisoner resistance, yet the institutional structures and management strategies actively induced prisoner frustrations and non-compliance. The event of resistance led to tighter security and discipline and more resistance, as the following chapters explore.

CHAPTER THREE

Contextualising Resistance: Prisoner Accounts of Power and Survival in the 'Pressure-Can'

Ex-Jika prisoner Peter Reed resisted the Jika system in numerous ways. During his confinement in Jika, Reed was on remand and not convicted of any crimes. As a remand prisoner he demanded his civilian clothing; he participated in hunger strikes and bronze-ups; he made formal complaints and lobbied for his rights; he continually appealed his classification and participated in a range of other tactics to survive the system. Reed took protests over his treatment in Jika to the courtroom during the 1988 trial over his alleged involvement in the 1986 Russell Street bombing.[18] During the trial Reed, Craig and Rodney Minogue all maintained their innocence over the bombing. On the first day of the trial Reed sat in the dock holding signs that stated, 'I am innocent', and 'Another Finch'. Reed was later acquitted of the bombing, but by this time Jika Jika had long been closed.

For Reed, resistance comprised a basic and unquestioned part of his daily survival in Jika. During our interview I asked him how he observed other prisoners to survive in Jika. He replied in a matter of fact tone, 'You have to be mad ... insane. You've got to be more

---

[18] On 27 March 1986, a bomb hidden in a stolen 1979 Holden Commodore was detonated outside the Russell St Police Headquarters Complex in Melbourne Victoria. The 'Russell Street bombing' caused considerable damage to the complex and surrounding buildings. Constable Angela Taylor was killed and 22 people were injured. The fatal bombing mobilised sensational media attention and public outrage, particularly in response to the death of Angela Taylor, who was at this time the first Victorian female police officer to die on duty. Such attention was maintained throughout the subsequent trial of accused Peter Reed, Stanley Taylor, Craig and Rodney Minogue.

insane or madder than those who are trying to control you, because they are the ones who are mad'. (P Reed Interview 15/5/04)

This chapter is concerned with prisoner accounts of life in Jika. Specifically, prisoner experiences of institutional power and management, and the alleged abuses inflicted by Jika staff are reconstructed and examined. Such conditions provide a context for prisoner non-compliance and the initiation of resistance campaigns in Jika during the 1980s. While previous discussions have focused on official rationalisations for the development of Jika, this chapter provides a subjective and unofficial account of the institution in practice based on available prisoner writings, complaints, letters, allegations and evidence given at inquests.

Traditionally, prisoners have resisted in many ways including self-education, letter writing, refusal to comply, hunger-strikes, sit-ins, riots, sieges, barricades and fires to name a few examples. Overall, acts of prisoner resistance are clouded by dominant, largely unsympathetic official representations that emphasise the dangerousness and individual pathologies of 'troublemaker' prisoners (Scraton et al 1991). As Scraton, Sim and Skidmore (1991: 63) state, the authorities, politicians or the media do not associate prison rebellion with meaningful behaviour:

> It is easily dismissed as 'mindless', 'drug induced,' or 'hysterical', thus negating any possibility that a prison 'riot' could be an expression of reason or a demonstration of desperate resistance.

Negative depictions of prisoner resistance are also used to direct attention away from conditions inside and fortify official calls for tighter disciplinary and security measures. Cohen and Taylor (1972: 129) comment that there is a popular sense of heroic romanticism associated with the plight of the 'political' prisoner of war who is allowed to fight back against his captors. Yet in stark comparison, the state prisoner who resists is by no means regarded as possessing qualities such as 'bravery' or 'character':

> Nor is he allowed anything like an acceptable set of motives – let alone an ideology – through which his behaviour could be comprehended ... When he tries to escape, goes on a hunger strike, makes a nuisance of himself by composing letters and

petitions, smuggles information out or refuses to accept the rules of the system, he is a "troublemaker" who "can't take his medicine". (Cohen & Taylor 1972: 130)

This point is relevant to prevailing official representations of resistance in Jika in the 1980s. However, it is also acknowledged that in addressing and documenting resistance, it would be incorrect to subscribe to rose-coloured romanticised images of collective solidarity. The Jika complex was filled with a disparate group of men and while there were defined groups who participated in transgressive activities both individually and collectively, many did not.

Most violence in prison cannot be unquestioningly characterised as resistance (Scraton et al 1991: 66-7). In Jika there were personality clashes, fractious arguments, petty disagreements, ongoing vendettas between prisoners and also between staff and prisoners, not to mention the frequent incidence of physical confrontation and violence. Jika was defined by a predatory, masculine culture of violence that is present in all male prisons. As discussed previously, violence and domination in prison must be understood not as a pathological manifestation of abnormal otherness, but as part of the normal routine which is sustained and legitimated by the wider culture of masculinity (Scraton et al 1991: 66-7; see also Sim 1994). As Sim argues, in prison socially instilled goals of male supremacy are enmeshed with the goals of the institution. In prison acts of violence and aggression are therefore acceptable vehicles of expression used to secure hierarchies and preserve individual dominance and male supremacy (Scraton et al 1991: 66-7; Sim 1994). Both prisoners and the state play a role in promulgating such values which has a formative impact on all relationships and aspects of institutional life.

As this chapter demonstrates, in Jika already existing conditions for violence were magnified by unaccountable power structures and the pressures created by the high-security regime and conditions. The manner in which violence between individual prisoners has been exploited by the authorities in both public and private contexts is also critical to understanding how violence is reinforced, institutionalised and represented in prison. As Scraton, Sim and Skidmore (1991: 67) argue:

> While the prison authorities denounce publicly the activities of a hard core of pathologically violent prisoners, their officers utilise privately the full potential of control which is rooted in their violence. This quite different expression of violence, which dominates interpersonal relations within prison, is also implicitly condoned, if not actively supported and exploited.

It was a common theme in prisoner accounts that behind the prison walls Jika officers actively encouraged, facilitated and utilised violence between prisoners as a means to intimidate, divide and control prisoners. However, when violence resulted in serious injury or death, officials reported incidents as evidence confirming the violent and dysfunctional identities of prisoners managed within and the need for tighter management and security. Thus, acknowledging the entrenched, complex nature of violent cultures, the role of penal power and how such conditions are magnified within high-security provides a more revealing picture of the institutional context in which certain prisoners existed and indeed resisted the Jika regime.

To comprehend the nature and form of prisoner resistance, it is critical to first examine how disciplinary power works to exacerbate resistance within the confines of high-security. This chapter therefore focuses on the prisoner experience within Jika and how such impressions stood in stark opposition to official assurances that Jika Jika was a secure, efficient and humane solution to housing high-risk prisoners. To consider acts of resistance in absence of this context would be to overlook the impact and experience of institutional power. It would result in the further discrediting and marginalisation of prisoner actions and representations, confirming simplistic and stigmatised images associated with criminality, violence, dangerousness and lack of social value. Most importantly, it is through the characterisation of prisoner acts of resistance out of context, as 'animalistic', 'mad', or 'violent', that attention is inevitably directed away from the violence associated with methods of institutional control and discipline in high-security, that Reed refers to as 'madness'.

Experiencing Power: Prisoner Accounts

Prisoner James Bazley was a high-security prisoner in Jika for 40 months from between 1983 and 1986. Even after his transfer, Bazley continued to write a series of monthly protest letters addressed to Attorney General Jim Kennan to draw attention to the 'harsh, brutalising, institutionalised torture' inflicted on prisoners in Jika. He stated, 'if I was to be asked the main difference between Jika and the infamous German concentration camps, I would say it is that there are no gas ovens in Jika' (*Telegraph* 24/11/87). He warned that if the authorities did not respond with decisive action, matters could deteriorate and serious trouble would be inevitable.

There is a marked disparity between the emerging prisoner accounts of life in Jika and the picture of institutional security and efficiency maintained by the authorities. Challinger's 1982 report represented an official attempt to document prisoner impressions of Jika. However, prisoner impressions and grievances were recorded after a relatively short time in the newly developed hi-tech environment, and therefore contrast considerably with later accounts. In addition, some favourable prisoner views of Jika were initially coloured by their time spent in H Division. As Jika prisoner John Dixon-Jenkins wrote:

> [I]f you were to see this place and look beyond the signs of very high-security that are everywhere, you would see a physical environment that looks better than any in any other part of Pentridge. This "humane" look belies the total insanity of what takes place in here. (Letter to Cliff Carrington 8/9/87 cited in *Bendigo Advertiser* 31/10/87 p 9)

Jika prisoners argued a variety of factors contributed to the creation of a 'pressure-can' environment. Overall, prisoners complained about the oppressive environment, the corrupt classification system, 'massive' abuses of power and 'mind games' played by prison staff (PRG 1988: 6). Prisoners also levelled allegations of officer misconduct and brutality. Ultimately prisoners expressed fear, desperation and frustration resulting from their alleged psychological abuse and intimidation by individual officers. Within this context, officers and prisoners became increasingly polarised. A culture of frustration, tension and fear built up and ultimately violence prevailed.

As discussed in Chapter Two, research and experimentation in the field of environmental psychology in the 1950s and 1960s documented the devastating impacts of extreme environments on humans. Noteworthy in this instance is Donald Hebb's famous 1951 sensory deprivation coffin experiment, which sought to document participant reactions of extreme anxiety and the onset of psychosis in response to the absence of sensory stimuli. Cohen and Taylor contend that experiences of long-term imprisonment remain starkly distinct from those of Hebb's subjects who had access to a 'panic button'. In this respect, Cohen and Taylor (1972: 47) argue that long-term prisoners experience a 'double deprivation' in so far as they endure the pains of imprisonment physically while being burdened with the knowledge that they will remain under such conditions for a lengthy period of time and there is nothing they can do. Such pains are again magnified for high-security prisoners who are held in extreme conditions for long and indefinite periods.

There are extensive prisoner reports, studies and clinical experience that document the detrimental effects associated with long-term periods of confinement in high-security and combined conditions of sensory deprivation and social isolation (see Haney 2003; see also Haney & Lynch 1997; Human Rights Watch 1999; Fellner & Mariner 1997).[19] In particular United States studies have drawn attention to the long-term debilitating effects of lock up, lack of privacy, the constant threat of brutality, ill-treatment, isolation, excessive noise, and sensory overload or deprivation associated with high-security confinement (Haney & Lynch 1997: 514). Haney and Lynch highlight that this research indicates it is not uncommon for long-term high-security prisoners to experience some or all of the following symptoms:

---

[19] For an appraisal of the effects of isolation and sensory deprivation associated with coercion, interrogation and political imprisonment see Physicians For Human Rights 2005: 60-1. For an Australian report in response to proposals to construct the Katingal Special Security Unit see Lucas 1976.

tension, irritability, sleeplessness, nightmares, inability to think clearly or to concentrate, and fear of impending loss of impulse control. Sometimes the anxiety is severe enough to be crippling. It interferes with sleep, concentration, work, and study and predisposes prisoners to brief psychotic reactions, suicidal behaviour ... it causes misperceptions and overreactions. It fuels the cycle of violence, leading to more violence and terror. (Study by forensic psychologist Dr Robert Slater in San Quentin Prison 1986, cited in Haney & Lynch 1997: 514)[20]

Physicians for Human Rights (2005: 60-1) also cite depression, anxiety, hypersensitivity to external stimuli, hallucinations, perceptual distortions, temporal and spatial disorientation, deficiencies in task performance, impaired motor coordination and paranoia. The long-term effects associated with such conditions have been likened to those experienced by survivors of torture (Haney 2003). In short there is extensive evidence confirming that sensory deprivation and social isolation can result in considerable psychic and physical pains for prisoners.

The above documentation of the harms and costs associated with high-security provide a vital context for prisoner impressions and reactive responses to the Jika regime. Most importantly these studies resonate with prisoner experiences of Jika throughout the 1980s and provide an insight into the acute experience of frustration, paranoia, fear and aggression that fed the spiralling institutional cycle of polarisation, violence and crisis.

Ex-prisoner Peter Reed argues that Jika was much worse than its predecessor H Division (P Reed Interview 15/5/04). While the disciplinary systems of both H Division and Jika sought to achieve full compliance, submission and control, through the systematic inculcation of fear and terror into prisoners, each subscribed to a different power play to achieve this. The authorities had used physical brutality to achieve compliance and submission in H Division. However, in Jika the nature of the power play changed

---

[20] According to Haney and Lynch, Slater was a former employee for the California Department of Corrections and was by no means sympathetic in any way to prisoners, nor was he readily convinced about the authenticity of 'prison-related syndromes'.

dramatically and prisoners were pressured into compliance via psychological methods of discipline and control. According to Reed, prisoners had become accustomed to H Division and knew what to expect when transferred there; that they would be subjected to a reception biff and then confined to an old bluestone cell. Reed stated that in H Division, prison officers could brutalise the 'toughest crim' but he could still survive because he retained control of his mind. In contrast, the strategies of the Jika disciplinary system focused on the prisoner's mind rather than the body and Reed believed that if the authorities 'can control your mind and abuse you mentally and break you that way, they don't need to abuse you physically' (P Reed Interview 15/5/04). Bazley commented that, 'in "the slot" [H Division] they might and probably would, knock you down occasionally, but it was preferable somehow. You were still a human being, not a goldfish, or a monkey strapped on a table for an experiment' (*Telegraph* 24/11/87).

For this reason conditions in Jika were a featured concern among prisoners. Like Bazley, Reed reflects that after his initial reception into the Division he felt as though he'd joined a concentration camp (P Reed Interview 15/5/04). He states that in Jika prisoners were surrounded by concrete:

> I know in the exercise yards, the caged ones, there used to be weeds growing between the crevices of the walls. We used to water those. Prison officers didn't like those, so they terminated or killed those plants. I call it a plant, it might be a weed to somebody else, but it was still a plant. To actually not be able to walk on grass or to feel grass ... your environment was totally controlled. (P Reed Interview 15/5/04)

Prisoners complained they were sometimes confined for more than 22 hours a day within the oppressive, controlled air-conditioned atmosphere with the same five to six prisoners. One anonymous prisoner stated, 'the problem that we are forced to endure is the psychological pressure of day to day living in this artificial environment. The psychological damage that is happening to prisoners in Jika is more intense than anywhere else in the prison system' (PRG 1988: 6).

Staff shortages, cost cutting and massive security breaches by prisoners, such as the 1983 escape, resulted in the further tightening of security. This translated into longer periods spent in cells. The corresponding psychological strain exacerbated by the conditions became too much for many prisoners. In 1986, prisoner Robert Wright wrote a formal letter of complaint stating:

> The units within Jika Jika are virtual echo chambers, as the minutest noise reverberates ... In the cells at night, one is able to hear the other prisoners using their toilets, flushing them, watching their television, even turning in their beds ... A degree of animosity will build up ... violence can and does erupt ... People such as yourself would never realise or understand the stress this place gives after a period ... you can find no way anywhere in the unit to escape all of this. (*Age* 29/7/89 p 27)

Prisoners complained matters were made worse by the fact they were given little work and had few activities to occupy their time. One prisoner claimed that prisoners in his unit put a proposal forward to the Governor that they be given a small wage in return for a thorough scrubbing of their unit (PRG 1988: 19). The Governor rejected the proposal and the prisoners scrubbed the windows and bars out of sheer want of something to do. The same prisoner warned forebodingly, 'the old adage applies here somewhere, "idle hands are the devil's playground". We can't even get a tennis ball to play with' (PRG 1988: 19).

Ongoing prisoner idleness, the tedium of the institutional routine and artificial conditions produced a psychologically surreal and damaging experience for prisoners. Prisoner Wayne King complained that due to the daily monotony of Jika, one day blended into the next; 'you'd spend the day in the day room reading newspapers or playing one of the two games on the computer. The cells are all open and we're free to go in and out. We are let into the exercise yard for maybe half an hour a day (sometimes less)'. Prisoner King characterised his time in Jika as 'a bad dream'; a 'mad experience' (Inquest 1988-89a 'Statement by prisoner Wayne King' 3/11/87). Such sentiments were common amongst Jika prisoners and particularly ex-prisoners who reported the negative effects stemming from their time in Jika. Ex-prisoner Maurie Dowdle reported during a press interview in 1987 after leaving Jika, he wished he 'could take off his head and rinse it under a tap ... after two years in Jika I have lost reality. I don't care about anyone or anything' (*Sun* 31/10/87 p 10).

Jika Jika: The 'Mind Games Capital of Pentridge'

Peter Reed commented that memories of his time in Jika remain vivid due to the fact there was an incident or disturbance every day (P Reed Interview 15/5/04). Jika Prisoners claimed that such occurrences were often fuelled by the psychological power play exercised by officers over prisoners to antagonise and provoke. More specifically, prisoners alleged that prison officers entertained themselves and exercised their control through the use of psychological 'mind games' (P Reed Interview 15/5/04). When giving evidence during 1989, prisoner Craig Minogue stated:

> Jika Jika was the mind games capital of Pentridge ... if any single thing could be done to frustrate, annoy, humiliate, degrade a prisoner, it was done. If you wanted a toilet roll, well 'five minutes', if you wanted a bar of soap, 'five minutes' ... anything they could fuck you around with they did. (Inquest 1988-89b: 689)

It was commonly asserted that when asked to open the remote controlled doors so prisoners could access the toilet or go to their cell, officers would either flatly refuse or delay the request as much as possible. Minogue further stated that:

> Of course, all these things generate some amusement for the prison officers in the spine of the units ... To leave the day room, you had to push a button in the day room ... they would just look up and then just look back and continue reading the paper. You'd press the button again and they'd wave to you or say 'five minutes', you know, and they'd be sitting probably five, six feet away from the control. This might not seem like a big thing, but in an environment like Jika it was definitely amplified. (Inquest 1988-89b: 688-9)

Remand prisoner Michael Dimitrovski commented that often during the day, when prisoners were engaged in activities, the unit doors slammed shut unexpectedly, trapping prisoners in their cells or in the day room for long periods of time. He referred to this as 'sneak-ellis' and was unsure whether the doors closed due to a mechanical malfunction or officers 'playing games' from the control spine. According to Dimitrovski this unexplained imposed 'lockdown' happened 'just about every day' he was in Jika (Inquest 1988-89a: 2005).

Prisoner Richard Light stated that it was often the case that if an officer refused to open the door for a prisoner to go to the toilet, they would eventually have no choice but to urinate on the day room floor in front of other prisoners. Additionally, Light complained, it was often impossible for prisoners to get time in the exercise yards, maximising their frustration at the amount of time spent in controlled conditions. According to Light, officers reportedly played on these frustrations by escorting prisoners as far as the yard airlock and then returning them to their cells (Inquest 1988-89a 'Undated notes and complaints by prisoner Richard Light'). Peter Reed also complained of this, stating that even when it was raining he was still desperate to get into the fresh air:

> There was no natural air going through there at all, and again that's why it was very important to have your one hour in that fresh air, even when it used to be raining or pissing down with rain I'd still want to get out there. Didn't care … it was rain! It was that fresh air. (P Reed Interview 15/5/04)

Prisoners also alleged that officers 'played' with the controls at the control panel for their own amusement. Light claimed certain prison officers toyed with the air-conditioning and heating so that during the summer the heating would be turned up while in winter prisoners were constantly ill with colds because the air-conditioning was on all the time. Prisoner Light also contended that prison officers sought to frustrate prisoners by interfering with the power supply to the day room. For example, if a prisoner turned on the television, the officers would turn the power off; if a prisoner began to cook toast, the power would go off (Inquest 1988-89a 'Undated notes and complaints by prisoner Richard Light'). Olaf Dietrich also complained that the power was turned off for extended periods and on one particular occasion in Unit 2 prisoners were deprived of power for nine days (Inquest 1988-89a: 2198).

Each unit was lit by bright fluorescent tubing and it was reported by Craig Minogue there were times where officers repeatedly switched the lights on and off for periods up to 10 minutes. He commented, 'Just little things like that sound petty ... but when you're in a situation like Jika, the situation becomes quite serious' (Inquest 1988-89a: 1132).

It was also complained that the hot water supply was turned off for long periods, leaving prisoners with cold water to shower and wash with.[21] Prisoner Sean Downie's wife Sally Downie raised her concern that Downie became highly aggressive and paranoid about Jika officers playing 'mind games' with prisoners. Downie allegedly complained to her that throughout the evenings prisoners could hear water running while they were trying to sleep and when they awoke to have their morning shower the water would be cold as if it had been done on purpose (Inquest 1988-89b: 16).

It was alleged that officers used food as an additional avenue to frustrate and provoke prisoners. Reed indicated that during his initial stay in Jika his meals were served containing all kinds of foreign objects. He stated:

> You're being fed your meal through a gap in the wall of, in the old scale about ten by eight inches. And you realise what you're eating isn't what's supposed to be what. Finding match heads, cigarette butts, sometimes like in a stew the meat or the stew itself will be like chewing gravel and when you examine that it was the sweepings off the floor. (P Reed Interview 15/5/04)

Reed attempted to avoid this by going on to a salad diet, because these meals were covered with plastic. However, he soon discovered this was by no means a deterrent and was consequently forced to use his monthly spend to purchase tinned and packaged foods from the prison canteen in order to feed himself (pers. comm. Bree Carlton & Peter Reed 24/8/02). Prisoner Olaf Dietrich stated that the problem of foreign objects in food was so frequent that prisoners rarely ate it and often it went straight in the bin, 'save the cakes or the bread', and prisoners would live on the 'canteen', which often entailed purchasing canned food such as fish and fruit (Inquest 1988-89a: 2158). An anonymous prisoner also complained

---

[21] Unpublished transcript of proceedings at Coroner's investigation into the death of John Williams, 1988, State Coroner's Office (hereafter 'Inquest 1988'), Unit 85 'Statement Peter Reed' 6/3/88.

that while in Jika he had seen prison officers eat prisoner meals, resulting in the prisoner receiving less (PRG 1988: 6).

In a more controversial example, the exercise of behavioural control over prisoners was alleged to have extended to the involuntary administration of drugs by prison staff. Craig Minogue made these allegations public during the fire inquest in 1988, stating his belief that prison officers drugged the food and milk of prisoners (*Herald* 5/12/88). Minogue reported that the drugs had the effect of making prisoners sleepy and feeling like they had a hangover. He told the coroner that because of the paranoia experienced by prisoners in Jika they did regular checks and dissected milk cartons and it was not unusual to find penetration holes (*Herald* 5/12/88).

The adequacy of medical care was an additional concern cited by Jika prisoners. It was alleged that when a health problem was reported medical attention was often deficient and in many cases delayed arbitrarily (P Reed Interview 15/5/04). Prisoners perceived such instances as an extension of the mind games administered by Jika officers, but with serious and potentially fatal consequences. For Peter Reed, such treatment led to long-term health consequences. During his apprehension and arrest by police, Reed sustained gunshot injuries and was therefore in a poor state of health when received on remand into Jika. In spite of this, Reed did not receive consistent or adequate medical attention. While physiotherapy had been prescribed as crucial to his full recovery, his appointments (scheduled within the prison) were frequently cancelled for seemingly spurious reasons such as insufficient staff on duty or security concerns. For Reed this lack of care resulted in long-term and continuing physical damage, pain and suffering (P Reed Interview 15/5/04).

Questions surrounding the immediacy and quality of medical care were also canvassed at the inquest investigations into the deaths of Sean Downie, John Williams and the Jika five (Inquest 1988 'Prisoner Statements' 10/9/87-12/3/88; see Inquest 1988-89a: Units 68-79; Inquest 1988-89b: Units 64-7). In the case of Williams, prisoners alleged the prison medical support officer (PMSO) on duty the night Williams died failed to investigate the prisoner's lack of response while administering treatments. Assuming he was asleep or 'high' the PMSO swore and abused Williams, leaving him unconscious in his cell where he subsequently died (P Reed Interview 15/5/04).

Prison officer mind games greatly affected the ability of prisoners to communicate with the outside world and this particularly involved prisoner access to personal mail and all visits to the division. Bazley alleged that it was not often that he would get mail, but when he did there were instances where officers would show it to him through the unit window, open and read, then laugh and show it to other officers (*Telegraph* 24/11/87). Outgoing mail was sometimes delayed up to two weeks after being sent: Craig Minogue reported that on one occasion he posted two letters on the same day and prison officers opened and swapped the envelopes resulting in the letters being sent to the wrong recipients (Inquest 1988-89a: 1132).

One of the most difficult challenges for Jika prisoners was their limited ability to maintain relationships with family, friends and loved ones while inside. While such an experience is common for prisoners across the board, it was further magnified for Jika prisoners who were subject to time-consuming and restrictive security stipulations. Families and friends of Jika prisoners commonly complained that when visiting the process was time-consuming and staff made things unnecessarily difficult. Sally Downie stated that on an average visit, from the time that she parked the car, until the time she got back outside the gate, it would take between two and two and a half hours (Inquest 1988-89b: 31). The actual time of the visit was on average 20 minutes and sometimes 'if you were lucky' visitors got an hour. Matters were made more difficult for Sally Downie because she had a baby. Due to security regulations she was prohibited from taking in clean nappies or any toys and books to amuse her son during the visit. She felt the staff were hostile toward her and would give dirty looks if the baby held the process up. She also complained that she was forced to make appointments at inappropriate times and that staff seemed to hold the attitude that if things were made 'uncomfortable and difficult enough you'll stop coming' (Inquest 1988-89b: 14).

The process for visits required prisoners to make an appointment and have visits approved by senior prison staff in advance. The details of the visit were recorded on a card and were forwarded to the visitor who was required to present the card on the day of the visit. Sally Downie reported that when she fronted for a pre-arranged visit two days before her husband's death, prison staff denied any knowledge of the visit and turned her away at the gates on the basis that she did not have her card (Inquest 1988-89b: 14). Distressed in hindsight that she was denied a last opportunity to see her husband, Sally Downie stated that on previous occasions sympathetic staff had allowed her to visit without the card.

In Jika it was a security requirement that officers supervise visits. Prisoners complained this was a violation of privacy affecting their ability to talk intimately with loved ones:

> The two screws sit right at the door, about four feet away, and just stare at you and listen to everything that is said. I get up to the visit and I can't concentrate. I can't communicate ... They [the screws] are the cause of relationships failing. And it's hard for the visitors to understand why we can't communicate properly. (PRG 1988: 8)

Sally Downie gave evidence that during her visits to Jika, Sean Downie became increasingly aggressive and paranoid. He believed that 'you couldn't trust anybody and you didn't say anything that they would listen to everything that you said' (Inquest 1988-89b: 16). This experience of paranoia was common among many Jika prisoners. One prisoner stated he found the process of visits so invasive and distressing that he refused to have them (PRG 1988: 8).

Prisoners believed that the mind games played by prison officers were used to deliberately push them to a point where they would react with abuse, threats or even violence. Prisoners who reacted in this way were immediately reported and charged or, for smaller infractions, had their names recorded in the 'black book' (PRG 1988: 8). Once a prisoner received four recordings in the black book he automatically lost his visits and phone calls for the next month. Prisoners complained that they were frequently recorded in the black book for mostly minor things. For example, one prisoner reported that, due to illness an outside doctor was brought in. Sedatives were issued and the prisoner was advised to rest in bed the following day. When the prison officers did the morning muster, they demanded to know why the prisoner was still in bed and despite his explanation he was recorded in the black book for breaching muster regulations. This resulted in the suspension of the prisoner's visits and phone calls for a month (PRG 1988: 10).

Staff and prison officials denied allegations that mind games took place. Jika Governor Herron stated he felt prisoners used the charge of mind games only when they were angered or upset at having been deprived of something they wanted (Inquest 1988-89a: 198). Supervisor of Classification Michael Ryan believed that the phenomenon of mind games constituted what prisoners 'imagined' as a type of psychological warfare (Inquest 1988-89a: 517). He maintained it was impossible for officers to control the air-conditioning as they would need to go beneath the floors of Jika to do so and then they would be placing themselves in a position of discomfort. In spite of official denials, some ex-prison staff alleged there was a group of younger officers recruited to Jika who often indulged in mind games. Former officer Ian Wright commented that 'six young stirrers' let the power go to their heads and tormented prisoners by playing with the air-conditioning and refusing prisoner requests, among other things (*Border Morning Mail* 21/3/89; see also *Advertiser* 21/3/89).

In many ways, prisoner accounts of mind games in Jika reflected the experimental push toward the implementation of behavioural modification and adjustment programs in United States and United Kingdom prisons during the 1960s. Such techniques were the subject of discussion at a 1962 seminar for prison officials and staff sponsored by the Federal Bureau of Prisons in Washington. Notable expert Dr Edgar Schein, Associate Professor of Psychology from the Massachusetts Institute of Technology, gave a paper titled 'Man against man: brainwashing', wherein he advocated techniques used in prisoner of war camps in North Korea during the 1950s. These included a systematic weakening and dislocation of close emotional ties; the segregation of 'natural leaders'; the punishment of prisoners who demonstrated uncooperative attitudes; the systematic withholding of all mail; preventing prisoners from writing home or to friends in the community regarding conditions of confinement; and, most important, 'placing individuals into new and ambiguous situations for which the standards are kept deliberately unclear and thus putting pressure on them to conform to what is desired in order to win favour and a reprieve from pressure' (Fitzgerald 1977: 64). Mike Fitzgerald notes that the implication behind such research was that these strategies would be appropriate for domestic prison systems. As discussed in Chapter Two, the subsequent effect was that they were in various forms implemented, particularly within high-security and control unit prisons in the United States and the United Kingdom during a time when prison authorities were experiencing significant problems associated with increases in prisoner politicisation and rebellion. Given the emphasis on overseas research and trends reflected in design briefs, it is highly likely such thinking had an impact on the development of disciplinary practices in Jika.

The practice of mind games in Jika magnified the negative impacts of restrictive conditions, exacerbated the deterioration of institutional relationships and fuelled the onset of conflict and violence. Such practices were experienced by prisoners as a form of psychological coercion, harassment and at times, terror. Prisoner allegations were nonetheless dismissed by officials as petty, non-existent or a product of prisoner paranoia. Contrary to official rationalisations, the above mind games represented a form of power play inextricably linked to strategies of control in high-security generally. While not strictly publicly countenanced, the exposure of state-inflicted abuse and misconduct in high-security is often disregarded or normalised on the basis of the dangerous and violent prisoner identities confined within. Moreover, when prisoner allegations are vindicated, such instances are attributed to individual officers or 'bad apples' who have acted outside official orders and institutional codes of practice. Such representations reflect a limited understanding of the embedded relationship between power structures and systemic violence in prison. As Joe Sim (1994: 108) suggests, in order to understand the mobilisation of violence and its intrinsic relationship to strategies of domination and subjugation, it is crucial to transcend commonsensical, state defined explanations which have focused on the role of inadequate individuals, psychopathic personalities and 'bad apples'.

The Sensation of 'Being Buried Alive': 'R&A' and Classification

It is noteworthy that many complaints by Jika prisoners with respect to the classification process, the role of the Review and Assessment Committee (R&A) and the Divisional Classification Committee (DCC) in Jika, reflected similar complaints about classification by H Division prisoners during the 1970s. It is an irony that such bodies and procedures were implemented as official responses to complaints about the arbitrary nature of the classification system in H Division.

As discussed in the previous chapter, the practice of segregating and classifying prisoners based on their perceived 'security risk' was initially devised and recommended by Mountbatten as a response to a series of high profile security breaches and escapes in British prisons during the 1960s (Fitzgerald 1977: 49). However, as the British experience suggests, its adoption quickly became problematic. Scraton, Sim and Skidmore (1991: 14) highlight that it became 'a contributory factor in the very problem it was designed to solve'. From a prisoner perspective, the very processes of classification brought contradictions that inevitably caused frustration and resulted in conflict. A central issue was the lack of provision for a prisoner to appeal and challenge his classification and his non-specific 'designation as a troublemaker' (Fitzgerald 1977: 52). This uncertainty is clearly linked to behavioural modification and control strategies in high-security that sought to instil compliance by placing prisoners in unclear and ambiguous situations. A key issue was that prisoners had no clear explanation as to why they had been classified to high-security, no consistent ground on which they could build a case for their reclassification and no certainty about how long they would remain

114

there. For these very reasons classification grievances comprised an ongoing source of tension and dispute between Jika prisoners and the authorities.

Jika Prisoners complained the R&A and DCC demonstrated a total lack of accountability, fairness and consistency. Prisoners argued these were powerful bodies operating with the primary objective of keeping long-term prisoners and those deemed 'controversial' in Jika for as long as possible. Prisoners reported they were frustrated by the impossibility of obtaining specific information regarding their classification status. They objected to the fact that they were denied access to their own classification files and to any verbatim accounts and minutes of R&A meetings (PRG 1988: 14-15). Moreover, prisoners were frequently disconcerted when, prior to a classification review, they were given hopeful advice regarding a possible transfer, only to be informed by the DCC that such a decision had been overturned and they would be considered again, good behaviour pending, in another six months.

Immediately after their reception, prisoners were informed, depending on their individual case, why they had been transferred to Jika. Prisoners complained that they were given little explanation and were often simply told they were classified under 'security', 'management' or 'suspicion'. With the exception of prisoners classified as 'protection', these were the three major categories used by the authorities during this time. The official classification category of 'security' applied to prisoners who had a history of escape and attempted escape within the prison system. 'Security' also applied to any prisoner 'felt [by the authorities] to be such a risk that they were a potential escapee' (Inquest 1988-89a: 10). The classification of 'management' was applied to any prisoner 'who will not conform with the system, who could be rebellious, who could incite other prisoners to go against the system, and generally cause problems to the management of the prison' (Inquest 1988-89a: 10). Prisoners charged with violent offences in other Divisions or who had allegations of violence made against them also came under the category 'management'. A further controversial classification category was 'suspicion'. Craig Minogue noted that when prisoners were transferred under this category, they were never given the 'opportunity to ascertain what the suspicion related to'. The implications of this were that if, for example, the authorities or staff suspected a prisoner's involvement in a conspiracy to escape or any activities that in their view threatened the good order of the prison, the prisoner could be transferred to Jika as a precautionary measure. Minogue also raised concern that there were instances where other prisoners would make unsubstantiated allegations resulting in another prisoner's transfer to Jika, and the classification bodies made no subsequent attempts to get 'both sides of the story' (Inquest 1988-89a 'Statement and further notes by Craig Minogue' 7/7/88). These specified categories allowed for broad interpretation by the authorities and many prisoners reported they could ascertain no justified reason for their transfer to Jika.

Prisoner Olaf Dietrich was transferred to H Division and then Jika after he had allegedly suffered a mental breakdown in the remand section of Pentridge where he destroyed his cell (Inquest 1988-89a: 2151). After allegedly receiving a beating from prison officers in H Division, he reported he was transferred to Jika Jika without any explanation. He stated he was at this time, 'a remand prisoner with no record of assault or even attempts, after all these events, I have never even raised a hand to these officers'. He demanded a formal explanation stating, 'please don't respond with a simple title of "management" ... please advise me, I am not a dangerous person and I am being put into a soul/mind destroying position' (Inquest 1988-89a 'Statement by prisoner Olaf Dietrich' 12/8/88).

Peter Reed referred to the frustrating and 'no-win' situation of classification in Jika and the prevalence of mind games within the classification and R&A process (P Reed Interview 15/5/04). The meetings were very brief, and if prisoners weren't 'bright enough, or astute enough to respond at the spur of the moment', they would find themselves stuck in Jika for a further three months. According to Reed, the R&A committee's standard line was 'we'll see you in three months time' (P Reed Interview 15/5/04). The categories of 'security' and 'management' were difficult to define and were open to official interpretation and subject to change. In Reed's own case he was initially classified to Jika under 'security'. Because R&A meetings were held every three months he consulted with his solicitor to build a case for his reclassification. However, when he attended the next meeting, he was informed his classification had changed to 'management', and so he had to go away and for the next three months prepare an appeal on the basis of 'management'. He stated:

> So you'd go away and you'd study that security reason and you'd write it all down and everything else so it was virtually bullet proof, then you would go in there and hit them with that three months that you've had to prepare your next case against them in relation to "security". They will then change from "security", your classification, to "management". Then you're put back in the same boat. You've got to then come up with the answers, hit them with whatever you can in relation to management. And again, that opens the Pandora's box because what does "management" mean? (P Reed Interview 15/5/04)

Reed noted that this process would go 'from three months to three months to three months' until suddenly a prisoner would realise they had been in Jika for 18 months.

Obtaining information regarding prisoner classification cases was a key issue for prisoners. If they wanted to appeal a classification decision they were required to await their review, working through the procedures of the R&A committee. Prisoners reported that the R&A and DCC denied them the right to access their classification files. Such access was critical for prisoners, as the absence of information used for the basis of recommendations and decisions by the R&A and DCC made the task of building an appeal case impossible. In 1987 a number of prisoners made formal Freedom of Information (FOI) requests to gain access to their files. Once the files were obtained prisoners expressed outrage at the fact that the R&A and DCC appeared to fabricate reports on prisoners (PRG 1988: 15). It was claimed that in the event that an officer or another prisoner had made allegations, these were placed on a prisoner's file. It was claimed there were instances where allegations were recorded without any formal investigation. In these circumstances such allegations informed decisions put forward by the R&A and DCC, regardless of the fact that prisoners had not been officially charged or given an opportunity to defend themselves (Inquest 1988-89a 'Statement and further notes by Craig Minogue' 7/7/88). One prisoner stated with respect to his file that:

> There are incidents recorded on my classo file (assaults on screws etc.) that I have never been charged with or investigated about. Allegations made against you by another prisoner or screw are a lot of the time placed on your file and treated as fact. The disturbing part is that you're never told of these allegations or given the chance to reply to them and have their validity tested. (PRG 1988: 14)

According to the FOI documents received by prisoners, the minutes of R&A meetings were selective in what had been recorded, while prisoner complaints were distorted and at times completely excluded. One prisoner claimed his complaints were listed as 'came before the committee and expressed bitterness' (PRG 1988: 14). Furthermore, prisoners claimed that the R&A and DCC had been known to take into consideration, when making recommendations about prisoner placements, charges on which they had been acquitted by judges in a court of law; '[they] tell us they don't recognise court decisions. They omit these statements from their recordings of meetings' (PRG 1988: 14). It was also found that prisoner complaints directed to the Minister for the Office of Corrections were also attached to some prisoner files. Prisoners believed that if the DCC was informed of prisoner complaints made specifically about classification this exposure could effectively leave them open to retribution by the DCC with respect to their cases. From this stemmed a strong concern that prisoners would feel intimidated and 'scared to lodge complaints' (PRG 1988: 16).

Several prisoners argued that their transfer to Jika was political and they remained classified to that Division due to their involvement in protest action inside. Such suspicions were not surprising. Zdenkowski and Brown (1982: 148) observe that 'prison activists attract an increasingly "dissident" classification and are subjected to a range of disciplinary practices, punishments and segregation aimed at neutralising their capacity to communicate and organise'. Prisoner Arthur Gallagher was involved in an ongoing dispute with the authorities over his classification case. He strongly believed that his inability to get out of Jika stemmed directly from his political involvement and engagement in protests while inside. Gallagher was considered by the authorities to be a 'controversial prisoner' and subsequently his case went above any recommendations made by the R&A and DCC to be considered by the Director-General. Governor Penter commented that Gallagher 'perceived' his political affiliations and activities served as driving justifications for his inability to get reclassified. While Penter admitted such affiliations could have constituted the reason why Gallagher's case was taken above the R&A and DCC, he would not openly admit this was the case (Inquest 1988-89a: 199).

With respect to the classification process, prisoners felt there was no accountability and that regulations were inconsistent and subject to interpretation. Craig Minogue stated 'it was almost as if the DCC decided to keep Jika Jika full to justify its ongoing existence' (Inquest 1988-89a 'Statement and further notes by Craig Minogue' 7/7/88). Some prisoners argued the very crux of Jika's problems rested with the classification system and they compiled a series of demands, later publicised through the Prison Reform Group *Doing Time Magazine*, that in their view would alleviate a large majority of Jika's problems (PRG 1988: 16). Among these were demands that all court decisions should be heeded by the DCC; charges laid against a prisoner on which they have been acquitted must not be used against them; all allegations made against a prisoner must be put to the prisoner and he be given a chance to answer them; should the allegations remain unsubstantiated they should not be entered on to his file; everything that is said at all R&A meetings should be taken down on transcript verbatim and prisoners should have access to a record of all transcripts; meetings should also be recorded; and independent representatives such as a non-prison employed doctor, psychiatrist or solicitor should be placed on the classification board for the purpose of increasing accountability. Prisoners argued that, given the long-term adverse effects of a sentence in high-security, legal limitations should be imposed on the maximum amount of time a prisoner could spend in Jika (PRG 1988: 16). This last demand served as a direct reference to prisoner Robert Wright, who at the time of his death in 1987 was the longest serving prisoner in Jika, having been confined there

119

since 1980. He had staged ongoing protests and disturbances with respect to his case and had along with other prisoners accumulated a lengthy conduct record over this period.

For many prisoners, keeping a clear conduct record while in Jika was impossible. Prisoners claimed this stemmed primarily from the fact that the divisional rules and regulations were inconsistent and subject to interpretation by administrators (PRG 1988: 5). This meant that rules could change from day to day, making it easier for prisoners to be charged. From the perspective of prisoners, such arbitrariness served as another example of mind games by staff and officials. Furthermore it was argued that staff and management used inconsistency and changeability as a form of power play upon prisoners, as if to provoke them so they then could charge them. As stated above, a prisoner's case for reclassification could be jeopardised by minor breaches of discipline. Overall prisoners indicted the disciplinary system within Jika as it appeared to function with the primary objective of keeping prisoners there.

Exerting Physical Power and Discipline in the Jika Regime: Cultures of Violence and Prisoner Allegations

Prisoners reported mind games were a daily reality in Jika and formed the basis for the struggle between prison officers and prisoners. Peter Reed contended that mind games comprised a psychological strategy aimed at breaking and provoking prisoners. He stated in hindsight, 'if you were paranoid, they made you super-paranoid and I suppose if you got super-paranoid would you be waiting for something to hit you over the head or would you do it first?' (P Reed Interview 15/5/04)

As stated previously, one of the earlier justifications for Jika focused on the objective of alleviating the alleged instances of brutality that marred the reputation of H Division in the Jenkinson Inquiry. The designers envisaged that through the physical separation of prison officers and prisoners, the safety of both parties could be ensured and violence prevented. Despite this, prisoner accounts suggested Jika had done very little to prevent the use of excessive and unacceptable force by prison officers or violence between prisoners. Disturbingly, prisoner allegations suggested that a renewed culture of violence had enveloped Jika. In early 1987 the Victorian Prisoners Action Group vindicated these claims when spokesperson Jeff Lapidos publicised statistics obtained through Freedom of Information from the Office of Corrections confirming that during 1985-1987 there had been 2500 incidents in Jika serious enough to report to the Director-General (*Herald* 30/1/87 p 8). Such violent incidents ranged from assaults between prisoners to the destruction of prison cells. Prisoner accounts suggested such incidents occurred on a daily basis, and that every day there was some altercation or abusive incident between staff and prisoners (PRG 1988).

It was alleged that certain officers engaged in standover tactics while subjecting prisoners to constant intimidation, verbal abuse, harassment and threats of violence (Inquest 1988-89a 'Statement and further notes by Craig Minogue' 7/7/88). Prisoners reported instances where officers rostered during the evenings drank on the job and, during routine security checks, disturbed prisoners who were trying to sleep by yelling insults and aggressively kicking cell doors (Inquest 1988-89a Exhibit 42). Further to this, Prisoner Richard Light complained that it was not uncommon during the evenings for officers to come in drunk and play football up and down the corridor outside prisoner cells to amuse themselves (Inquest 1988-89a 'Undated notes and complaints by prisoner Richard Light'). Such displays of aggression escalated already existing feelings of fear among prisoners. Subsequently, if a prisoner raised his concerns via formal official channels, it was often the case that he was informed such fears were unfounded and he was merely being paranoid (PRG 1988: 10).

Prisoners charged that some prison officers went further than the usual verbal displays of aggression and actively sought to pit prisoner against prisoner for their own entertainment. An anonymous prisoner wrote, 'I have seen [the prison officers] go from the sublime to the ridiculous. They've set up prisoners to attack other prisoners' (PRG 1988: 19). In one circumstance this prisoner reported that two prisoners took to two other prisoners with cricket bats. The same prisoner also reported he was involved in a similar incident where an officer gave a stanley knife to a fellow prisoner who in turn attacked him, slashing a 14-inch cut across his stomach (PRG 1988: 19). Peter Reed also commented on prisoners being pitted against one another, commenting that he could recall numerous incidents and name officers where this had taken place (P Reed Interview 15/5/04).

Contrary to the official rationale for Jika, prisoners alleged they had experienced and witnessed 'bashings' by prison officers (PRG 1988: 5). It was reported that these commonly occurred during unit transfers. Unit 2 was a smaller section of Jika that prisoners claimed was used as a punishment or isolation section. This was denied by the authorities who argued the only factor distinguishing Unit 2 from other units was its size. Craig Minogue stated that when a prisoner was taken to Unit 2, a group of four to six officers would remove him and take him into the central circle of Jika called Unit 7. As in H Division, Minogue claimed that during the transfer the prisoner would be stripped, roughed up, threatened and abused (Inquest 1988-89b: 683). Thereafter he would be placed in a cell with only a mattress.

Prisoner Olaf Dietrich alleged that after his transfer to Jika's Unit 2 he had been brutalised, placed in shackles and tortured with an electric cattle prod. He alleged that six officers entered his cell and when he offered resistance he was placed in restraints. Dietrich reported that he was left in this state for a number of days, until officers returned with a 24-volt cattle prod, which they 'shoved' into his buttocks for 'lunchtime entertainment' (Inquest 1988-89a: 2270-2). According to Dietrich this form of abuse or torture was quite common in Jika. He reported instances where officers had thrown effigies of nooses into prisoner cells and said, 'hang yourself' (Inquest 1988-89a: 2269). He also alleged that there were instances where officers turned fire hoses on prisoners in their cells. He stated:

> There's procedures down there, and methods that they use as a form of management. Some are warranted some are not. Some are used in vengeance ... They actually ridicule you when you're curled up on the floor in pain and you're shackled after a beating. You're degraded. Sometimes you've got no clothes on

for days lying on the concrete floor. It's just disgusting. Nobody will ever know the torture of that institution down there. (Inquest 1988-89a: 2271-2)

During 1987, prisoner John Dixon-Jenkins described his experience while held in Unit 2. He wrote that settling in was extremely difficult, as his cell had changed four times in 12 days and he had been completely isolated, spending between 22 and 24 hours a day confined to a cell (PRG 1988: 9). He had only managed to talk to other prisoners through locked doors, bars and bulletproof glass. On the day of writing, Dixon-Jenkins alleged that two prisoners called out from their cells that they feared they might be 'bashed or killed by prison officers, and asking if I would try to keep an eye on them and please notify someone (anyone) on their behalf if the worst were to happen' (PRG 1988: 9). Within two hours Dixon-Jenkins stated he saw a number of prison officers go into the cell of one of these prisoners and shortly after that the prisoner emerged appearing 'dazed' and 'holding his head' (PRG 1988: 9). The Governor allegedly informed Dixon-Jenkins the prisoner had merely fallen and hit his head on the floor:

> The Governor told me I could repeat what I saw to the Ombudsman or anyone else if I chose, but that no one would believe me. Unfortunately, I know that is true. There are always plenty of prison officers to swear the "official line" ... I was told the prisoner would confirm that version of the "accident"; and I am sure he would. The man was terrified, practically cowering in fear. (PRG 1988: 9)

The combination of Jika's oppressive environment, the psychological pressures created by security and management procedures and controls and the alleged mind games, threats and brutality by prison officers had a cumulative effect, pushing some prisoners to breaking point. Olaf Dietrich characterised his experience in Jika as 'oppressive' and 'soul-destroying'. He stated, 'I consider myself to be a fairly tough person mentally, but after three months, the place started to get to me' (Inquest 1988-89a 'Statement by prisoner Olaf Dietrich' 12/8/88). Reed seconded this in his description of the psychological pressures prisoners experienced:

> You were always being pushed ... it was total control of everything. As I said if you were in H Division you went to

> smash something you'd smash it. In Jika ... what could you
> smash? The concrete? The bars? The bulletproof glass? I mean,
> your bed was a concrete bed, the shelving there was stainless
> steel. (P Reed Interview 15/5/04)

This chapter has presented prisoner experiences of life in the Jika
high-security complex while highlighting the disparity between
such accounts and the views of staff and officials. Prisoner accounts
in their raw form reveal much about the nature of institutional
power structures and coercive strategies of control in operation.
Perhaps most importantly they provide a vital context for
understanding the disintegration of institutional relationships, the
reoccurrence of abuse and violence (from both sides) and
subsequent prisoner campaigns of non-compliance and resistance.
Traditionally, state-centred responses to disorder and crisis either
deny prisoner allegations or attribute institutional problems to the
individual pathologies of prisoners. Such a narrow focus precludes
any real understanding of the institutional forces and cultures that
give rise to internal conflict, disorder and violence. Moreover, in the
context of high-security, a focus on individual pathologies leads to
security based responses to problems and an increasingly punitive
regime, which only serves to exacerbate conditions and give rise to
more extreme and violent forms of prisoner transgression and
resistance.

CHAPTER FOUR

'Rebelling Against the Dictatorial Regime in Jika'[22]:
Acts of Prisoner Transgression and Resistance

On the evening of 30 July 1983, prisoners Robert Wright, David McGauley, David Youlton and Timothy Neville escaped from Unit 3 Side 2 of the Jika Jika High-Security Unit. The prisoners escaped by crawling through open security locks along the Unit corridor until they reached the external security yard. They exited the security yard by forcing off external facia panelling on the facility's exterior and crawled through the area located between the ceiling and roof until they reached the perimeter of the facility. The escapees managed to elude the hi-tech monitoring cameras and microwave detectors and scaled Jika's perimeter razor ribbon fence. They then proceeded to the northern wall of Pentridge, and climbed over with the use of blanket strips and a grappling hook fashioned from the frame of a Unit 3 noticeboard. At the time of escape electronic screening devices were out of operation. Despite the absence of the prisoners Unit 3 staff recorded the evening muster as correct.

Investigating police believed that the escape had been planned three months in advance. At the time of the escape, Unit 3 prisoner Jolly was engaged in leatherwork hobbies and the escapees were watching television in the day room. Unit 3 prisoners had

---

[22] Quote from Inquest 1988-89b: 694. The following italicised account is based on the unpublished transcript of proceedings at the Coroner's investigation into the deaths of James Richard Loughnan, David McGauley, Arthur Bernard Gallagher, Robert Lindsay Wright and Richard John Morris, 1988-89, Public Records Office Victoria, file number 1989/680 (Inquest 1988-89a), Unit 75, Police Commander PH Bennett 'Report to Chief Commissioner of Police Re: 30/7/83 Jika Breakout' 19/10/83 pp 1-2.

complained of the noxious sealant spray fumes used by Jolly and requested the security locks be opened to the exercise yards to clear the fumes. Prison officers Scott and Van Oosten had months earlier granted permission for the opening of the doors while Jolly was engaged in hobby work. By the evening of the escape Unit 3 officers on duty automatically opened the doors as soon as Jolly's spraying commenced. Police reported that the noise of Jolly's compressor and spraying served as a cover for the escapees who had crouched under Jolly's workbench, making their way, one by one, through the opened corridor security lock.

The entire incident caused embarrassment to the authorities. An official stated, 'When you spend so much money making a place escape-proof and four men get out with such apparent ease there is something very seriously wrong' (Herald 1/8/83 p 4). The officers on duty were publicly reprimanded for allegedly failing to carry out musters accurately and for making false and misleading entries in the Unit 3 diaries. Prison officers, angered by these allegations, threatened industrial action, while departmental officials publicly stated the need for tighter security measures and stricter discipline. Perhaps even more embarrassing was the fact that the escapees were at large for well over two months. Secretary for the Police Association Tom Rippon publicly stated his concern that 'once again' police were out 'risking their lives' looking for fugitives. In an appeal for tighter security he further stated that the department had 'listened too much to rehabilitation officials when deciding policy on the prison ... those in Jika are not rehabilitation material – they are incorrigible hardened men' (Herald 1/8/83 p 4).

Conceptualising Power and Resistance as Institutional Text

The 1983 escape drew attention to the fallibilities of the hi-tech security devices, and the fact that not one but four prisoners could elude even the most 'advanced' technology of an 'escape-proof' prison complex. The manner in which the escape took place demonstrated the ease with which prisoners were able to subvert the daily routine and transgress the physical boundaries comprising the basis of their confinement in high-security. Ultimately, the escape signified the opening up of a 'gap' or 'space', where strategies of the powerful were rendered vulnerable by challenges and tactics of the non-powerful.

The exertion of disciplinary power and corresponding acts of prisoner resistance are a dynamic arising from the fundamental structures, operations and functions of high-security imprisonment. Power and resistance, though diametrically opposed, are inevitably intertwined and comprise a fierce institutional dynamic of struggle further heightened by the physical and psychological pressures of an oppressive 'high-security' regime and environment. Deeper exploration of such a struggle, perennially obscured by institutional secrecy, serves to illuminate grittier, hidden aspects of life in Jika from a prisoner's perspective. This view remains antithetical to representations by the authorities who sought to depoliticise prisoner resistance, presenting it as a mere disturbance and confirming the violent nature, dangerousness and incorrigibility of high-security prisoners. Subsequently, each act of aberrant behaviour by individuals or breach of security was systematically represented and used by the authorities to fortify justifications for tighter security, stricter discipline and ultimately longer periods spent in Jika by prisoners. Conversely, Jika prisoners found ways to publicly challenge these official views while heightening individual and collective campaigns of resistance. However the price paid for this was an ever-expanding sentence in Jika and the ongoing denial of prison 'privileges'.

The tactics used by Jika prisoners were diverse and numerous. These ranged from acts of passive resistance such as refusal, to intellectual actions associated with the publicity, politicisation and pursuit of prisoner rights, to more extreme measures of bodily resistance and violent protests such as fires and barricades.[23] A

---

[23] While prisoner disobedience and rebellion constituted an essential part of the daily routine in Jika, it is also recognised that not all prisoners resisted. Prisoners with partners, wives and children often adapted to and accepted the system in order to retain contact with the outside world, while others chose not to challenge the system for their own personal reasons. The prisoner accounts used have emerged as those of active prison campaigners

general list of Jika prisoner tactics include the hunger strike; refusals to comply with officer orders or daily routine; refusals to work; refusals to participate in daily activities; refusals to wear prison uniform; refusals to wash; refusals to move. If an incident occurred where a prisoner was intimidated, abused or threatened, prisoners in that unit kept diaries and records documenting events. In some units mutual support was provided between prisoners on upcoming legal trials or reclassification, along with other grievances. These same prisoners lobbied collectively for a public inquiry or Royal Commission into conditions and allegations of brutality within Jika. They lobbied staff for legal and educational materials. They painted, drew pictures and political cartoons and composed poetry and writings about their experience. They wrote letters to family members, friends, prison advocates, legal representatives, and journalists about conditions inside. They smuggled out unauthorised information and produced and circulated prisoner publications detailing their experience and concerns. Many made formal complaints to the ombudsman and some prisoners pursued human rights litigation against the department. It should be acknowledged that some of these men, still in the prison system, continue with this work in different institutional contexts nearly 20 years on.[24]

Militant and violent forms of resistance included the erection of barricades; lighting fires; threats and abuse towards officers; use of physical resistance against officers; the destruction of cell and/or prison property; bronzing up,[25] banging up,[26] yelling and making

---

who have specifically sought to get information out about their experiences, conditions, views and actions. This chapter therefore represents a very specific experience of resistance in the high-security wing of Jika.

[24] Craig Minogue is a well-known anti-prison activist and published writer who has initiated numerous actions. He has litigated in the Australian Federal and High Courts in an attempt to establish whether prisoners have enforceable protection from human rights violations in prison. See Craig Minogue, 'An insider's view: human rights and excursions from the flat lands' in Brown & Wilkie 2002.

[25] The 'bronze-up' is a method of protest, which involves prisoners using their own bodily refuse, specifically excrement, to paint cell walls. Bronze-ups can occur as an individual expression of protest or form an ongoing collective

noise; attempted escape and escape; self-harm; the fashioning of weapons and concealment of contraband. Irrespective of the fact that prisoners were confined six men to a unit, they managed to communicate through windows by using obscure codes, sign language and by yelling. Such communication led to the organisation of collective protests that culminated with the 1987 fire.

For Jika prisoners, the act of resistance, regardless of its form, had limited capacity for creating permanent change within a high-security prison. However, it did serve a number of purposes for prisoners. For some prisoners, resistance served as a bargaining tool and a means of resolving what Keith Carter (2000: 365) refers to as the 'crisis of visibility'. For others it served as a vehicle for self-expression or a way of venting feelings of frustration and desperation. For most, the act of resistance was a key component of short-term survival. The acts listed above are by no means exclusive to high-security imprisonment. Many were and are commonplace resistance tactics prevalent across the mainstream prison system. What the case study of Jika Jika demonstrates is that the oppressive psychological and physical realities of high-security compounded prisoner experiences of disempowerment and feelings of loss of control, thus evoking more extreme, desperate and sometimes violent measures of resistance. It is within such a context that the prisoner's mind and body came to comprise renewed sites of struggle upon which the institutional dynamics of power and resistance were played out.

This chapter critically examines the various ways prisoners resisted within the constraints of high-security. It is argued that a combination of restrictive conditions and an inflexible and uncompromising regime in Jika gave rise to desperate and in some

---

campaign. Sometimes referred to as 'smearing', bronze-ups are a common and effective method of protest by prisoners in so far as there is little the authorities can do to prevent prisoners from participating. It also elicits reponses of revulsion by staff, as cells must be cleaned each day in the interests of institutional hygiene. (see Rhodes 2004)

26 'Banging up' refers to individual and collective prisoner protests where noise is made by banging cell doors.

cases violent forms of prisoner resistance. Moreover, and building on discussions in the previous chapter, it considers how prison power structures, based on domination and subjugation, teamed with the overarching official objective of coercive control in high-security, only serve to fuel polarisation, violence and disorder. Resistance by Jika prisoners is considered in the context of Cohen and Taylor's (1972: 134) pioneering model for conceptualising resistance, which includes 'self-protective', 'campaigning', 'escaping', 'striking' and 'confronting' types of resistance. For the purpose of this discussion, transgressive acts and modes of bodily resistance are also addressed in order to provide an examination of prisoner responses to the high-security environment in Jika. It is hoped that through a discussion of different types of resistance, the potentialities for resistance from the perspectives of both prisoners and the authorities within the limitations of a high-security prison will be illuminated.

Conceptualising Resistance in Jika

Resistance within high-security is pervasive, subversive, and requires prisoner ingenuity. It incorporates a broad variety of actions and attitudes. While many prisoners resisted for their rights in Jika, many did not perceive their actions as ideological or political. Transgressive acts often serve simple needs such as letting off steam or creating a situation to break the monotony of the daily routine. As Bosworth and Carrabine (2001: 507) argue, forms of resistance or 'counter-conduct' in prison are 'motivated as much by anger, rage, exploitation and injustice as by pleasure, play and boredom'. Thus in order to grasp the nature and extent of prisoner tactics in Jika during the 1980s it is necessary to distinguish between acts of resistance and unintentional or intentional acts of transgression.

Cresswell has addressed the distinctions and overlaps between transgression and resistance. He states, 'transgression is judged by those who react to it, while resistance rests on the intentions of the actor(s)' (Cresswell 1996: 23). This can be better illustrated through everyday prisoner responses within Jika, where daily regimes and routines were unselfconsciously subverted and defied. Rather than stemming from broader political objectives (although sometimes they did), these everyday actions can be characterised as reflexive and unselfconscious; organic responses to 'let off steam' and survive the stringencies of lockdown. In Jika, such acts included heated exchanges between prisoners and prison officers; prisoner refusal in its many forms, or attempts by prisoners to communicate with one another through the bulletproof glass. This is not to suggest that transgressive acts do not at times intentionally challenge or provide 'potentials' for resistance. In prison the case is quite the opposite. The moment a reaction or response is drawn from the institution, the meaning of the act correspondingly transforms, thus providing new possibilities for future struggle. Cresswell (1996: 23) clarifies this point, stating that 'intentional transgression is a form of resistance that creates a response from the establishment – an act that draws the line on a battlefield and defines the terrain on which contestation occurs'.

Cohen and Taylor's (1972: 134) model for resistance is particularly useful for categorising and understanding prisoner actions within the institution. They identify five 'types' of resistance: 'self-protecting', 'campaigning', 'escaping', 'striking', and 'confronting'. Perhaps most critical to the experience of high-security are 'self-protective' types of resistance, which encompass a range of active and passive refusals to cooperate with prison staff, prisoner intransigence and challenges to rules. Also included is the use of intellectual engagement, or what Cohen and Taylor (1972: 138) refer to as 'mind building', where prisoners use study as a coping mechanism to make sense of their own experience and assert themselves. This is accompanied by a rise in self-consciousness, which is characterised as a realisation of the individual self 'against' the institution rather than 'within' it (Cohen & Taylor 1972: 138).

'Campaigning' is a mode of fighting back that involves the formalising of responses such as 'moaning, niggling, complaining and making a nuisance of oneself' into professional campaigns (Cohen & Taylor 1972: 140). These campaigns encompass both individual grievances and collective campaigns about prison conditions. The role of 'campaigning' is particularly significant to Jika as many of the emerging prisoner accounts and experiences were products of ongoing and unrelenting complaints procedures used by prisoners considered 'troublemakers' by both staff and other prisoners. The category of 'escaping' involves prisoners physically transgressing the bounds of the institution. Cohen and Taylor note that a successful escape requires particular prisoner ingenuity and in some cases a certain amount of collaboration, particularly in a high-security unit. 'Striking' refers to modes of resistance such as hunger strikes designed to attract outside attention and humanitarian responses. These protests comprised an important form of collective and individual protest in Jika throughout the 1980s.

Lastly, modes of 'confronting' signify a last-resort willingness to take chances in a powerless situation. As discussed with respect to H Division, these acts are collective, encompassing barricades, cell-destruction and fire. The Jika fire constituted a significant example of such desperate actions. Cohen and Taylor note 'the localised nature of these disturbances, their irregular appearance, and their sudden conclusion suggest they depend more upon the insensitivity of the authorities than upon any growing political consciousness amongst the inmates' (Cohen & Taylor 1972: 146). This was in fact the case with Jika prisoners, as their responses were determined and amplified by the refusals on the part of staff and the authorities to address their grievances.

Another form of resistance not specifically addressed by Cohen and Taylor is bodily resistance, which is particular to prisoner reactions and responses within extreme conditions of long-term confinement. Bodily Resistance takes place in both collective and individual circumstances and involve actions such as the 'bronze-up', no wash protests, self-mutilation and in the case of asylum seeker detainees in recent years, lip-sewing. Acts of bodily resistance encompass distinctive responses to definitive and open-ended sentences in high-security conditions and particularly during periods spent in solitary confinement. Bodily resistance involves the symbolic subversion of power structures imprinted on the prisoner's body by processes of institutionalisation. As Rhodes (1998: 287) argues:

> In an intensive management unit, the circularity of the relationship between the mechanism of domination and the act of resistance is blatant; the inmate is able to make the constraints of prison "play spontaneously upon himself" in unexpected and inverted ways. He discovers that his body, the very ground of the panoptical relation, is also its potential undoing.

Acts such as the smearing of bodily refuse and self-mutilation can serve as a desperate vehicle for resistance when other external paths have been removed. Acts such as self-mutilation can also result in a temporary reprieve from conditions when prisoners are transferred to hospital. Most importantly, bodily resistance presents an avenue for prisoners to assert self-determination and control over their imprisoned bodies. Scraton, Sim and Skidmore (1991: 62) note that in high-security the choices open to prisoners to air their grievances and make complaints are limited and when 'faced with harsh regimes, threats and violence, prisoners respond in different ways'. They characterise self-harm by prisoners as a direct product of the violent institution. This presents a contrast to the authorities who often transfer the responsibility for such acts by prisoners on individual inadequacies and weaknesses caused by 'personality disorders', 'depression', and 'hysteria'. Ironically prisoners displaying symptoms of such pathological disorders are subjected to punitive 'treatments', such as solitary confinement and longer periods in high-security (Scraton et al 1991: 63). Specific acts and forms of bodily resistance will be addressed in further detail shortly.

While it is clear that prisoner resistance and transgression led to an increased dynamic of institutional struggle in Jika, such actions are distinct from other direct instances of resistance self-consciously or collectively geared by prisoners to defend prisoner rights, raise awareness and publicly challenge the legitimacy of the institution. In this way, resistance in Jika, which culminated in the 1987 fire, marked a decisive progression that escalated possibilities for disorder within the distinct topographies of power integral to high-security. This progression responded directly to the changing functions and exertions of disciplinary power in Jika. As the regime became increasingly unaccountable, restrictive and coercive, prisoner actions in turn echoed such extremities, drawing attention from the outside and thus making prisoners and their plights increasingly visible, if only temporarily.

Transgression and Resistance in Jika

> Even as the body is bounded and imprisoned, it can exercise a power that will elude the mechanisms of repression and the desire for absolute control.
>
> **Joseph Pugliese** (2002: 3)

As the picture of the Jika disciplinary regime suggests, prisoners had little control over their environment. They were subject to constant surveillance and scrutiny and were placed in a position where they were forced to rely on prison officers for basic things such as opening doors to allow access to the toilets or cells. The added ingredient of alleged mind games further magnified prisoner experiences of powerlessness and frustration. As Peter Reed stated, one of the most profound challenges for a Jika prisoner was to rise above the institutional psychological pressures designed to break him. For this reason, Jika prisoners often retaliated against their treatment by imposing their own system of mind games directed at prison officers. As Craig Minogue explained:

> If someone imposes a punishment on you, you have only got two choices: beg for mercy and break down and cry so they know the punishment has had some effect, or to laugh in their face. We simply laughed in their faces. (Inquest 1988-89b: 711)

The notorious 'black book' was used by officers to record minor disciplinary infractions by prisoners. If prisoners received a certain number of entries, they would lose certain privileges. Prisoners complained that prison officers used the book frequently and often when prisoners had not committed any offences. As Craig Minogue recalled, 'one didn't have to make a deliberate nuisance of oneself, it was quite easy to get into the black book' (Inquest 1988-89b: 710). Unit 4 prisoners held a competition to see which prisoner could get his name recorded into the 'black book' the most times. Sean Downie wrote:

> They have a black book system here. It's a joke, if you are not wearing the white shirt, bed's not made, or something trivial like that, they put you in it. The thing is to see who gets in it the most. It really is a pathetic joke. The screws really think they are holding it over us. It only gives us a carte blanche to fuck up more. (Inquest 1988-89b: 710)

Craig Minogue commented that once prisoners got four black book entries and lost their visits and phone calls for the month, it would make little difference to then go on to get 50 or 60. Subsequently, prisoners 'would constantly come out on muster with one shoe on, or a singlet on, or a shirt on backwards, or your bed unmade or stay in bed while [officers] were trying to do requests' (Inquest 1988-89b: 711). The act of refusing medication and food and refusals to comply with orders constituted a fundamental non-violent basis for passive resistance by prisoners in Jika. Unit 4 prisoners created a system where if an officer gave an order to a prisoner, that prisoner would refuse and another prisoner would then later fulfil the order. For example, if an officer demanded that a prisoner make his bed or clean up a mess in the day room he would refuse and one of the other Unit prisoners would then later make the bed or clean up. When asked what purpose this served, Minogue replied, 'the basis for that is rebelling against the dictatorial regime in Jika' (Inquest 1988-89b: 694).

It was often recorded in the Jika unit diaries that certain prisoners were on self-imposed loss of privileges or lockdown. Self-imposed loss of privileges (LOP) was a common response by prisoners to prison staff periodically cancelling visits or confiscating various privileges such as activities equipment, televisions or radios with little or no explanation. Self-imposed LOP was a self-conscious form of buying out of or 'resigning from the system' (Mooney 1978). As Reed stated, after going on self-imposed LOP a prisoner became harder but at least:

> There was nothing else that could be held over their heads by the prison officers ... Take your T.V., take your radio, take it all. Then what else have you got left? There's nothing, there's no more games. Then you cut yourself off from the outside world, don't worry about the visits. (P Reed Interview 15/5/04)

Prisoners also responded to prison officers 'playing' with the doors and unexpectedly locking the units down for long periods during the day, thus denying prisoners access to various sections of the units including the toilets. Dimitrovski reported that to avoid being trapped he would often place a chair in the doorway as a barricade, enabling him to move from the day room to his cell if the officers elected at any point to shut the doors (Inquest 1988-89a: 1997).

The above examples of refusal and subversion comprised retaliatory responses by prisoners who sought to exert control in their interactions with prison officers by 'upping the ante', welcoming the prospect of retribution and demonstrating they remained unbroken by the system. Such campaigns by prisoners to treat the Jika disciplinary system as a joke no doubt frustrated officers and fuelled a growing sense of mutual antagonism.

Jika prisoners devised ways to communicate with one another through the ventilation vents and bulletproof glass windows. These unauthorised conversations, dubbed by the authorities 'Jika talk', were based on different codes of sign language between prisoners from the divided sides of the units (Inquest 1988-89a: 2024). Craig Minogue stated that prisoners used the sign language because 'we had the belief that Jika Jika was electronically bugged with listening devices, so anything of any great importance was said via sign language' (Inquest 1988-89a: 1106). The codes used varied. Prisoners sometimes fogged up the glass and wrote letters backwards to spell out words to the other side. Although this process was time consuming, Peter Reed believed it was the most effective means of communication because prison officers never sustained an interest for long enough to ascertain the nature of the message (P Reed Interview 15/5/04). In addition to writing letters prisoners would mime words and use prison-devised sign language. For example, to signal a barricade, prisoners mimed placing an object through the bars. While 'Jika talk' was used in some circumstances to organise collective protests such as the 1987 fire, it often served as a general mode of communication. Unit 4 prisoner Dietrich commented that there was constant 'talk' between the two sides of Unit 4 in regards to all sorts of events and issues (Inquest 1988-89a: 2141).

In this context, the use of codes and sign language served as fundamental tools for survival in that they enabled a medium for prisoner conversation to occur unmonitored by prison officers and other hi-tech surveillance devices. 'Jika talk' also enabled prisoners to sustain a sense of collectivism despite the conditions and pressures of lockdown. In some of the units, namely Unit 4, after the deaths of prisoners Downie and Williams in August 1987, a certain level of solidarity built up and there was a growing culture of 'looking out' for one another. Communication formed an essential component of this.

Through the use of their bodies, Jika prisoners were able to engage in forms of resistance over which the authorities and prison officers had no control. While prisoner self-harm was reported to take place readily, there is too little publicly available documentation to establish its prevalence in Jika. However, a regularly recorded example of bodily resistance was the prisoner bronze-up. In Jika, the bronze-up involved prisoners collecting their own faeces and smearing it throughout the cell areas. Not only did it create a hygiene risk to staff and other prisoners; the act of smearing aggravated non-participating prisoners because of the discomfort associated with the smell within a non-ventilated and confined area. The bronze-up served as an effective bargaining action for prisoners. Its appeal and effectiveness lay quite simply in the fact that the prison officers and the authorities could not stop the supply (Rhodes 1998: 296).

On a number of occasions in 1987, Jika prisoners bronzed up specifically in response to conditions and classification grievances in various units. The campaign was frequently disruptive to the daily running of the prison and caused havoc with the placement of prisoners. Peter Reed recalled his involvement in a Jika bronze-up, 'I remember it clearly, I mean the smell, the dry-retching ... and then you become immune to it, the smell just went. And to actually see the screws and how they acted and everything else, was great' (P Reed Interview 15/5/04). While the specific details and timelines of each bronze-up campaign are difficult to document, it seems that they were a recurring mode of resistance that peaked during 1986 and 1987. Republican prisoners in Northern Ireland throughout the late 1970s also used the bronze-up during the notorious Long Kesh H Block blanket protests and hunger strikes (see McKeown 2001; Campbell et al 1994). Jika prisoners were aware of the H Block protests and cited the actions of the Irish Republican prisoners as a source of inspiration for their own campaign. During one ongoing bronze-up, prisoners were transferred to a separate unit where they maintained their campaign. They wrote:

> We have turned this unit into another 'H Block' as prisoners in Ireland did protest at the inhumane treatment they had to suffer in H Block over there by covering their surroundings with excreta ... The unit must be virtually dismantled for it to be sterilised as the shit is in many places they cannot get to. It is a very tense atmosphere in this unit between us and the screws. (PRG 1988: 13)

In June 1987, prisoners Robert Wright and David McGauley were reported for instigating a bronze-up where they smeared a series of slogans to protest against their classification. Duty prison officers thoroughly documented the protest and photographed the slogans, which named individual officials high up in the classification process believed by prisoners to be corrupt (Inquest 1988-89a 'Prisoner Incident Report Form' 15/6/87, 'K Division Incident Reports: March-September 1987'). Other general slogans included 'set up after set up in the human zoo'; 'welcome to hell'; 'No more cover ups'; 'The monster factory Jika'; 'Animal House'; 'No more verbal on classo and investigate the lot' (Inquest 1988-89a 'Photographs of bronze-up, vandalism and graffiti'). The intentions and objectives of this protest did not seek to raise awareness beyond the units of Jika. Rather, the intended audience were prison staff and officials. The campaign itself signified a defiant assertion by prisoners that if they were going to be treated like animals, they would in turn respond by behaving like animals. As Reed reflected, it was a case of 'who turns who into an animal?' and it served as an ideal form of passive resistance as officers were unable to retaliate in the immediate circumstances (P Reed Interview 15/5/04).

Rhodes (1998: 296) documents the fears and disgust of prison officers in United States supermax prisons confronted with the throwing and smearing of bodily refuse. In the eyes of prison staff, such acts of 'primitivism' merely confirmed the aggression, unpredictability and dangerousness of prisoner behaviour. In this way prisoner bronze-ups are not officially regarded or represented as resistance because such acts are located outside the 'protocols of rational and reasonable behaviour', and it is through the logic of official rationalisation that the perpetrator of institutional violence becomes the victim (Pugliese 2002: 2). Therefore to present the occurrence of bronze-ups outside the context of the administration of power and discipline in Jika is to omit the dynamics of struggle over institutional control; a defining feature of high-security.

Campaigning and confrontation also took place in Jika. Immediately before the protest fire in 1987, classification representatives informed prisoner Robert Wright that his reclassification had been unsuccessful and that he should attempt to 'make a life for himself in Jika' (Inquest 1988-89a: 1092). This decision angered Wright; after almost seven years of confinement in Jika, the fear that he would remain 'buried' there became a reality (Inquest 1988-89a: 1109). An examination of the Unit 4 official incident and conduct reports between 1986 and 1987 reveals that prison officers were exhaustive in their documentation of every prisoner infraction and suggestion of suspicious behaviour. As highlighted in the above discussion regarding classification, gratuitous reporting and black book recordings by officers had far-reaching impacts on a prisoner's prospect for reclassification. This further magnified existing tensions, exacerbating additional forms of active resistance. As Craig Minogue stated:

> It is difficult to explain in words the inhuman conditions that we were expected to live in in K Division. It is simply not possible to "make a life for yourself in K Division." The conditions ... were simply indescribable and I saw people's personalities change after only a short period of time ... Paranoia set in and so did thoughts of violence. (Inquest 1988-89a: 1092)

Just as prisoners devised many ways to transgress the boundaries of the Jika disciplinary regime on a daily basis, they additionally drew upon numerous tactics to publicise their grievances and concerns to the outside public. In this manner prisoners can be seen to have used tactics encompassed within Cohen and Taylor's modes of 'self-protecting', 'campaigning' and 'confrontational' modes of resistance. They utilised both their bodies and intellects as vehicles to reconcile the profound crisis of visibility and resist the 'open-endedness' of their sentence in Jika. Prisoner campaigning and confrontation were both non-violent and violent.

Like their H Division counterparts, many Jika prisoners wrote letters detailing their experiences and complaints to legal representatives and advocates, friends, family and the media. Others pursued official lines in their various complaints, and these were directed to the State Ombudsman, prison officials, government bodies and representatives such as the Attorney General. As stated above, prisoner James Bazley continued to write protest letters to the Attorney General after he was transferred from Jika. His ongoing concerns were also reflected in a later appeal to Coroner Hallenstein, during the Jika fire inquest of March 1988. He wrote, 'I do hope you find the key to the Pandora's box of Jika Jika which obviously, the OOC want buried with the victims of the Jika fire' (Inquest 1988-89a 'Letter from James Bazley to State Coroner Hallenstein' 6/3/88). There are, in addition, extensive examples of other Jika prisoners writing letters to draw attention to their grievances. Prisoner John Dixon-Jenkins was well known for his desperate letters to journalists and the media detailing his experiences in Jika and alleged suspicious circumstances surrounding the death of Sean Downie. Arthur Gallagher and Robert Wright also lobbied government agencies regarding their classification cases.

Prisoner grievances were independently compiled, published and distributed by outside advocates in the form of various prisoner publications. In 1988, the Victorian Prison Reform Group (PRG) published an edited collection of prisoner letters titled *Jika Jika Revisited* (PRG 1988). The editors of the publication acknowledged in the preface: 'These letters are highly emotive. They indicate the anguish and despair of imprisonment and the varying perspectives of what prison means to each individual' (PRG 1988: 4). In this way the collection provided a confronting and subjective account of life in Jika that took an antithetical departure from the rationality of official reports and inquiries and gave prisoners an opportunity to have their views published and distributed. The PRG published a number of prisoner publications and was a driving force behind the 'Doing Time Show', which sought to allow prisoner access to the media via the airing of relevant news stories and commentary each week on local community radio station 3CR.

Prisoners corroborated complaints and allegations regarding incidents occurring in the units by compiling notes, multiple prisoner witness statements and their own 'incident reports' detailing any instances of ill-treatment, mind games or abuse. In this way prisoners tactically sought to maintain an unofficial body of evidence that specified times, names and events. For example, notes and statements were compiled after an incident where prison officers allegedly entered Unit 5 noisily during the night, abusing prisoners and kicking their doors. In this case, prisoners Ian Murdon, Peter Reed, Craig Minogue, Rodney Minogue and Gareth Thornton documented specific details of the incident and then made formal complaints to the Ombudsman (Inquest 1988-89a Exhibit 42). This practice is extensively documented within prisoner multiple statements and 'notes' following significant incidents including the deaths of John Williams, Sean Downie and the Jika fire (Inquest 1988-89a Exhibit 79; see also Exhibit 80). After the death of John Williams, Unit 5 prisoners documented the times and corresponding actions by prison staff and officials and how they dealt with the body of the deceased and responded to subsequent prisoner requests (Inquest 1988 'Unit 5 Side 2 Prisoner Notes' 22/8/87). These notes were submitted to the coroner as formal evidence during the subsequent inquest.

Peter Reed relied on his 'prison diaries' to document the times of every meal, every request and every interaction on every day with officers to provide a formal reference point for his experience in Jika (P Reed Interview 15/5/04). Craig Minogue also kept a record of signed and witnessed statements on all major incidents occurring in Jika. These formed the basis of numerous submissions to the Jika inquests. While some prisoners struggled with their literacy skills, others provided assistance and mutual support. The act of collating and documenting prisoner evidence was crucial in that it sought formally to contest the seemingly monolithic block of 'official' evidence and representation by using the same methods as the authorities. Given the propensity of prisoner complaints and allegations regarding prison officer violence and abuse, it is not surprising that with the exception of those in high ranking positions, Jika officers refused to disclose their names to prisoners. Minogue stated, 'It's the situation where a prison officer's name is a pretty guarded secret. If you ask a prison officer his name, he won't tell you' (Inquest 1988-89a: 1115).

Prisoners reported that the official processes and avenues for making requests and complaints in Jika often resulted in delays and ongoing bureaucracy, making them ineffective. Minogue stated that he perceived the process of requests to be a 'pretty pointless' exercise at the time. He gave the example that if a prisoner wanted something simple like a tennis ball, 'you had to see the activities officer who had to see the storeman, who had to see this bloke, had to see that bloke, and it was sort of like an endless chain' (Inquest 1988-89a: 1130-1). However, despite this knowledge among prisoners, they stubbornly persisted in their use of official avenues to lodge requests and complaints. Prisoners were often acutely aware that the outcomes of their campaigning would not in most cases achieve their ends, but as Cohen and Taylor (1972: 142) recognise, campaigns are principally calculated to annoy.

Prisoners were required to air their complaints or grievances through the chain of command. They were required to raise the issues with a duty prison officer, and then approach a senior and then a chief. They then had to take the issue before the Governor, and then the Grade III Governor until finally the issue would go to 'Head Office'. If the issue at this point remained unresolved, their only remaining official avenue was to make a formal application to the Ombudsman. As Peter Reed stated, 'all of those avenues are like going to the toilet and wiping your arse ... totally useless' (P Reed Interview 15/5/04). Nonetheless, prisoners persisted and this often resulted in small victories. An example of this related to the request by remand prisoners Reed, Craig and Rodney Minogue in Jika in 1986 for their civilian clothing, which was a legal right for remand prisoners. In Jika, this right was disregarded and remand prisoners were forced to wear the regulatory prison greens. Reed stated that

The 'Jika Five', an undated photograph taken in Jika Jika, from left to right: David McGauley, Robert Wright, Arthur Gallagher and James Loughnan. Inset above left: Richard Morris.

Interior of prisoner accommodation unit taken prior to opening during a press tour in July 1980. The Age Archives/Courtesy of *The Age*.

The bronze-up was a recurring protest action initiated by prisoners in Jika during the 1980s. Officials documented these incidents with written reports and photographic records. The above undated Polaroids show the interior of accommodation areas where prisoners engaged in a 1987 bronze-up campaign. (Inquest 1988-1989a: Exhibit 19) Courtesy Public Records Office Victoria

Jika Jika interior of spine leading to Unit 2 taken during the aftermath of Sean Downie's death. (Inquest 1988-1989b: Forensic Photographs 24/8/87) Courtesy Public Records Office Victoria

Staff control area and entry to Unit 2 taken during the aftermath of Sean Downie's death. The trolley pictured in the foreground holds Downie's property which was not distributed by officers after his transfer to Unit 2. (Inquest 1988-1989b: Forensic Photographs 24/8/87) Courtesy Public Records Office Victoria

The controversial so-called 'suicide-proof' grille in Downie's cell was not produced as evidence during the inquest. (Inquest 1988-1989b: Forensic Photographs 24/8/87) Courtesy Public Records Office Victoria

The scene in Unit 2 cell five where Downie was alleged to have taken his life by hanging. (Inquest 1988-1989b: Forensic Photographs 24/8/87) Courtesy Public Records Office Victoria

Door of Unit 2 cell 5 where Downie allegedly lit the fire taken during the aftermath of the emergency response. (Inquest 1988-1989b: Forensic Photographs 24/8/87) Courtesy Public Records Office Victoria.

Unit 2 corridor leading to prisoner cells taken during the aftermath of Downie's death. (Inquest 1988-1989b Forensic Photographs 24/8/87) Courtesy Public Records Office Victoria

Unit 4 corridor taken during aftermath of the October protest fire and emergency response.
(Inquest 1988-1989a: Metropolitan Fire Brigade 1987 Exhibit 109)
Courtesy Public Records Office Victoria

Interior prisoner day room area taken during aftermath of fire and emergency response. (Inquest 1988-1989b: Forensic Photographs 24/8/87) Courtesy Public Records Office Victoria

Interior of Unit 4 prisoner accommodation area taken during the aftermath of fire and emergency response. (Inquest 1988-1989b: Forensic Photographs 24/8/87) Courtesy Public Records Office Victoria.

he told officers that he was unconvicted and therefore he wanted his own clothing, 'that fits, that makes me a human'. He recalled that it took him three months of requests and letter writing to the authorities, until finally the Ombudsman agreed and ordered Jika staff to allow civilian clothing to be worn by remand prisoners. However, as Reed stated, it was in fact a rare occurrence for prisoners to achieve wins or receive recognition for their complaints through the Ombudsman's office. Such avenues were extraordinarily lengthy and often resulted in the vindication of the authorities and prison staff (P Reed Interview 15/5/04).

When official avenues failed, and they usually did, a further method used by prisoners to bargain with the authorities and raise publicity surrounding their grievances was the hunger strike. Like the bronze-up, the hunger strike signified a form of protest where prisoners self-consciously put themselves as risk, using their bodies as a brittle medium for non-violent resistance. However, the major difference between the bronze-up and hunger strike was that the latter sought to attract public sympathy and attention to conditions inside. There was a series of individual and collective hunger strikes in Jika between 1986 and 1987. A number of prisoners participated in a collective hunger strike during March and April in 1986. One of these prisoners was Arthur Gallagher and his particular case received extra publicity due to a 'sympathy' hunger strike undertaken by his brother outside Pentridge. Gallagher's brother 'Billy' marked the size of a Jika cell on the grass outside Pentridge at the time, informing the press that prison staff had punished Gallagher for his participation in the hunger strike (*Courier-Mail* 7/4/86). This kind of outside support and representation was critical for prisoners who had no access to the media but wanted to publicise their grievances.

Reed recalled his successful involvement in a collective hunger strike aimed at getting better conditions in Jika. The strike received significant attention and resulted in officials attending Jika to inquire about grievances and what they could do to get prisoners to cease the protest. Reed noted that after this:

> Things started to slowly change. I mean we wanted carpet in the cell instead of standing on the concrete floor and they gave us a

strip of carpet. I mean they were only small things … but then we were promised bigger and better things. (P Reed Interview 15/5/04)

Craig Minogue also referred to the Jika hunger strikes and how such wins resulted in prisoners getting extra furniture and computers in the Jika units (Inquest 1988-89a: 1125). In other examples, some Unit 4 prisoners, including Craig Minogue, Olaf Dietrich and Richard Morris, refused meals after the death of Sean Downie in 1987. It was documented in official incident reports that prisoners would persist with refusals until there was a formal inquiry into the circumstances surrounding the death (Inquest 1988-89a 'SPO Cain, Incident Report Form', 25/8/87, 'K Division Incident Reports: March-September 1987'). The outcome of this action was not specifically documented within available official sources. Prior to the eruption of crisis in Jika, prisoners used the hunger strike as a bargaining tool over a range of grievances relating to conditions and classification. However, such negotiations were stalled by the Jika deaths and subsequent closure of the Division in 1987.

Many Jika prisoners broke under pressure and reacted with violent outbursts. Under these circumstances there were instances where some affected prisoners, internalising their pain, sought to deal with their situation by attempting suicide or through self-harm.[27] The occurrence of violent incidents peaked in 1987 (*Herald* 30/1/87 p 8). There were extensive instances of cell and property destruction, prisoner barricades, fires and the reporting of violent threats made by prisoners to officers. Prisoners also referred to the pressures that pushed them towards violence. One anonymous prisoner stated, '[m]ost violence [in Jika] happens when a prisoner reaches the end of his tether and decides to take no more' (PRG 1988: 5). Dixon-Jenkins echoed this observation; 'such are the never-ending mind games and overt suppression of my work … as

---

[27] While the occurrence of self-harm and attempted suicide in Jika Jika was frequently referred to in prisoner accounts and specifically in the Prison Reform Group publication *Jika Jika Revisited*, actual cases of self-mutilation were not documented in the inquest files in any detail that would allow the collation of precise statistics or enable the detailing of specific cases.

terrible as it sounds, I sometimes have the urge to let go with just one potent blow' (letter 1/10/87 in *Bendigo Advertiser* 31/10/87 p 9). Extensive incident reports were documented and compiled by prison officers in relation to these incidents during 1987. However, official reports presented a one-sided view of the polarised atmosphere during this time and failed to account for prisoner allegations that such instances were provoked by abuses and threats made by other officers. Another common prisoner claim was that prisoners known to be 'political' were subjected to 'extra special' treatment. Such feelings further intensified prisoner responses and exacerbated the explosive descent into crisis.

Power Meets Resistance: A Crisis-Inducing Cycle

Every act and indeed the very anticipation of transgression or resistance confirm the need to implement tighter security, harsher disciplinary strategies and the deployment of official force (Pugliese 2002: 6; see also Rodriguez 2006: 145-84). According to Jika prisoners, prison staff responded to prisoner resistance campaigns by imposing a tighter regime on those involved, limiting their privileges and playing mind games.

The underlying basis for such complaints was the accusation that officers demonstrated double standards through their open favouritism toward 'protection' prisoners over those classified as 'security' and 'management'. Protection prisoners were confined in Unit 6, and there was an intense rivalry between Unit 6 and all other Jika Units. According to most prisoners, Unit 6 comprised the 'show unit' of Jika where outside visitors were taken. It was nicely set up and prisoners were happy because they had access to various activities (Inquest 1988-89a: 1128). This affected other Jika prisoners in a number of ways. Above all this system of favouritism underpinned the extension of existing mind games by officers. Prisoners complained that if they expressed an interest in an activity or particular program, it would be passed on to Unit 6 prisoners instead. It was also alleged that prison officers would then inflame the situation by informing prisoners of this fact. For example, Unit 4 prisoners devised and proposed a program to the authorities that included the packing of all basic prisoner rations. Such a menial task was proposed to alleviate ongoing boredom and idleness and initially the Governor expressed enthusiasm for this idea. However, Unit 4 prisoners were later informed the task had been referred on to Unit 6. This was despite the fact prisoners there were already responsible for most Jika 'jobs' including the library, washing and ironing (Inquest 1988-89a: 1127).

Prisoners reported that officers played the usual mind games and further denied access to exercise yards. Prisoner privileges such as electric kettles, toasters, computers, televisions and typewriters were confiscated for no reason and then given back and then confiscated again for the amusement of the officers. This underpinned the reasoning behind prisoner self-imposed LOP by Wright and Gallagher (Inquest 1988-89a 'Statement by Rodney Minogue' 24/3/88). Most significant among prisoner complaints were allegations that prisoners were subjected to frequent and indiscriminate cell searches or 'ramps', ravaging prisoner cells and property. While such searches were customary, prisoners alleged that they had property stolen or interfered with. More seriously, prisoners engaged in work on upcoming legal and classification cases and those known for their lobbying and litigation actions against police and the department had their paperwork interfered with and in some cases stolen. Dietrich complained he had documents stolen, which he later saw in the hands of the prosecution during his legal trial (Inquest 1988-89a 'Statement by Olaf Dietrich' 12/8/88). Dixon-Jenkins, Reed, Light and the Minogue brothers all complained similarly of documents being interfered with or stolen. Craig Minogue alleged that during cell searches, there were instances where officers had grabbed handfuls of paper and thrown them into the air and when prisoners complained, the authorities took no disciplinary action (Inquest 1988-89a: 1133).

Unit 5 Side 2 prisoners had also complained during August 1987 that they received 'special treatment' from officers, while in contrast Side 1 had been receiving additional privileges (Inquest 1988 'Statement by Peter Reed' 6/3/88; see also 'Unit 5 Side 2 Prisoner Notes' 22/8/87). Prisoner Reed alleged prisoners had their supply of hot water turned off for almost an entire month, their meals were served cold and their tennis table and hobby equipment had been confiscated without reason and given to Side 2 prisoners. Furthermore, prisoners allegedly suffered ongoing abuse and threats by officers along with triple the amount of searches where cells were turned upside down and property was damaged. Reed stated that after one of these cell searches, 'one would think a tornado had struck' (Inquest 1988 'Statement by Peter Reed' 6/3/88). Resisting prisoners perceived they were singled out, intimidated and threatened by staff. Unit 4 prisoner Richard Morris wrote a formal complaint to the Ombudsman alleging his intimidation over the ongoing protests occurring in Jika. He reported being transferred from Unit 4 to Unit 5 where he was subsequently placed on lock-up and LOP. He alleged that officers refused to grant him permission to mix in Unit 5, and when he protested, they sprayed a fire hose through the cell door trap. Morris further alleged CPO King threatened him with violence. According to Morris, King's threats constituted a common campaign against Jika prisoners, and when they retaliated by making formal complaints, he would threaten to come down on them harder. Morris characterised King's threats as frightening, stating they caused him to fear for his life (Inquest 1988-89a 'Notes and letter to the Ombudsman by Richard Morris' 6/87).

This alleged 'special' treatment by staff precipitated reactive responses by prisoners in the form of violent threats, abuse and the destruction of the Units. On 22 August, Unit 4 Side 2 prisoners initiated a barricade. Barricades in Jika were considered to be a last resort and sometimes served as an effective bargaining tool (Inquest 1988-89a 'Statement by Richard Light' 6/11/87). Prisoners Olaf Dietrich and Sean Downie allegedly tied the doors of the Unit shut and Richard Light obscured the windows of the unit with newspaper. Prisoners demanded to see the Governor to discuss conditions. Much was made of the barricade and it was alleged prisoners threatened the lives of duty officers (Inquest 1988-89b Exhibit AX). The situation was short-lived and the Governor successfully persuaded prisoners to end their protest. However, the barricade was a warning of the crisis to come. Within two days, prisoners Sean Downie and John Williams died in unrelated yet controversial circumstances.

The Jika Jika High-Security Unit comprised a series of powerful disciplinary strategies, directed at both prisoner bodies and minds and designed to curtail resistance in its many forms. However, rather than preventing or limiting resistance, each strategy of discipline and control opened up new spaces, tactics and possibilities for prisoner transgression and resistance. These tactics served numerous and diverse personal objectives for prisoners, but above all they constituted necessary responses for prisoner survival in high-security. As demonstrated, acts of resistance and expressions of non-compliance were used by the authorities to further fortify tighter security and discipline. These 'crackdowns' in security and discipline and 'special treatment' aimed at non-compliant prisoners merely created an atmosphere of frustration, fear and paranoia, which inevitably fuelled a growing crisis. As John Dixon-Jenkins commented forebodingly:

> Some days there must be dozens of provocations, many very small and petty but they add up. Little things like getting a "special" meal covered with foil which when I opened it up was only boiled potatoes and spinach (but there were no green leaves on the spinach, only the thick white stems), I looked up to see three prison officers grinning at me from behind the bullet-proof glass and bars. Violence, not on my part, is growing closer and more obvious almost each day. It must be coming soon … I may somehow die in here. (Letter 11/10/87 cited in *Bendigo Advertiser* 31/10/87 p 9)

Keith Carter (2000: 364) refers to the dangerous dynamic that can develop in prison when discipline and security are maintained by forcible methods that exceed acceptable legal boundaries (see also Edney 1997). The deployment of forcible methods and continuing exertions of unaccountable power within the restrictive context of high-security merely serves to build mutual resentment and antagonism while leading to the occurrence of serious abuses, violent outbursts, riots and a descent into general crisis. It was this dynamic that led to the Jika deaths and the subsequent barricade and fire in 1987.

CHAPTER FIVE

Descent into Crisis: The Deaths of John Williams and Sean Downie[28]

On 22 August 1987, John Williams became the third prisoner to die in Jika. Williams was reported to have died of a drug overdose in his cell during the night and was found the following morning by Unit 5 Side 2 prisoners. During the morning, duty officers recorded the morning muster as correct. Unit 5 prisoners found Williams' body after the Unit had been opened up for the day. Senior prison officer Wall gave a statement alleging that when he opened up the trap door to Williams' cell during morning muster, he saw Williams sitting on his bed, and said 'Good morning John'. Williams did not answer, yet Wall was not concerned as, based on his experience in Jika, it was not uncommon for prisoners to ignore officers. Governor Davis commented that the incorrect muster caused him 'concern', though he was convinced Wall had believed Williams was dressed and ready at the time of morning muster.

Prisoners contested official accounts, alleging their concern about Williams' welfare the night before. They reported that during the previous evening, the prison medical support officer (PMSO) responsible for administering 'treatments', refused to tend to Williams due to his lack of response. According to prisoners he stated, 'fuck him, he's nothing but a fucking junky'. This caused

---

[28] The following italicised account is based on transcript and statements comprising investigations into the death of John Williams 1988 (Inquest 1988) Unit 85, including, 'Statement Governor A Davis' 22/8/87; 'Statement SPO J Wall', 22/8/87, 'Statement Peter Reed, 6/3/88, 'Statement Paul Anderson', 10/9/87, 'Statement Dennis Quinn', 11/3/88, 'Statement Prison Officer Debney', 22/8/87, 'Statement Gareth Thornton', 12/3/88.

concern to neighbouring prisoners who alleged they called to Williams, receiving no response. At that stage they assumed he was asleep. However, their concern increased when he failed to respond to their calls the next morning. Prisoner Paul Anderson stated that despite prisoners calling to officers and pressing the emergency buttons in the cells there was no response. It was alleged officers did not conduct the customary morning muster and the cells were not opened until 8.30am rather than the usual time of 7.45am. After the cells were opened prisoners found Williams sitting on his bed fully clothed, bent over a piece of paper holding a biro, his face purple. When distressed prisoners attempted to inform duty officers of the situation, it was alleged they were ignored and so they began to throw chairs and tables at the glass to get the officers' attention. Prisoner Paul Anderson stated, 'I raced down to the enunciator and called the prison officers. I said 'There's a bloke in here, you need to get the [health attendant]'. One prison officer came to the glass and looked at me in a stupid way and walked off. I got upset and banged a chair against the glass, yelling 'get in here you dogs there's a bloke dead in here'. Prison officers submitted statements alleging the delay to attend to the situation stemmed from a need for backup due to outwardly aggressive threats made by prisoners who had called them 'fucking scum dogs' and blamed them for Williams' death.

Prisoners believed Williams died from an overdose because he continually stockpiled his prison medication in order to 'get high'. They made allegations against the officers and one of the PMSOs. In their view, Williams' drug dependency was common knowledge around the Division yet, they claimed, the prison medics fed Williams Rohypnol 'as if they were lollies', and failed to ensure he took the drugs. The authorities refuted such allegations and Chief Prison Officer King gave evidence at the inquest alleging Williams had smuggled drugs into Jika during a contact visit with his mother and these drugs had been found in the toilet of the cell during investigations following his death. During the inquest a toxicology report suggested that the substance found in Williams' body was not a prison prescribed drug.

Oppositional Accounts: Reconstructing the Case Studies of Downie and Williams

> I was asked on one occasion as I was leaving, 'Name one prisoner who's unhappy in this division at the moment? Things are running smoothly' and I named two prisoners: Sean Downie and John Williams and, within a few weeks, both of them were dead.

HM Pentridge Prison Chaplain Peter Norden (Inquest 1988-89b: 74)

August 1987 marked the ultimate descent into institutional crisis in the lead up to the October fire. Within the space of two days, two prisoners, John Williams and then Sean Downie, died in different Units of the division. The accounts, events and circumstances surrounding these deaths were controversial. Evidence put forward by prison staff and the authorities was vehemently contested by prisoners who alleged that officer negligence, ill treatment and in the case of Sean Downie, criminal conduct and abuse, directly contributed to and caused the deaths.

The Williams inquest commenced on 1 March 1988, only to be adjourned after prison advocate Jeff Lapidos made representations on behalf of prisoners in the unit where Williams died. He argued to Coroner Hallenstein that prisoners had been excluded from the inquest even though they were direct witnesses to circumstances surrounding the death. He requested that the inquest be adjourned and prisoners be allowed to make submissions. Coroner Hallenstein reluctantly agreed but warned:

> I'm mindful ... that prisons constitute an issue which, probably, has no relevance to the matter that I'm considering. If it is considered that these proceedings are going to be used as a public forum for expressing personal views then they're not going to be. (Inquest 1988: 55)

These comments were prompted by Unit 5 prisoners who, in their statements, documented a series of complaints relating to their treatment in Jika. The transcripts pertaining to the recommencement of the inquest proceedings and the coroner's findings were not available in the file. Staff at the Coroner's Office were unable to locate the files, believing them to be lost. It is for this practical reason that the case of Sean Downie, rather than that of John Williams, provides a central focus in this chapter. The known circumstances surrounding the Williams' death and the subsequent death of Sean Downie are significant as they contributed directly to the powder keg atmosphere and the growing sense of crisis in Jika during this time.

Despite the contested circumstances surrounding the deaths, the respective inquests received very little media attention or public scrutiny. In contrast, and only weeks afterwards, the October fire and later inquest into the related deaths gained considerable media coverage. This exposure, in conjunction with Jika's closure immediately after the fire, created an illusion of accountability. Under these circumstances the unresolved circumstances surrounding Downie's death in Jika were lost in the furore over the fire. It is therefore the purpose of this chapter to redress the silences by piecing together the accounts, events and circumstances surrounding Downie's death. This reconstruction serves as a precursor to an examination of official responses to deaths in custody in Chapter Six.

Accounts of Downie's death reveal conflicted, oppositional views of events. Rather than attempt at this point to mediate or reconcile these representations, this chapter provides an overview of evidence that reflects the views of the various parties represented at the inquest. These include the 'official' summary of events; prison officer reports; prisoner accounts and allegations; and evidence put forward by the Downie family, friends and 'other' representations.

Flashpoint: Sean Downie 24 August 1987

The official records[29] indicate that at approximately 4.55pm prison officers were alerted to an activated smoke alarm in Unit 2 of Jika Jika. Prison officers Wales and Gough were sent by control room operator senior prison officer (SPO) Jones to investigate and on entering the Unit confirmed via radio that smoke was coming from

---

[29] For the purposes of this discussion 'official records' refers to those accounts based on statements, memorandums and documents by the Office of Corrections authorities, staff and the Victoria police.

a fire lit in one of the cells. At 5.00pm SPO Jones notified security officers at the East Gate and staff at the lodge in order to get reinforcements. Several officers attended the emergency situation in Unit 2 and ascertained the smoke was coming from cell number 5, remand prisoner Sean Downie's cell.

During evacuation procedures, officers decided to evacuate cells 4 and 6 prisoners, Read and Warburton first before attending cell five. Prison officer Macdonald stated that this was because Sean Downie had a violent reputation and was known to have previously threatened the lives of certain Jika prison officers. Officers reported that attending Downie's cell first could have endangered the lives of prison officers and other prisoners if he proceeded to attack (Inquest 1988-89b: 457-61). Side 2 prisoners Read and Warburton and Side 1 prisoner Dixon-Jenkins were evacuated to the exercise yards. On entering Sean Downie's cell, prison officers found their visibility was obscured by thick black smoke. Still expecting to be attacked by Downie, they kicked through the small fire built against the door from chunks of mattress and other ripped bedding and found Downie's burned body hanging from a sheet at the back of the cell.

Sean Downie: An Official Summary of Events

Sean Downie was a 23-year-old remand prisoner charged with murdering a taxi driver in January 1987. Prior to his arrest and remand he had not done time in prison, and at the time of his death his case had not been heard. From the time of his reception to his death, official records indicate Downie was struggling to adapt to prison life and that he committed a number of minor and major infractions against regulations that culminated in an attack on another prisoner and his classification to Jika Jika.

The official records document a number of incidents involving Downie's non-compliance and alleged involvement in violent scuffles in D Division over April and May 1987. These incidents resulted in Downie's transfer first to H Division and then to Jika as a last resort. The final straw related to an incident in May 1987 where Downie was accused of stabbing another prisoner in D

Division (Inquest 1988-89b: Exhibit AX). The incident was reported to police and Downie was charged with attempted murder. Downie was temporarily moved to H Division while matters were investigated.[30] The above charges had not been heard at the time of his death.

The Review and Assessment Committee (R&A) in conjunction with the Divisional Classification Committee (DCC) considered Downie's placement on 6 June and recommended Downie be transferred to Jika under the classification, 'management' (Dessau 1989: 3). Chairman of the R&A Cliff Shackson stated:

> Given Downie's propensity for violence and the fact that he has been involved in at least two fights, one that may have resulted in the stabbing incidents [sic]. The nature of the charges that he is awaiting trial on, plus his attitude of non-compliance when being questioned on matters, lends to the belief that he should be housed in a Division where maximum surveillance can be maintained. (Inquest 1988-89b: Exhibit AX)

Downie was subsequently transferred from H Division to Jika on 15 June. On his reception, R&A advised him of the reasons for his transfer. Downie told the R&A that he preferred to be in 'H' Division as he had a job and got along with the other prisoners there (Inquest 1988-89b: Exhibit AX). The department's view of the situation was that despite the fact that Downie was a remand prisoner, the decision was justified:

> Given the nature of the offences for which Downie had been remanded, murder and assault with a weapon, and his involvement in violent incidents within 'D' Division, Downie's placement in 'K' Division [Jika Jika] was appropriate. (Inquest 1988-89b: Exhibit AX)

When initially received in Jika Unit 5, Downie put himself on self-imposed isolation due to personality clashes with other prisoners. Downie's behaviour quickly deteriorated and staff reported he posed increasing management problems. This deterioration was believed to correlate directly with Downie's eventual placement in

---

[30] Coroner Linda Dessau, *Finding of Inquisition upon the Body of Sean Fitzgerald Downie*, 21/9/89, Public Records Office Victoria (hereafter 'Dessau 1989'), pp 2-3.

Unit 4 with controversial prisoners such as Craig Minogue and Olaf Dietrich, who were seen as 'troublemakers' by the authorities (Inquest 1988-89b: Exhibit AX). Throughout August, Downie was involved in a number of incidents that finally led to his transfer to Unit 2 the day of his death. These included refusals to work; insolence and abuse towards staff; refusing lawful orders; the alleged making of violent threats towards staff; his alleged involvement in a barricade with others in Side 1 Unit 4 on 22 August; and throwing his food on the floor on 24 August. Governor Davis reported his concern in a memorandum:

> I am of the opinion that prisoner Downie is becoming more and more aggressive and threatening towards staff and this may require he be returned to another unit or kept on "lock-up". (Inquest 1988-89b: Exhibit AX)

During his time in Unit 4, a major source of Downie's grievance stemmed from unanswered demands to wear his civilian clothing. In Jika all prisoners were required to wear prison greens, until earlier that year when other remand prisoners in the Unit successfully obtained authorisation to wear their own clothing. After moving into Unit 4 Downie observed other prisoners wearing their own clothes. He was thereafter encouraged by these prisoners to make requests for his own clothing. His first recorded request was on 21 August and at the time of his death, the clothes were still on request and waiting to be obtained from the store.

On 24 August, Downie was transferred out of Unit 4 and placed in Unit 2 at approximately 1.00pm by CPO King, SPO Cain and prison officers Keating, Fitzsimmons and Robertson. Upon being strip-searched, he refused to get dressed in his prison greens, making further demands for his own clothes. SPO Cain reported that Downie was placed in his cell wearing his underwear and CPO King spoke with him, stating the issue of this clothing would be sorted the next day (Inquest 1988-89b: Exhibit AX).

Prison officer Bezanovic brought Sean Downie's cell property from Unit 4 to Unit 2 at approximately 3.30pm (Inquest 1988-89b: 1471). He left it in the corridor. Due to staff shortages and the early close of the prison, Unit 2 duty officers Robertson and Keating stated there was no time to search the property and therefore it could not be handed out to Downie that afternoon. Before the close of the Unit, Downie requested permission to speak to Governor Penter who was doing his rounds in Jika Jika that afternoon. After speaking with Downie, Penter subsequently gave orders to staff that Downie's property should be searched and distributed. Despite Penter's orders, prison officer Robertson left a note on the property stating, 'Downie is a [sic] lock up. His gear is not to be handed out to him until further notice' (Inquest 1988-89b: Exhibit AX). Robertson stated the intended purpose of the note was to communicate with staff between shifts and watches. The failure of unit staff to search and hand out Downie's property was not intended as an unauthorised punishment or victimisation of Downie, though it was later accepted by the department with hindsight that some of his gear could have been handed over in order to placate him (Inquest 1988-89b: Exhibit AX).

At approximately 5.00pm staff were alerted to a fire in Unit 2. A number of officers attended the scene. After Sean Downie's body was recovered, the Governor of the Metropolitan Prison observed:

> It appears that Downie cut up his mattress into small pieces the size of footballs and placed a sheet, his chenille bedspread and a blanket in a pile, directly in front of the door, set fire to it and that he then stood on the bench near the air-conditioning vent and hung himself with a knotted sheet. (Inquest 1988-89b 'Statement Governor Edgar Penter' 24/8/87)

The CIB Arson Squad reported the fire occurred at around 4.55pm, activating the alarm in the Divisional control room, prompting the rescue operation that followed (Inquest 1988-89b 'CIB Arson Job Sheet Case No. 3696: Current Position of Inquiry' 24/8/87). Sean Downie was pronounced dead at approximately 5.48pm by the prison doctor, and the Coburg police arrived at the scene by 6.10pm (Inquest 1988-89b 'Statement Governor Alan Davis' 24/8/87). At no time were the Metropolitan Fire Brigade (MFB) notified of the fire. They attended the scene at 6.35pm after a press inquiry prompted District Officer Peter Eagan to lodge an emergency call himself (Inquest 1988-89b: 1698). During this time there was no direct transmission of fire calls linking Jika to outside emergency services.

The OOC maintained that despite adverse publicity generated by the Fire Brigade on this point:

> The staff on duty in 'K' Division [Jika Jika] were in fact acting in accordance with the Unit's Standing Orders, which require that the officer in control assess the fire risk and act accordingly. In the case of cell 5 of Unit 2 the fire had been extinguished and could cause no further harm or damage. (Inquest 1988-89b: Exhibit AX)

An internal inquiry conducted only months after Downie's death by Assistant Directors of Prisons Paul Delphine and Norman Banner summarised the departmental view of Downie's death. Delphine and Banner highlighted issues requiring further investigation, such as staff miscommunication in relation to the distribution of Downie's clothes and property, and a lack of accountability in the form of written records in the Unit and Governor Diaries for prisoner placements within Jika. Despite these noted inadequacies, Banner and Delphine stated that the offences for which Downie had been remanded and his conduct in other Pentridge divisions vindicated his classification as a remand prisoner to Jika. They additionally concluded that an examination of all reports and personal observations pertaining to emergency procedures confirmed that, 'staff acted quickly and professionally in the management of the emergency situation' (Inquest 1988-89b: Exhibit AX).

Prison Officer Representations

Most officers alleged that while in Jika, Sean Downie's behaviour and attitude deteriorated and he became increasingly aggressive and hostile toward staff (Inquest 1988-89b: Exhibit AX). This was reinforced by a number of reports relating to incidents in which Downie was involved during August 1987 involving insolence and abuse to officers (Inquest 1988-89b 'OOC Memorandum' 12/8/87; see also 'OOC Memorandum' 21/8/87), refusals to comply with the daily routine and regulations (with specific reference to his campaigning for clothing) (Inquest 1988-89b 'OOC Incident Report' 21/8/87), and outbursts of violence and violent threats made to officers specifically.

The most serious incident occurred two days prior to Downie's death, Saturday 22 August, and involved the initiation of a barricade by Unit 4 prisoners (Inquest 1988-89b 'OOC Incident Report' 24/8/87). Prisoner Olaf Dietrich was at this time engaged in a campaign where he refused visits due to regulations requiring prisoners to change into overalls during visits – a process they argued was dehumanising. On this particular day Dietrich refused the overalls and was therefore refused visits. A protest was initiated and all prisoners participated in smashing the cameras and barricading the Unit doors. During this protest Downie was alleged to make a razor action across his throat, which was directed at prison officers. Downie was also reported to invite prison officer Ryan to come in with the 'goon squad' and said that 'he was going to have him' (Inquest 1988-89b 'OOC Incident Report' 24/8/87). The standoff and destruction of the Unit 4 day room continued throughout the afternoon. Acting Governor Davis eventually attended and ended the protest guaranteeing prisoner concerns would be dealt with the following day.

After the barricade staff reported Downie's behaviour and subsequent management was becoming an increasing issue. Much of this deterioration was attributed to the behaviour and influence of the prisoners in Unit 4 during this time. Deputy Director of the Prisons Division Michael Ryan later commented in a departmental report:

> Certainly it appeared that Downie quickly joined in this display of non-conformity and unruliness and in fact his behaviour seemed to become even less tolerable than the others. Therefore, in retrospect, placing Downie in Unit 4 was probably not a good decision and may have provoked a great deal of trouble that he was involved in the days leading up to his death. (Inquest 1988-89b Exhibit BH)

Ryan further commented that Downie's aggressive and volatile behaviour in the lead up to his classification to Jika, and his subsequent behaviour within the Division, suggested the 'workings of a very troubled and disturbed mind' (Inquest 1988-89b Exhibit BH). In contrast, there were prison officers who gave evidence during the inquest that Downie was quiet and generally cooperative. Prison officer Robertson had no problems with

Downie, and saw him as a 'yes sir, no sir' cooperative type of prisoner (Inquest 1988-89b Exhibit AX).

On 24 August, after lunch was delivered to Unit 4, prisoners Downie and Minogue complained to staff about the quality and quantity of the food and Downie registered his protest by upending his meal on the corridor floor (Inquest 1988-89b 'Statement Prison Officer Reading' 24/8/87). Prison officer Fitzsimmons, who had earlier issued prison clothing to Downie, informed him that if he cleaned up the meal no charges would be laid. Downie refused and went into his cell. Fitzsimmons then saw the prison clothing he had issued being thrown out the door of Downie's cell. He then reported matters to the Governor (Inquest 1988-89b: 328).

On this same day CPO King received authorisation to move Downie from Unit 4 to Unit 2 from Governor Davis, based on the reasoning that Downie's behaviour was steadily deteriorating and his attitude was becoming more aggressive. At 1.15pm, Governor Davis and Governor Penter attended Unit 4 to inform Downie of the move. There are inconsistencies in the prison officers' statements relating to the actual identities and number of the officers enlisted to move Downie. During the inquest, the officers involved were unable to recall the specifics of the operation. The coroner ascertained that the group consisted of CPO King, SPO Cain and prison officers Keating, Fitzsimmons and Robertson, though prisoner accounts suggest there may have been other officers involved (Dessau 1989: 319).

Downie refused to leave Unit 4 voluntarily (Inquest 1988-89b: 1320). King instructed Fitzsimmons to order Downie to come out and that if Downie refused he should go and get the cell assault mattress.[31] CPO King informed the inquest a mattress was taken down but not used (Inquest 1988-89b: 1330). Officers reportedly forcibly carried Downie out of Unit 4 holding his arms and legs. Unit 4 prisoner allegations that officers, and particularly CPO King,

---

[31] The mattress was allegedly used to subdue prisoners during cell extractions and was described as a little round cushion with two straps to put your arm through and it measured approximately a diameter of 76cm (2 1/2 feet) (Inquest 1988-89b: 321).

swore at Downie were denied. CPO King stated that this would never happen under his charge. Words were carefully selected and spoken to avoid a retaliatory situation with the prisoner and officers carried out their duties with 'professionalism' at all times (Inquest 1988-89b: 1332). Fitzsimmons found the suggestion amusing; 'you wouldn't use that language … especially in earshot of other prisoners' (Inquest 1988-89b: 320). Robertson and Keating also denied the use of foul language (Inquest 1988-89b: 1119; see also 1162). It is difficult to ascertain the manner by which Downie was carried from the cell, though it seems that when Downie refused to leave the cell voluntarily, each officer grabbed an arm and a leg and he was carried out. Robertson could not remember whether any strategies for Downie's removal were discussed beforehand (Inquest 1988-89b: 1119). Downie was carried up to Unit 7 and strip-searched. When issued with prison clothing he refused it and so Officers left it in Unit 7. Downie was then placed in a cell and left wearing only his underwear (Inquest 1988-89b: 1162).

That afternoon, Unit 2 duty officers reported that Downie displayed no signs that he might commit suicide (Inquest 1988-89b: 1116). Downie had allegedly requested his property, although this was not given to him as officers stated there was no time to search it properly prior to lockup (Inquest 1988-89b: 1094). The Unit was subsequently locked down early at approximately 3.46pm (Inquest 1988-89b: 1135).

On 26 November 1987, more than three months after Downie's death, CPO King made an additional police statement wherein he admitted to a visit he made to Downie's cell after lockdown at approximately 3.55pm. SPO Jones was on duty in the control room and knew of the visit, yet he did not make any record of the visit in the Unit diary. CPO King was officially off duty at the time of the visit. This visit was made with officers Marten and Cain. Cain was also off duty. Cain first made a mention of the visit to police two years after Downie's death in August 1989 (Dessau 1989: 11).

King alleged the visit was prompted by noise coming from Downie's cell, and that he and the other officers attended to 'calm' the situation.[32] King stated he could see bedding on the floor but had no recollection of any ripped mattress materials. He told Downie that if he had any problems during the night he should press the emergency alarm button:

> I believe after we finished chatting with the prisoner, he seemed quite calm and collected and no great dramas, and we left it at that and I said, "The chances are you'll get all your gear tomorrow". (Inquest 1988-89b: 1328)

When asked during the inquest why he didn't record the visit in any police statements or reports relating to Downie, he replied, 'the conversation as I can remember ... was pretty much a nothing thing at that time' (Inquest 1988-89b: 1346).

Cain and Marten were not involved in the conversation and could not recall why specifically they went down to see Downie. They did, however, recall that King did not open the cell door and spoke to Downie through the trapdoor only. Cain could not say what was said nor was he close enough to see any of Downie's ripped bedding on the floor. His view was that King was his superior and dealing with the situation; 'there was no need for all of us to traipse down and stand in front of the cell and talk to Downie' (Inquest 1988-89b: 1044). When pressed during the inquest about not reporting the visit at the time of Downie's death, Cain replied, 'I'm not trying ... we're not trying to hide anything in this case. It's just that sometimes you remember things and sometimes you don't' (Inquest 1988-89b: 1058).

Officer Marten could not recall specifics either, but he did recall King saying something to the effect that 'If you want to treat your bedding like that you can sleep in it' (Inquest 1988-89b: 863).

Prison officer Noel Gough knew little of Sean Downie: 'He was a pretty quiet sort of fellow. He did say to me one day that he had lost everything. I think I asked him how he was doing and he said that he'd lost everything ... He was the least of our problems' (Inquest 1988-89b: 832-3). Officer Fitzsimmons also raised concerns at this time because Downie had placed himself in isolation to avoid

---

[32] Prison officers were able to monitor sound in prisoner cells via audio surveillance devices installed in the control room areas in each Unit.

other overbearing prisoner personalities in the unit. He appeared to Fitzsimmons to be depressed as he refused to leave his cell even to have a shower. One day Fitzsimmons alleged he went in and opened Downie's cell door:

> Sean was just lying in bed, I don't think he'd had a shower or anything. I said, "How long are you going to stay in here?" and he shrugged his shoulders again. I knew what the problem was and I said, "Why don't you put it in writing then?" I said, "Let me make a report and you just sign a protection form?" And he just said, "No, I just want to stay here". (Inquest 1988-89b: 317)

Fitzsimmons found it extraordinary that Downie refused his help, 'If it was me I'd be going crazy ... I'd be banging my head against the wall but Sean ... he wouldn't show any emotion whatsoever' (Inquest 1988-89b: 317).

On the fateful afternoon of Downie's death, prison officers attending the emergency situation in Unit 2, Macdonald, Morton, Hill and Ryan, reportedly responded promptly and efficiently. The decision was made to first evacuate other Unit 2 prisoners before attending to Downie in case of attack. Macdonald stated, 'from past experience, when prisoners fire up in their cells, upon opening the door officers are assaulted whether with knives, boiling water or other things. This was what I was concerned about at the time' (Inquest 1988-89b 'Statement Prison Officer Iain Macdonald' 24/8/87).

Officer Gough was deeply affected by the fires and deaths during 1987 in Jika. He was on duty during Williams' death, Downie's death and the fatal October fire. When giving evidence he stressed that he found it hard to remember things as each event became mixed up with the others (Inquest 1988-89b: 827-8). Gough was on duty and involved in the emergency situation surrounding Downie's death, and after debriefing with support representatives he was told to take sick leave for a couple of days. On coming back to work he was told that he would not be paid for those days. He said that consequently after the October fire, 'I went home in a taxi, got out of the taxi, threw up in the bush, went home and six hours later I went to work again because I wasn't going to get tricked on that one again' (Inquest 1988-89b: 828).

Gough alleged that on the day Downie died, he overheard a conversation between CPO King and other officers along the lines that 'that guy [Downie] should be up in observation' (Inquest 1988-89b: 830). This was after King, Marten and Cain visited Downie's cell. Though Gough played a significant role in the Downie emergency situation he was unable to recollect the specifics of the operations due to his involvement in other traumatic incidents of the time. He was also plagued by feelings that he could have helped Downie:

> I suppose the question I'm asking myself is that – could I have earlier, when I spoke to Downie, done something, or Mr King have done something or is the system not allowing that to happen. Can those matters be looked at and fixed so that it doesn't happen again? (Inquest 1988-89b: 860)

During the aftermath of the rescue operation, Gough was present in Unit 2 with Governor Penter. He alleged that Penter was annoyed when finding Robertson's note on Downie's gear, which contravened a direct order to officers that afternoon to search and distribute the property before the close of the prison (Inquest 1988-89b: 834).

Gough compiled a later statement where he appealed to the coroner to investigate the Downie matter closely. He stated his concern that during the Williams inquest the statement read out during proceedings was not his own. He also claimed that he and other officers had been approached by an 'unknown' official from 'Head Office' who informed him 'I can tell you what to say in court' (Inquest 1988-89b 'Statement Prison Officer Noel Gough' 4/8/89). It should be noted it was unclear whether this allegation by Gough related specifically to the Downie, Williams or fire inquests. However, Gough expressed his hope that the Downie inquest would not be a repeat of the Williams inquest, as he believed serious questions needed answering. He stated his belief that the leadership of the prison 'left something to be desired'. He also commented that the 'wrong' men were rising through the ranks to higher positions in the division and there were instances where such power was 'abused' (Inquest 1988-89b 'Statement Prison Officer Noel Gough' 4/8/89). Gough's concerns appeared to signify some form of a 'split' between new and older generation prison officers in Jika, but other officers did not echo such concerns during the Downie inquest. It is significant that beyond brief consideration of these concerns during the inquest, the coroner did not pursue the allegations in any depth.

Prisoner Representations

Prisoner Olaf Dietrich had known Sean Downie since he was transferred to Unit 4 in late July 1987. He assisted Downie with legal preparation for his upcoming case and believed that such help, not offered prior to his admission to Pentridge, gave him hope and restored his motivation (Inquest 1988-89b 'Statement Olaf Dietrich' 24/8/87).

Like the other prisoners in Unit 4, Dietrich heard officers entering Downie's cell to transfer him to Unit 2, but was unable to see anything while locked in his cell. He alleged he heard a scuffle but no response from Downie. He later made inquiries into what happened to Downie but received no response. Dietrich maintained in his police statement that he believed Sean Downie was the target of a victimisation campaign by CPO King (Inquest 1988-89b 'Statement Olaf Dietrich' 24/8/87).

Prisoner Rodney Minogue was also in Unit 4 when he heard the commotion. He looked out the crack between the wall and the door. He viewed two officers going into Downie's cell while another went away and returned with a white mattress.[33] The officer went into the cell with the mattress and the other officers followed. He saw Downie brought out soon after. It was unclear to Minogue what was happening, 'I wasn't sure … it seemed a bit of both bragging and carrying on. When they got him in the foyer I heard someone say, "Not here, in the circle"'.[34] Prisoner Richard

---

[33] It was unclear whether a white mattress was used in Jika Jika to subdue prisoners. In this particular case, the existence and usage of such a weapon was contested by CPO King and other officers, though Prison Officer Fitzsimmons first drew attention to its existence (Inquest 1988-89b: 320).

[34] The circle referred to Unit 7 which was a central area where a number of corridors stemmed off to become populated Units. Strip-searching

Light also heard the commotion and alleged that CPO King made threats. He pressed his ear against his cell wall so he could hear better but could not see anything (Inquest 1988-89b 'Statement Richard Light' 24/8/87).

Prisoner Craig Minogue recalled that prior to lunch prisoners were informed the division was short-staffed and they would be locked down between 11.40am and 1.15pm (Inquest 1988-89b 'Statement Craig Minogue' 24/8/87). After lunch Minogue went into his cell, turned his radio on and fell asleep. At 1.10pm he alleged he was woken by the voice of CPO King:

> "On your feet arsehole, on your feet." Then he said "Are you going to clean that up?" He then again said "On your feet." He then said "Right drag him out ... my officers will fix you. You've got an attitude problem." (Inquest 1988-89b 'Statement Craig Minogue' 24/8/87)

Minogue could hear commotion and went to the crack in the door but could not see much. He could only guess at this point that Downie had been dragged out.

Later Minogue observed one of the officers getting his watch back from the panel operator and surmised that this was a good indication the officers coming in to remove Downie had been looking for trouble. Minogue went to clean up the meal Downie had thrown in order to avoid any confrontations with CPO King. Later when Minogue had been informed of Downie's death he recorded his own statement to give to police:

> I decided to write this statement after I was told by another inmate on Side 1 of the Unit that Bluey was dead. I think he was told by a hospital attendant who was in the Unit at about 10.30pm. I was told through the toilet vents which allow you to communicate between sides, I have been in this Unit with Sean for some weeks now and he was a nice quiet bloke who would go along with no worries but the last week he's got the "right royal stuff around" because he wanted to wear his own clothes because he is a remand inmate. (Inquest 1988-89b 'Statement Craig Minogue' 24/8/87)

---

traditionally took place in this area (Inquest 1988-89b 'Statement Rodney Minogue' 24/8/87).

Minogue reiterated his belief that Unit 2, to which Downie was transferred just hours before his death, was used as a punishment unit. Minogue alleged that prison officers transferred prisoners to Unit 2 and on the way it was customary for them to be taken into Unit 7, strip-searched, roughed up, threatened and abused before being thrown into a Unit 2 cell with only a mattress: 'You were often left in the cell with nothing for days or weeks and the discipline was a lot harsher. You were very often locked away from other prisoners and were on your own all the time' (Inquest 1988-89b: 693-4). When Minogue was asked during the inquest whether he believed King had a particular problem with Downie, he replied that King just had a problem with everyone (Inquest 1988-89b: 690).

Minogue also raised his doubts about any prisoner being able to thread a sheet noose through the suicide proof grilles, particularly without any property in the cell. He and the other prisoners in Unit 4 were so certain of this that they conducted a test run to see if they could thread a noose in their own Unit:

> We had the use of nail clippers and all types of pens, pencils, combs, everything that one wouldn't have in Unit 2 because of the set-up in Unit 2 being a punishment unit. We tried for a good hour to make any successful go of it and we decided that it couldn't have been done. (Inquest 1988-89b: 683)

Like Unit 4 prisoners, Prison Chaplain Peter Norden also raised the question of how Downie could have threaded the noose when he had no property with him on being moved to Unit 2. Norden reported prior to Downie's death, no prisoner in Jika had hanged themselves:

> In contrast to the old prison cells in other parts of Pentridge it was designed in such a way that it was difficult for people to damage themselves, including suicide or, for instance, particularly, in hanging. (Inquest 1988-89b: 89)

Norden emphasised the vents in the division were designed to prevent the concealment of contraband. A prisoner would need a strong piece of metal or material to thread a noose because the grille within the vent had little holes less than a quarter of an inch in width making it impossible to get fingers through (Inquest 1988-89b: 89).

In addition to Norden and prisoner witnesses, counsel for the deceased also raised the issue of the suicide-proof grille. Police and forensic investigations immediately after Downie's death did not raise any questions relating to the grille being used as a suicide point. However, it is noteworthy that during the inquest there was no formal inspection of the grilles in response to conflicting evidence. Additionally, there was no admission of a Jika grille as evidence before the coroner in order to test the threading of a sheet noose, although this would have been relatively easy to organise.

Craig Minogue was the only Unit 4 prisoner to give evidence at the inquest. The other prisoners from that particular unit refused when brought before the coroner. The reasons given for this were that the witnesses feared repercussions. Dietrich stated:

> Your Worship, with the utmost respect to this court and its jurisdiction, this court or the highest court in the land cannot offer me protection whilst I'm out there. I've suffered greatly since the Jika Jika inquest and I will not suffer anymore … [Being a witness] doesn't mean a thing when I'm out at Pentridge, with prison officers locking up and feeding you three times a day … Unfortunately the person will get away with it yet. (Inquest 1988-89b: 742-3)

Prisoner John Dixon-Jenkins was classified to Jika in August 1987. Prior to his classification to high-security Dixon-Jenkins took nine hostages within Bendigo Prison. At the time of Sean Downie's death, Dixon-Jenkins had only been in Jika for two weeks. He had also been placed on isolation in Unit 2 Side 1.

Dixon-Jenkins' police statement was tendered as evidence, yet he was not called by the coroner to give verbal evidence during the course of the inquest. Dixon-Jenkins alleged that he witnessed Downie being brought 'roughly' into the unit on 24 August (Inquest 1988-89b 'Statement John Dixon-Jenkins' 23/4/92). He stated that once in his cell, Downie claimed that officers, including CPO King had beaten him during his transfer between units. After lock-up and the departure of unit staff, Dixon-Jenkins alleged that he heard the footsteps of officers coming into the unit so he went to the door and looked through the crack, which meant he could see down the passageway to the corridor connecting the two sides of the unit. He claimed that he saw four or five officers going into the other section of Unit 2. Because he was new to Jika, Dixon-Jenkins was unable to identify the officers. However, he later recognised one of the officers as CPO King. He allegedly heard a door open and then yelling and screaming; 'the screaming came to an end in a choked off sound. Aside from that choked off end to the noise this sounded a lot like other times I have heard prisoners being beaten by prison officers' (Inquest 1988-89b 'Statement John Dixon-Jenkins' 23/4/92). Everything then went quiet and as Dixon-Jenkins found his position uncomfortable he left the door and lay on his bed.

He fell asleep and shortly after, a prison officer wearing breathing apparatus shook him awake. The room was smoky and black ashes had been tracked over the cell floor. Startled by the abrupt shaking, his initial anxiety was that officers believed he was responsible for the fire and that he would be beaten. He was assured that this was not the case and on being escorted out of his cell, he surmised from the position of the sunlight in his cell that no more than half an hour could have passed since he fell asleep. On coming out of the unit, Dixon-Jenkins met with a scene of chaos:

> There were a number of prison officers there, some of them very agitated. One of them kept repeating, "I've got pieces of him on my hands". One of them joked, "He didn't smell as bad burning as the last one". Another told me that if I knew what was good for me I would tell no one about what had gone on. I wasn't sure what he meant at that time because I didn't realise the fire had been connected with Sean Downie. (Inquest 1988-89b 'Statement John Dixon-Jenkins' 23/4/92)

Distressed, Dixon-Jenkins was taken by officers into a visiting box area and given a television. It wasn't until after hearing about Downie's death on the news that he put all he had seen and heard together:

> It is my belief that the prison officers who came back to unit two that afternoon went into Downie's cell and did give him a beating. I do not believe that after this beating Downie did, was able to, could have, had the means to or had the time to start a fire, hang himself and burn himself and his cell ... I believe Downie was not only beaten but also strangled to death by prison officers (whether this was the original intention of the prison officers or not, this could have been a beating that got out of hand). I believe that Downie was then hung and burnt in his

cell by prison officers to cover up the evidence of their wrongdoing. (Inquest 1988-89b 'Statement John Dixon-Jenkins' 23/4/92)

After a few days John Dixon-Jenkins was moved into Sean Downie's cell. He alleged that he was forced into the cell by several prison officers wearing riot gear and carrying plastic riot shields. The cell smelled strongly and there were still pieces of burnt flesh all over the walls, cabinets, table ledge, mirror and bed. The fire damage by the door had been painted over and the floor partially mopped, but on the whole the cell had not been cleaned properly. After repeated requests Dixon-Jenkins was given cleaning materials.

While Dixon-Jenkins was mentioned during the inquest investigations and proceedings, he was never called as a witness. This was the case even though prisoners such as Craig Minogue from Unit 4 were called. There is little discussion or explanation in the transcripts and available exhibits to suggest why this was the case other than the fact that Dixon-Jenkins was 'unavailable' during the inquest. In order to investigate Dixon-Jenkins' allegations, additional forensic and medical 'second' opinions were sought. These forensic examinations reported that the lack of physical marks on Downie's body confirmed the alleged use of violent force by prison officers was 'inconceivable' (Inquest 1988-89b 'Victorian Institute of Forensic Pathology Medical Opinion Re: Sean Downie'). The matter of John Dixon-Jenkins' allegations and the significance of the forensic reports will be subject to further discussion in Chapter Six.

Prisoner Mark Read, more popularly known as 'Chopper', was next door to Downie in Unit 2 the day he died. He offers a conflicting account to allegations made by Dixon-Jenkins and accounts by Unit 4 prisoners. Read was called as a witness to the inquest in 1989 and appeared on two occasions to give evidence before the coroner.

Read was in his cell on the day in question when Downie was brought down wearing only his underwear into Unit 2 by officers. Read alleged that Downie was quite distressed but he also reinforced that it was not 'an uncommon sight' for prisoners to be dressed only in their underwear in Jika (Inquest 1988-89b: 659). According to Read, Downie was concerned and worried about his future. He described him as 'paranoid' about prison officers, feeling he was hardly done by (Inquest 1988-89b: 660). That day Read had access to the day area and corridor outside his cell, and due to the fact that Downie was brought down to Unit 2 a few hours before lock up, Read was able to communicate with him through the door. Read alleged that he passed Downie some cigarettes, four matches, a piece of strike and an *Age* newspaper under his cell door in order to placate him (Inquest 1988-89b: 658).

After the afternoon muster and lockup Read was in his cell when he heard noises from Downie's cell. He claimed Downie was making a racket by kicking his door and yelling. He heard tearing noises, which he believed to be Downie ripping up his bedding. According to Read, four officers came to investigate the noise and to ask what Downie was making the racket about. Read believed the door to Downie's cell was not opened by officers during the course of their inquiries; he couldn't be sure, because he stated, the doors in Jika were noisy when they were opened or closed. With doors opening and closing all the time throughout the unit, he became oblivious to which doors were being opened or closed or if in fact they were being opened or closed at all (Inquest 1988-89b: 669). Read's overall account of the cell visit was that officers spoke briefly, but calmly, with Downie about the state of his cell and then left. He did not think that the cell visit was irregular or unusual. He claims that at the time he was on medication and went to sleep. Read woke to find his cell smoky (Inquest 1988-89b: 664-5). He could not give any indication that he heard Downie building a barrier to light the fire because his medication enabled him to sleep heavily. Read found no delay or problems with the evacuation process by officers (Inquest 1988-89b: 673).

An important aspect of Read's account related to the question of the grille in the cell where Downie allegedly hung himself. His views conflicted with those prisoners in Unit 4 who questioned the possibility that a sheet could be threaded through the tiny holes. Read argued that he used both grilles regularly to string up a washing line throughout his cell (Inquest 1988-89b: 671). He also outlined in detail methods by which the sheet could have been threaded and how prisoners could use materials such as cotton from bedding or clothing, the plastic out of a biro, shoelaces or wire to make the task easier.

> If you've got a thin piece of cloth and you wet the cloth and run it out nice and thin and fold it over in half and chew it with your teeth and push it up ... pull it down and the other bit drops through the other hole, you grab hold of that and thread it through. (Inquest 1988-89b: 664)

Prisoner Sean Warburton was also in Unit 2 in a cell opposite to Downie. After lock up Warburton alleged he heard tearing noises coming from Downie's cell; 'I wasn't sure whether it was a protest and he was trying to damage his cell' (Inquest 1988-89b: 1641). He also heard noises suggesting Downie was attempting to damage the toilet and sink in his cell. He did not hear anything to suggest he was building a fire.

On recalling the final cell visit before Downie was later found dead, Warburton alleged that the prison officers, who he could not identify, all spoke to Downie and swore about the fact that his mattress had been torn up, calling him a 'stupid cunt' (Inquest 1988-89b: 1633). Warburton did not think the cell visit irregular or unusual in any way. When pressed during his evidence, he stated he felt fearful on hearing the officers coming down to the unit; 'it's left over from the bad old days, a fear of nightly visits from prison officers and I feel very uncomfortable if I hear any noises' (Inquest 1988-89b: 1666). He also stated that even if he did hear something he preferred to turn a blind eye in order to protect himself. When asked whether this way of thinking applied to the visit to Downie's cell that afternoon, Warburton replied that he was locked in his cell and that he knew his presence in that unit would be noted by officers 'I just didn't want to go anywhere near where the front of the door was or anything' (Inquest 1988-89b: 1667). When asked if he could recall the doors to Downie's cell being opened by the officers on this visit, he responded in a similar way to Read:

> All I heard was – the doors are pretty noisy when they're opened, they're all electronic and compressed air sort of situation and they open up – I can't say whether they were in there or not, or at the door, or inside, or whatever, but they

> never removed the mattress, I know that. (Inquest 1988-
> 89b: 1640)

Warburton did not explain and was not asked to explain how when locked in his own cell he could know that officers did not remove Downie's mattress which was later used as fuel for the fire. Warburton was in his cell writing a letter when he smelled smoke. He heard knocking on the wall coming from Downie's cell and thought at the time it was a protest. Warburton did not see it as his role to report what was occurring, because, he stated, 'in prison informing just isn't on, so it didn't matter what he [Downie] was doing next door' (Inquest 1988-89b: 1641).

Officers opened Warburton's cell soon after he smelled smoke. As he was being escorted to the safety of the exercise yards, he looked back and allegedly saw 'a big burn mark, a black mark where someone or something had been dragged outside' (Inquest 1988-89b: 1642). The mark was smudged through the doorway of Downie's open cell door. Warburton's allegations contradicted accounts by officers who maintained that Downie's cell was attended last during the evacuation procedures due to the threat he posed to the safety of officers and prisoners.

Warburton referred to conversations and reactions by an officer he saw in the exercise yard:

> After we were in the exercise yard, we were talking with the prison officer; the prison officer was pretty upset, he had tears in his eyes and [said] that, he had probably never seen nothing like that before and he told us they were unsure who to grab first, whether to grab this man and they probably thought he was too far gone anyway or to take us first and in the end, they grabbed the other bloke. (Inquest 1988-89b: 1643)

Prisoner Shane Ward was present in Unit 5 with prisoners Chopper Read and Danny James after the Unit 2 fire and evacuation. Ward alleged that he overheard conversations in Unit 5 between James and Read, 'Mark Read said he knew Downie was a dog and Downie had just come from Unit 6 and that Mark Read was doing his own thing by calling out' (Inquest 1988-89b: 1839). The implication here was that Mark Read was verbally harassing Downie prior to his death in Unit 2. Furthermore, Ward allegedly overheard Read telling James that he was planning on informing the police that he slept right through the incident (Inquest 1988-89b: 1848). The implication being that he heard or in fact knew more than he indicated in his evidence.

Shane Ward had spent some time in Unit 5 with Sean Downie during the period where prisoners were on self-imposed isolation due to problems of harassment from problematic prisoner personalities such as Danny James, and constant protests and bronzing up were the order of the day. He stated that he got to know Downie quite personally during this time:

> I want to stress that Sean Downie appeared to me, at all times, sane and he didn't mind being in his cell alone ... my impressions of Sean Downie as a person was that he was sane, polite, easy going and truly there was a lot of harassment. (Inquest 1988-89b: 1849-50)

He also added in his statement that the allegations CPO King had attacked Downie were fabrications made by prisoners 'out to get King' (Inquest 1988-89b: 1849-50).

While the purpose of this section is to offer an overview of accounts, rather than assess their reliability and credibility, it should nonetheless be noted that Shane Ward had a psychiatric history and due to many incidents, a reputation among other prisoners and the authorities for reporting falsities. When questioned on Ward's evidence against Read, Read stated:

> Like none of us know who Shane Ward is, do we? ... The same bloke who told them he knew where Azaria Chamberlain's body was buried once, and he told them he knew where Donald McKay was buried. He was going to the Stewart Royal Commission to give them his in depth knowledge on international drug dealings. (Inquest 1988-89b: 2005)

The Downie Family and Other Representations

Sean Downie's wife Sally Downie was the main representative from the Downie family to give evidence at the inquest. She drew attention to a number of management issues in Jika and the subsequent physical and mental deterioration of her husband. Sally Downie noted a considerable change in her husband after his transfer to Jika. While in H Division, she believed Downie was at his best because he was working and staff members were flexible about visiting procedures (Inquest 1988-89b: 25). In contrast, and as outlined in Chapter Three, Sally Downie registered her distress at the fact that due to the security requirements of Jika, things were made difficult for her to visit with her and Downie's son (Inquest 1988-89b: 16).

Sally Downie reported that after coming to Jika Downie became increasingly paranoid about prison officer mind games (Inquest 1988-89b: 16). Sally Downie was also concerned about Downie's health and the adequacy of medical care he received. After his reception to Jika Downie had the flu and was given antibiotics for an infection. Sally Downie was a nurse and told the inquest she was surprised that the amount of Amoxil allegedly administered to her husband for this affliction was 250mgs, a dosage appropriate for an eight- to ten-year-old child (Inquest 1988-89b: 24).

According to Sally Downie, after being in Unit 5 for a brief period Downie was, along with other prisoners in the Unit, having difficulty with prisoner Danny James. When telling staff of his inability to mix with James and his need for alternative placement, Downie was transferred to the stricter security regime of Unit 2, which made him extremely angry. Sally Downie stated:

> In one of the letters he does say that he'd been told on admission to Jika, that if he had any problems, to approach the appropriate people, and when he did that, basically ... he was the one that was given a hard time about it. (Inquest 1988-89b: 27)

Prison Chaplain Father Peter Norden got to know Downie during his stay in H Division and on keeping up with Downie after his transfer he was also made aware of problems posed by James, who was a loud and intimidating character. In Unit 5 James was given the run of the unit while other prisoners were locked up. This created tension and bad feeling among the other prisoners. Downie confided to Norden that he was disturbed that it was he who was put into isolation as a result of his complaining to staff of James' behaviour. While Downie was in Unit 2, Norden made a number of representations to CPO King about this issue, which he felt were largely ignored (Inquest 1988-89b: 65).

Norden felt this was because in Jika 'matters of security were a paramount concern and matters of personal need were overlooked and the consequence of that was that serious management problems arose' (Inquest 1988-89b: 66). Norden was surprised at Downie's classification to the high-security unit originally designed for terrorists (Inquest 1988-89b: 71). He had conversations in which Downie confided he felt he was going mad, and that he didn't feel he could talk to anyone. Aside from representations made to CPO King, Norden approached Chairman of the DCC Michael Ryan asking for Downie's placement to be reconsidered. The response was apologetic but there was little that could be done. Downie was classified to Jika for good reason and as to his placement within that Division, staff had to balance many factors such as prisoner personalities, security and cell vacancies, which meant that sometimes these situations arose (Inquest 1988-89b: 82). Norden stated:

> If there was any concern with the security of that division, you could get a change in 24 hours, but where there were concerns of other sorts to do with human and social needs, you could make representations for weeks on end, as I did, without getting any response. (Inquest 1988-89b: 102)

While there was no formal action taken in response to Norden's requests, Downie was eventually moved to Unit 4 where Norden perceived that 'he was doing better and there was light at the end of the tunnel, there were possibilities' in relation to preparing for his case and interacting with other prisoners (Inquest 1988-89b: 115). Norden believed that Downie's transfer back to Unit 2 on 24 August would have troubled him due to his previous experience and so he would have resisted the move, viewing his situation as 'being buried there' (Inquest 1988-89b: 88).

CHAPTER SIX

Exonerating Institutional Liability: Official Responses to the Death of Sean Downie[35]

The inquest into Sean Downie's death commenced proceedings before State Coroner Hallenstein on 19 April 1988, only to be adjourned the same day. The reason for this was that solicitors acting on behalf of the Downie family alerted the coroner to the existence of documents reportedly withheld by the Office of Corrections from the coronial investigation. The documents were obtained through Freedom of Information and passed on to Hallenstein who commented:

> [T]his is perhaps one of the most troubling of matters I have ever seen while I have been a State Coroner … one could say that the institution of the Coronial Service, the position of the Coroner under the Coroners Act, has been treated with something less than one might expect of an institution that should carry some respect for it, if it is going to be of any value to the community at all.

Amongst the OOC documents was a vital report resulting from an internal OOC investigation into Downie's death conducted by Assistant Directors of Prisons Norman Banner and Paul Delphine. Hallenstein stated that the information reflected facts and circumstances surrounding Downie's death previously unknown and unreported to him. He further commented that whether or not these circumstances caused the death of Sean Downie was not the issue, 'the issue is that they are relevant circumstances

---

[35]   The following italicised account is based on the unpublished transcript of proceedings at the Coroner's investigation into the death of Sean Fitzgerald Downie, 1988-89, Public Records Office Victoria, file number 1989/664 (Inquest 1988-89b), 19/4/88 pp 1-2; 19/9/89 p 2033.

surrounding the death; and they are facts which, for whatever reason, had been withheld from a Coroner'. The failure to pass on the information constituted a serious breach of OOC responsibilities set out in the 1985 Coroner's Act. Under the Act the OOC is statutorily bound not only to report the death of any person held in care immediately, but also to provide the investigating coroner with any information that may help the investigation (Coroners Act 1985 (Vic) ss 13.5, 14.1). Hallenstein elected to adjourn proceedings until the documents were submitted through the formal channels and the existing inquest brief updated. Due to the nature of the material contained in what were essentially non-public documents Hallenstein chose to stand down, stating his belief that it would be inappropriate for him to continue in his role as investigating coroner for the Downie inquest.

In August 1989 proceedings resumed under Coroner Linda Dessau and further information was unearthed. It was not until this time that three officers, King, Cain and Marten, came forward to reveal they had visited Downie's cell one hour before his death (Dessau 1989: 10-11, see also 29). The previously unreported and unrecorded cell visit, in conjunction with the apparent failure by the OOC to volunteer information to the investigation, posed serious issues that clouded the proceedings of the inquest. The Director-General of the OOC, Peter Harmsworth, maintained that all information deemed 'relevant' by the department had been provided to the coroner's investigation. In addition, he defended the OOC's initial failure to prepare properly for the inquest, claiming the OOC had never been formally advised by the State Coroner's Office of the inquest starting dates. Dessau stated in her findings that the inquest date and notification were irrelevant; 'the statutory obligation is clear ... the Coroner was not given a clear and honest account of the events integral to a proper investigation of this death'. Dessau's findings subsequently recommended that the unreported cell visit by officers and the broader conduct of the OOC during the inquest be subject to further independent investigation outside the proceedings of the Downie inquest.

Dessau handed down her findings more than two years after Sean Downie's death on 21 September 1989. Dessau found that Downie set fire to his cell and caused his own death by hanging (Dessau 1989: 26). She further found that despite the delay in contacting the Fire Brigade, prison officers involved in the emergency operations had gone quickly to the scene, performing an efficient and competent rescue. She praised their teamwork, quick thinking and bravery, but the OOC did not escape criticism (p 24). Perhaps most significantly, Dessau found that Downie's treatment by duty staff in Unit 2 contributed in part to his suicide:

> In the last hours before his death he was locked in a cell for what would be more than 16 hours. He was wearing only underpants. He was entitled to his cell property. He had requested it. He had been promised it. He did not receive it. He was entitled to his civilian clothing. He had been requesting it over a number of days ... He did not receive it. He was visited by a group of officers about one hour before his death. The officers did nothing towards righting these wrongs. There is no doubt that these deprivations could have led him only to despair ... His spirit was broken by the cumulative effect of the deprivations suffered and in this sense those responsible for his care, those responsible in combination for such treatment and the structure that permitted it have made a contribution to his death. (p 27)

Dessau stated that the OOC had as part of its employ, a number of staff from base grade to senior ranks 'who together and separately acted improperly, inappropriately or unfairly' (p 27). She found that due to this fact the OOC through its employees, agents and servants contributed to Downie's death. Dessau made a number of recommendations relating to existing operational and classification procedures in Jika.

It must be emphasised that Sean Downie's death cannot be considered in isolation from the deaths of John Williams and the Jika five. All these deaths were symptomatic of a system and institution failing to function as it was intended to. Linda Dessau's findings did express some criticism of the OOC. However, in light of the contested circumstances, inconsistencies in the available evidence and the conduct of the OOC throughout the lengthy inquest, Dessau's ultimate finding of suicide as the immediate cause of death left a range of uncomfortable questions unanswered.

Perhaps most troubling was the apparent lack of rigour and thoroughness exercised throughout the inquest in adequately testing evidence that suggested Downie did not commit suicide. These inadequacies are attributable to two fundamental factors. The first is external to the coronial process and refers to a significant lack of openness on the part of the OOC. Broadly speaking, this lack of openness stemmed from deeply ingrained processes of institutional secrecy that functioned to obscure the inner workings of prison from the outside world, while hindering public accountability. The second factor, which forms the basis for discussion in this chapter, broadly refers to the insufficiency of the coronial inquest as a form of official inquiry to investigate deaths in custody. Such insufficiencies stem from: the State Coroner's limited ability to investigate beyond the immediate circumstances of the death; the primacy acceded to the official account over other non-official accounts during the inquest process; and a lack of systematic and scientific rigour in testing evidence throughout the course of investigations.

The Jika Jika fire and the subsequent closure of the division in November 1987 propelled the Victorian OOC into a significant 'crisis of legitimacy'. This crisis stemmed from the high number of deaths and prisoner allegations of officer misconduct, ill treatment, brutality and corruption within the official and organisational ranks of the OOC. Even after the Jika fire and the seven deaths in 1987, the Victorian Government and OOC refused to address the seriousness of the situation. No independent inquiry or Royal Commission was appointed. Consequently, the inquests served as the only avenue for institutional accountability and scrutiny. In spite of this, throughout the inquests the OOC maintained a refusal to cooperate fully with the process. OOC officials instead actively thwarted certain aspects of the investigation while attempting to control and limit what aspects of Jika's managerial and institutional routine would be subject to investigation.

The central purpose of this chapter is to review Dessau's finding and also provide a critical examination of the official investigations and inquiries that followed Downie's death. Questions are posed as to the adequacy and effectiveness of the coroner's powers to investigate and make findings with respect to deaths in custody and the *Coroner's Act* 1985 (Vic). More specifically, it assesses the extent to which the inquest served the need for institutional accountability and public scrutiny with respect to the contested circumstances surrounding Sean Downie's death. Ultimately this chapter demonstrates that the official investigations conducted into Downie's death prioritised the interests of correctional officials and staff over efforts to provide a full and thorough investigation into and explanation for Sean Downie's death.

Investigating Prisoner Deaths in Custody: Deficiencies in the Inquest Process and the Victorian Coroners Act 1985

Historically the inquest was established as a principal public forum, functioning, when held in relation to state agencies, on the premise that deaths involving such agencies are matters of significant 'public interest' (Hogan 1988: 117). The independent powers of investigation afforded to the coroner distinguish the coronial inquest from other forms of official inquiry. The inquest is intended to serve as a critical forum with the central purpose of rendering state institutions and agencies subject to public scrutiny and accountability in the event of a death in custody. The need for public accountability in this context is further heightened by the fact that the conduct of law enforcement agencies, such as police and custodial staff within prisons, is often obscured and protected by institutional processes of secrecy. Such public accountability is critical and proportionate to the vast powers allocated to state agencies. As Michael Hogan (1988: 116) argues:

> The state has at its disposal enormous coercive powers, both physical and legal. When someone comes into contact with the state, the state assumes responsibilities for the wellbeing of that person. If someone dies in the custody or through the actions of state officials, a heavy burden must rest with the state of satisfying us that its actions have been beyond reproach. Accordingly, the standards and mechanisms by which this is determined are of great importance.

Much has been made of the independent status and uniquely broad powers of investigation legally afforded to coroners as investigators. In the public eye, coroners are seen almost universally as state officials independent of the police, the prisons and criminal courts (Scraton & Chadwick 1987: 220). Despite the predominance of this view, the idea that the coronial process serves as an impartial mechanism of accountability constitutes a hotly debated area in the United Kingdom and the United States. In Australia it is an area of inquiry in great need of further scholarly research and critical consideration. Vital to the thrust of this chapter is the argument that the legal avenues and mechanisms for post-death investigations, particularly the inquest, are seriously limited. Relevant to this discussion is a general examination of deficiencies in the coronial process in Australia. Consideration of broader theoretical approaches to explaining and understanding the occurrence of deaths, particularly suicides, in custody is also provided.

Central to this discussion is the landmark 1987-1991 Royal Commission into Aboriginal Deaths in Custody (RCIADIC), which was established in response to increasing public concern at the high number of Aboriginal deaths in custody and the inadequacies of official explanations for the deaths. While the Commission focused upon the deaths of Indigenous Australians, the findings in the National Report remain significant for all deaths in custody in that they drew attention to serious deficiencies within existing official and legal frameworks for post-death investigations and avenues for institutional accountability. The RCIADIC stands as the only national formal inquiry of its scale appointed to scrutinise investigations into deaths in custody in the Australian criminal justice system. Commissioner Elliott Johnson stated in his 1991 National Report that there may not have been a need for a Royal Commission or at least the terms of reference may have been quite different:

> had there been adequate objective and independent investigations conducted into each of the deaths after they occurred and had those investigations examined not only the cause of death – in the medical sense – and whether there had been foul play but also questions of custodial care and the issue

of responsibility in the wider sense. (RCIADIC Report 1991: Overview & Recommendations p 3)

Significant amongst Johnson's concerns were the limited scope of the inquest investigation; the undue reliance placed by police and coroners on misleading or inaccurate evidence without critical examination; the failure to call relevant witnesses; and delays in the scheduling of inquests and the delivery of inquest findings (RCIADIC Report 1991: vol 1 ss 4.5.5, 4.5.8). Johnson also charged that in the case of the deaths subject to the RCIADIC terms of reference, the immediate post-death investigations by police lacked rigour and thoroughness. He maintained this stemmed from the fact police often approached the investigation with the preconceived and unquestioned notion that the death was a suicide. The result was that important evidence was lost, omitted or not tested and the investigation failed to reveal a complete account of the circumstances surrounding death. Hence Johnson recommended that whether or not a death appeared to be a suicide, all deaths in custody must be investigated as though they were homicides in order that all evidence be accounted for and tested (RCIADIC Report 1991: vol 1 s 4.1 Rec 35a). Johnson stated:

> The public should be satisfied that the prisoner or confinee came to his death by the common course of nature, and not by some unlawful violence or unreasonable hardship put on him by those under whose power he was while confined. There should not be given an opportunity for asserting that matters with regards to deaths in public institutions are "hushed up". (RCIADIC Report 1991: vol 1 s 4.7.2)

When a death occurs and allegations of mistreatment or brutality are raised and circumstances are contested, it is only natural that suspicions on the part of fellow prisoners, friends and family are magnified. While the thoroughness of police post-death investigations signifies a crucial starting point in the overall process, there remain very few avenues open to the coroner during the inquest to exercise a matching level of rigour in testing evidence. As Scraton and Chadwick (1987: 216) highlight, it is not the role of the inquest to serve as:

> a court in which people are on trial. It is an inquiry and its procedure is inquisitorial and not adversarial, as in other courts.

In that sense "guilt" is not at issue and no one is accused. Should liability, civil or criminal, be raised then the inquest should be adjourned and the issue of liability resolved in the appropriate court.

Furthermore, evidence is not treated with the same stringency as evidence presented during a criminal court hearing. Victorian Coroner Graeme Johnstone argues that this approach better suits the inquest's integral role, which is ultimately to search for truth. He contends that the 'strict application of the adversarial rules of evidence and procedures would severely curtail this role and unduly hamstring a coronial inquiry, effectively "marginalising" its community importance and effectiveness' (Johnstone 1988: 145). Despite Johnstone's concern, the fact remains that the inquest often serves as the only public forum where evidence can be heard, cross-examined and state agencies held accountable. It is therefore a most significant process for the friends and families of those who have died. In the event that serious allegations are made, the meticulous testing of evidence, while essential, is hindered by the predominantly inquisitorial nature of the inquest and the narrow scope of investigation afforded to the coroner.

Freckleton and Ranson (2006: 662) state prison deaths represent one of the most contentious and difficult topics canvassed in coroner's courts. Issues such as conditions of confinement and provision of adequate care, particularly for prisoners considered 'at risk', are paramount to circumstances surrounding death, particularly suicide. In spite of this it is not the role of coroners to determine criminal liability; 'instead, the coroner is to find the facts from which others may, if necessary, draw legal conclusions' (Freckleton & Ranson 2006: 629). There is therefore a tendency in modern investigations and findings by Australian coroners to avoid legally defined terms such as 'suicide', homicide', 'natural causes' or 'accident', and instead mediate evidence and describe in detail the medical causes and circumstances leading to death (Freckleton & Ranson 2006: 629). Australian coroners in all jurisdictions do not have powers to commit individuals to public trial. In the event that irrefutable evidence arises to suggest staff misconduct or violence has led to a death, the only option open to coroners is to refer the case to the Department of Public Prosecutions (DPP). The DPP then makes a decision about whether formal charges will be laid and the matter referred to trial.

In some Australian jurisdictions, including Victoria and Tasmania, coroners are able to make findings of contribution. As Freckleton and Ranson (2006: 645) acknowledge, it is an integral part of a public inquiry to establish how a death occurred through the agency, intervention or involvement of another person or entity'. In this respect, coroners are mandated to make findings identifying any person, body or agency who may have contributed to the deceased's death (2006: 644). Contribution is not concerned with the direct causes of death, as Freckleton and Ranson (2006: 648) establish, 'the more derelict in duties the person is found to be, the closer to the foreground of events preceding the death, and the more likely it is that he or she will be found to have contributed to the death'. Contribution constitutes a contentious finding that has been subject to legal criticism in the past, in so far as judgments of fault and or blameworthiness can determine criminal and civil liability, which it has been argued exceed the coroner's powers (2006: 644-6). However, coroners continue to make findings of contribution. In the context of prison and police deaths in custody, such a finding is one of the few avenues amounting to a form of public accountability for state agencies. In Victoria, findings of contribution are often accompanied by the incorporation of criticisms and recommendations in the interests of preventing future similar deaths. This is particularly relevant to issues surrounding adequacy of institutional care in cases where prisoners identified 'at risk' have died in custody (2006: 663-4).

A significant deficiency pinpointed by Commissioner Johnson in the National Report of the RCIADIC was the issue of 'narrow focus'. Generally speaking, the issue of 'narrow focus' refers to the limitations imposed on the coroner's power to investigate the immediate circumstances and causes of death only. In this sense it is common that a coroner's finding will ultimately focus on the immediate medical causes and circumstances surrounding death. Consequently, Johnson recommended that coroners be required by law 'to investigate not only the cause and circumstances of the death but also the quality of the care, treatment and supervision of the deceased prior to death' (RCIADIC Report 1991: vol 1 s4.7.4, Rec 12). To illustrate this by way of example, if a prisoner is found to have committed suicide, the coronial process often relies on 'discovering intent', thus 'focusing on a rationale for suicide over the gathering of information concerning the circumstances of death' (Brown 1988a: 52). Such an approach is problematic in that it fails to consider the impact of imprisonment upon the deceased, and in what manner this experience may have contributed to suicide. David Brown (1988a: 52) has identified two conflicting theoretical models for understanding prison suicides. One, 'importation theory', looks upon prison suicide as random in its occurrence, arguing that the experience of imprisonment has a limited influence on prisoner suicidal behaviour. The second model, 'deprivation theory', emphasises the role of the experience of imprisonment. As Canadian researchers Reasons and Bray argue:

> Let us view the prison suicide as violence produced by the nature of the procedures, policies and practices of the prison, rather than focusing upon the inmate as both offender and victim (cause and consequence). (Canadian researchers Reasons & Bray cited in Brown 1988a: 52)

In a coronial inquest there is an attempt to balance these two approaches to finding cause for prison suicides, though often it is the case that the coroner is limited and circumspect in investigating beyond the immediate circumstances of death (Freckleton & Ranson 2006: 664). With respect to the RCIADIC, Commissioner Johnson asserted that the narrow focus of the inquest often resulted in a direct failure to examine broader custodial issues external to the immediate circumstances and causes of death particular to Indigenous prisoners.

Just as there are distinctive factors and issues implicated in the cause and effect of Indigenous deaths in custody, so are there in deaths in high-security institutions. In the case of the 1987 Jika deaths, the narrow focus of the inquest presented barriers to attempts by the coroners to investigate how the custodial regimes and practices particular to Jika may have given rise to these deaths. Instead, large amounts of time during the inquests were dedicated to establishing the non-compliance, violence and criminal identities of those who had died. The link between deaths in custody and custodial conditions in high-security is little documented in Australia during this time. This constitutes a significant omission given that Jika Jika was one of the first institutions in Australia designed on the premise of controversial behavioural modification and sensory deprivation principles.

In 1987 the Australian Institute of Criminology conducted a national review of deaths in custody that revealed in statistics only, that maximum-security prisoners were 'grossly over-represented' (Brown 1988a: 56). Brown (1988a: 57) highlights that the report failed to formally recognise this correlation, let alone make any attempt to identify any common factors among the deaths associated with the custodial and disciplinary regimes of maximum-security confinement. Particularly troubling was the fact that there was no information given as to whether the deaths occurred in general maximum-security sections or in special isolation, segregation or disciplinary cells (1988: 57). As can be seen with the case of Sean Downie, the role of his confinement within Jika Jika cannot be downplayed as a contributing factor in the lead up to his death. It is arguable that in one sense Coroner Dessau did address the issue of his personal treatment, even if she was not able to fully inquire into the psychological impacts of Downie's transfer as a remand prisoner to high-security conditions in Jika. However, the manner in which this was dealt with by Coroner Dessau in the 1988 to 1989 inquest cannot be addressed adequately without a brief consideration of the structures and processes informing Victorian coronial structure and process.

While there are consistencies in the administration of the coronial process across Australian States, Victoria remains distinctive in that it was subject to significant reforms that took a major departure from English law in 1985. It was the implementation of these reforms that significantly distinguished Victoria's coronial functions from other Australian States. The *Coroners Act* 1985 (Vic) reformed legislation to create a centralised State Coroner system. It was the first time in Australia that such an integrated coronial structure was established (Waller 1998: 4). The

1985 Act entailed a 'State-wide service under the direction of a legally qualified State Coroner combining the independent offices of the coroner with that of medical and scientific expertise in the Institute of Forensic Pathology' (Johnstone 1988: 143). The changes had a number of implications. Significant was the emphasis on prevention and in this context it was believed that:

> [The] marriage of the law, in the guise of the Office of State Coroner, and the medical and scientific professions in the institute would create the best climate for death investigation and its contribution to prevention. (Johnstone 1988: 142)

While aiding the coroner in the investigation of deaths, the Institute was also empowered to conduct formal research in the interests of preventing future fatalities.

Under the 1985 Act the Office of the Coroner is empowered to investigate and examine all reportable deaths and to make findings with respect to the identity, cause and circumstances of death and the identity of any person found to contribute to the death (Johnstone 1988: 143). It is also the jurisdiction of the coroner to investigate fire. Perhaps most notably, the coroner is empowered to comment and make recommendations on public health and safety, or 'the administration of justice which relate to the death' (Johnstone 1988: 143). The Office of the Coroner's power to commit for trial was also removed, the implication being that any matter before it that relates to criminal law is beyond its jurisdiction. As stated above, if during an investigation a coroner believes an indictable criminal offence has been committed their only remaining role is to refer the matter on to the Director of Public Prosecutions (Johnstone 1988: 143). Victorian State Coroner Hallenstein summarised the key objectives of the Victorian coronial service as:

> to draw together the expert materials and conclusions, to see if anything, and if so what, can be learned from the event and its investigation and to see if there is anything which could be done to avoid repetition of unnecessary tragedy. (State Coroner Hal Hallenstein cited in Johnstone 1988: 143)

In sum, during this time the newly reformed Victorian coronial system was distinguished from other States in that it integrated a range of bodies and organisations to comprise a comprehensive post-death investigation system under the umbrella of the State Coroner's Office and the centralised authority of the appointed State Coroner. With the exception of New South Wales, the coroner's power to make recommendations within inquest findings presented an additional distinction between Victoria and other States at this time.

In the National Report of the RCIADIC, Commissioner Johnson praised the revamped Victorian system as the most 'innovative and efficient in Australia' (RCIADIC Report 1991: vol 1 s 4.5.18). In addition, critics such as Hogan (1988: 123) referred to the changes as 'radical and comprehensive'; an 'overhaul' of existing legislative frameworks and administrative arrangements. However, it must be emphasised that such acclaim and praise stemmed exclusively from an evaluation of the legislative changes, rather than the actual translation of reform into practice. Commissioner Johnson has acknowledged there is often a gulf between the implementation of legislative reform and the realisation of those changes in practice (RCIADIC Report 1991: vol 1 s 4.5.60). Despite the changes within the *Coroners Act* 1985 (Vic), the reality was that many of the core deficiencies described above remained. As Johnson reported, it was a result of these deficiencies that coronial structures and processes subsequently failed to 'supply the critical analysis which is needed of the reasons for custodial deaths' and that in the few cases where coroners did pursue these matters, 'the issues raised were frequently not brought to the notice of the relevant authority and certainly not to the notice of the public' (RCIADIC Report 1991: Overview & Recommendations p 3). Presently all Australian jurisdictions have been amended and provide for coronial recommendations. However, it remains that there are few formal mechanisms or procedures put in place to ensure recommendations are addressed and where practicable, implemented (Freckleton & Ranson 2006: 662).

As illustrated through the Sean Downie case, the intended function of the inquest to provide institutional accountability and scrutiny remains limited and tokenistic. This is because the inquest is essentially an official inquiry. Its structure and processes are determined by the same official discourse that functions in the interests of the very state agencies subject to scrutiny.

Performing Accountability and Scrutiny: The Coronial Inquest as 'Public' or 'Official' Inquiry?

As I have argued elsewhere, rather than producing any real avenues for accountability, reform or change, official responses to prisoner deaths in custody are tactical in that they function to reinforce the institutional power and legitimacy of the prison authorities (Carlton 2001: 50-6). The role and power of official discourse as a legitimising tool for state agencies whose conduct is subject to public question, is essential in this respect. Carlen and Burton (1979: 48) have characterised official discourse as 'the systemisation of modes of argument that proclaim the state's legal and administrative rationality. The discourse is a necessary requirement for political and ideological hegemony'. In other words, when discreditable episodes occur, creating what Carlen and Burton refer to as 'legitimacy crises', authoritative modes of official inquiry ultimately function to exonerate the state agencies being held to account for such episodes (1979: 44). In this way, official investigations, reports and inquiries can be seen to represent:

> a system of intellectual collusion whereby selected, frequently judicial, intelligentsia transmit forms of knowledge into political practices. The effect of this process is to replenish official arguments with both established and novel modes of knowing and forms of reasoning. (1979: 7-8)

For Scraton (2002: 28), 'the production of truth and the exercise of power are inextricably interwoven'. He states that it is through the very processes of official truth making and denial that, 'not only does the state claim legitimacy for the operation and function of power, it proclaims and confers legitimacy on truth' (Scraton 1999: 275). It is thus through the powerful discourses of law, epistemology, social science and commonsense, encapsulated within the processes of official truth making, that the official view is institutionalised and accepted as 'formally sanctioned knowledge' (Scraton 2004: 175-94).

Central to the maintenance of ideological and political hegemony is the prominence given to the official version of events as authoritative, rational, truthful and in most cases, 'the facts'. As Carlen and Burton (1979: 44) highlight, it is a central function of official discourse to redeem the legitimacy of state agencies and institutions through the 'confrontation and appropriation of unofficial versions of discreditable episodes'. This is a fundamental tactic of those dominant and powerful groups who claim 'commonsense' or 'truth' as their own (Hogg & Brown 1998: 18-44). Official versions are thus bolstered and legitimated at the expense of other critical accounts, which are relegated outside the realm of 'commonsense'. Moreover, such accounts are neutralised, marginalised and silenced through their treatment as 'other' or 'untruth'. In this way, official representations maintain their dominance within Becker's (1967: 242-3) 'hierarchies of credibility' and are thus received and relied upon unquestioningly as 'the truth'.

In the case of prison post-death investigations and inquests, the primacy of the official account is established from the moment the investigation begins. This stems from the fact that the major and trusted witnesses to the events surrounding the death are prison officials and staff – the very gatekeepers of institutional prisoner discipline, management and secrecy. Witness statements by duty staff and prison administrators are thus extensively supported by corroborative, 'official' documentation including prison officer memorandums, governors' reports, diaries, prisoner musters and incident reports. Moreover, such 'facts' comprise the very basis for the coroner's inquest brief and are thus relied upon to piece together a picture of the immediate events leading to the death of the prisoner. In this way, 'the account of "the facts" or "what happened" is taken from the mouths of the institutionally most powerful, the "primary definers" – police and prison officers' (Brown 1988b: 38). Conversely, the response to non-official allegations or accounts contesting the official version of events are questioned and treated as 'unreliable', 'agenda' or 'value-driven'. As Scraton and Chadwick argue, such accounts are represented as 'political', comprising strategic attempts to undermine authority.

Perhaps the most pervasive and powerful tool state agencies have in the event of a death in custody is the criminal record of the deceased. During inquest proceedings it is common that counsel representing the interests of state officials set out to direct attention away from the actions and behaviour of prison staff and officials, while focusing on the character of the deceased as unmanageable, non-compliant and in particular, violent. As Jack Henry Abbott (1981) famously stated of his own experience in the United States prison system:

> If I were beaten to death tomorrow, my record would go before the Coroner's jury – before anyone who had the power to investigate – and my "past record of violence" would vindicate my murderers. In fact, the prison regime can commit any atrocity against me, and my "record" will acquit them.

During Sean Downie's inquest, counsel representing the OOC and prison officers spent much time establishing Downie's 'violent' tendencies: his 'violent' disregard for authority, 'violent' outbursts, alleged 'violent' threats made to officers, and his continual involvement in 'violent' protests. Downie's prison record was produced and counsel for the authorities catalogued a range of incidents including alleged violent assault, threats to officers and barricades, along with further minor disciplinary infringements, to demonstrate a steady deterioration in his behaviour and attitude. With the exception of a few, many prison officers agreed Downie demonstrated an aggressive disposition. This was supported by a series of internal investigations conducted in the aftermath of Downie's death. Deputy Director-General of Prisons Michael Ryan observed that Downie's 'pattern of behaviour over the preceding eight or nine months, both criminally and in the prison environment suggests the workings of a very troubled and disturbed mind' (Inquest 1988-89b: Exhibit BH). Further to such official reconstructions of Sean Downie during the inquest, was a focus on his demonstrated inability to 'adjust' to prison life, his growing depression, psychiatric instability and desperation (Inquest 1988-89b: 1668).

The official documentation to support the official view of Downie's character was thin. Some of the officers alleging Downie was a dangerous and unpredictable prisoner had no specific dealings with Downie on a day-to-day basis, and had only 'heard' things from other officers regarding his conduct (Inquest 1988-89b: 465). In addition there were Jika duty officers who gave evidence to the effect that in their dealings, Downie was quiet, kept to himself and was not a difficult or troublesome prisoner (Dessau 1989: 20). In this context it is significant that the contents of Downie's classification file mainly comprised documentation pertaining to minor prison disciplinary infringements and pending assault charges that led ultimately to his transfer to Jika. This is because the stated purpose of Jika was for 'unmanageable' and long-term prisoners, particularly those posing a security risk. To make an informed and justified decision to place a 'first-timer' who was on remand into a high-security section like Jika with long-term prisoners, clearly required further documentation.

Downie's file did include a series of newspaper clippings reporting his capture and arrest for murder prior to his imprisonment (Dessau 1989: 27-8). However, while the decision to reclassify Downie to Jika depended partly on these charges, no police records relating to this investigation were included to support the transfer. This was a considerable omission as Downie was reportedly suicidal at the time of his arrest. Perhaps most disturbingly, the R&A Committee did not have any documentation on Downie's involvement with psychiatric services while in prison, and as the inquest progressed it became clear that Downie's psychiatric and medical records were inconsistent and incomplete (Dessau 1989: 27). Such information was crucial given Downie's transfer to high-security. Prison Social Welfare Officer Paul Hamilton gave evidence stating that after Downie died he had indeed 'lost' or most likely 'destroyed' Downie's files documenting their meetings (Inquest 1988-89b: 191). Claims by prison officials and staff that records and files have been 'lost' or destroyed constitute typical responses devised to protect institutional and official secrecy.

Coroner Dessau (1989: 27-8) commented on some of these omissions and inadequacies, and stated they demonstrated poor prison management, inadequate record keeping and communication, though she did not go as far as to question the official depiction of Downie's character. On the contrary, the construction of Downie's character as aggressive, violent and unstable permeated Coroner Dessau's findings. At the time of his death Downie was a remand prisoner and his charge of murder was yet to be heard. However, Dessau made reference to his alleged murder of a taxi driver in what she described as 'cold blooded circumstances' (p 17). She concluded on the second page of her findings that Downie was a 'troubled man responsible for an impulsive and senseless act of violence' (p 2). The ultimate effect of this was to find guilty and publicly serve judgment on the deceased who was at the time of his death a remand prisoner and had yet to be given the opportunity to defend himself in court.

Scraton and Chadwick argue (1987b: 220) that the construction of 'reputations', through the use of imagery associated with social inadequacy and violence, can be used as a means to legitimate and justify deaths in custody, whilst minimising the seriousness of allegations of negligence, brutality or misconduct. A further troubling, yet logical implication here for Sean Downie was that due to his dangerousness, non-compliance and instability he was in a way expendable – as though he had no value as a human being. Moreover, such a view suggests Downie's death could not be deemed controversial due to his status as a prisoner and more particularly a high-security prisoner. Michael Hogan (1988: 130) further supports this view stating that:

> The effect is to blame the victim: they, and they alone, are the problem. Attention is diverted from the officials and agencies, and from the law and practice which gave rise to the death. The context of the death is ignored or denied.

This view of Sean Downie as 'violent' and 'dangerous' was largely supported and echoed in the public arena by the daily tabloids at the time of his death. The Sun proclaimed in its headlines, 'Jika hanging, cabbie case man' and reported that at the time of his death, 'Downie was on remand for the brutal slaying of Melbourne taxi driver John Robinson' (*Sun* 25/8/87 p 1). Such newspaper reporting was also prevalent during the aftermath of the Jika fire two months after Downie's death wherein the complete criminal and prison records were published alongside photographs of deceased prisoners Arthur Gallagher, James Loughnan, David McGauley, Richard Morris and Robert Wright (*Herald* 30/10/87 p 22). The construction of criminal reputations and use of violent imagery to support the notion that there may be an 'acceptable' death in custody further reflects the prevailing dominance of official versions of events. It also demonstrates the powerful effectiveness of official discourse, which seeks to focus on the dangerous and violent nature of those who have died in custody in order to divert attention away from, and legitimate, the behaviour and conduct of state agencies subjected to scrutiny.

Imprisoning Prisoner 'Truths': Hierarchies of Credibility and the Official Discrediting of Prisoner Evidence

> The prisoner, you've got to remember, is always the liar. He can't be believed.
>
> **Ex-Jika prisoner Peter Reed** (Interview 15/5/04)

During inquests, prisoner evidence is subjected to significant scrutiny, interrogation and scepticism by the authorities. In particular criminal records and reputations are raised and used to discredit and delegitimise prisoner accounts that challenge the official version of events as unreliable. Moreover, it is a strategy applied most rigorously to prisoners considered to be 'troublemakers' or 'political' while inside, thus easily dismissing and silencing their complaints as vexatious and largely dishonest. This constitutes a further example of the way attention is diverted from the behaviour and conduct of state agencies and focused upon pervasive fear-inducing stereotypes associated with the 'criminal', the 'dangerous', the 'inadequate', the 'mad' and the 'deviant'. Such imagery is located outside the commonsense world of 'respectability, conformity and genuineness', and provides powerful justification for the management and 'marginalisation of identifiable groups' (Scraton & Chadwick 1987: 213). As Scraton and Chadwick (1987: 213) have noted, such constructs have throughout history been institutionalised and transmitted as powerful ideologies forming the basis 'for the political management of crime, "social problems" and a whole range of social policy and criminal justice responses'. They further argue, 'They are not merely analytical constructs but are powerful definitions present in the discretionary use of state power by the police, Department of Health and Social Security officials, magistrates, judges and prison officers'.

Therefore, it is not surprising that the coroner does not intervene or place any limitations on lengthy lines of questioning aimed at establishing the criminal identities and reputations of prisoner witnesses during cross-examination. This is because notions of 'reliability' and 'credibility' comprise 'officially' constructed or 'commonsense' notions informing the very structures of the criminal justice system. They are privileged and unquestioned and positioned against the reputations and identities associated with criminality that are conversely, constantly interrogated and challenged.

However, when a prisoner gives evidence supporting the official version of events, this evidence is often uncritically privileged as 'truth' over other prisoner evidence. This raises the question as to whether the presentation and testing of evidence during the inquest process is subject to double standards that privilege the views and interests of state agencies over the importance of institutional accountability. It also raises the question as to how such adversarial lines of questioning find a place within a process officially celebrated for its inquisitorial focus and quest to uncover 'truth'. It is difficult to see or justify how the personal criminal and prison records of prisoner witnesses are relevant to the process of investigation and making findings in relation to the cause of death and circumstances surrounding death. Selective official strategies to discredit or indeed use prisoner evidence can be well demonstrated through the comparison between the treatment of prisoner Craig Minogue's evidence and Mark 'Chopper' Read's evidence by counsel acting for the authorities in the Downie inquest.

The official view that Downie's steady deterioration in attitude and demeanour was partly attributed to his placement in Unit 4 was largely accepted by Coroner Dessau. As particularly stated, it was considered that Downie's impressionable nature led him to be influenced by other 'trouble-making' and 'non-compliant' prisoners well known for their 'views' of prison officers and Jika generally. Craig Minogue was considered to be one of these prisoners. He gave evidence during the inquest proceedings, alleging officers had verbally abused, threatened, brutalised and subsequently murdered Sean Downie the evening he died. He further alleged such threats and brutality by officers comprised a common experience for prisoners in Jika. While Minogue had not been a direct witness in Unit 2 where Downie died, he alleged witnessing the threatening and rough-handed transfer of Downie by officers from Unit 4 only hours before his death. He also alleged that another prisoner, who he refused to name, provided him with a first-hand account of the circumstances surrounding Downie's death in Unit 2. In addition, he strongly disputed that it would have been possible for a prisoner to thread a noose through the perforated grilles located in the roofs of prisoner cells. During the inquest proceedings, counsel for the authorities, Mr Thomas, spent little time clarifying the details surrounding Downie's death, choosing instead to focus almost exclusively on Minogue's reliability and credibility as a witness. In making extensive reference to Minogue's criminal record, Thomas pressed him to reel off his convictions and charges (Inquest 1988-89b: 700-1). In particular, Thomas sought to capitalise on Minogue's recent and well-publicised alleged involvement in, and conviction for, the Russell Street bombing,[36] and went as far as to directly quote the sentencing judge:

> I could not consider that it is an exaggeration to state that you struck a blow at society itself, expressing by that action your contempt for the institutions and values upon which ordinary decent members of the community depend. You expressed complete disregard for what is and must remain the central tenet of our community, that is that human life must be treated as inviolable. (Inquest 1988-89b: 698)

---

[36] Despite his conviction, Craig Minogue maintains his innocence, alleging he was framed. He remains in prison to this day.

Thomas also pursued Minogue's conduct while in prison, asking questions about his involvement in prisoner rights campaigns and his participation in protests such as the October fire. In particular he questioned him over his recent attack on a Jika prison officer with a can of fruit in a sock (Inquest 1988-89b: 704). Thomas dismissed Minogue's allegations that the officer in question had attempted to threaten and stand over him. Furthermore, he rejected Minogue's allegations that Jika prison officers used mind games and abused prisoners, drawing attention instead to Minogue's record of involvement in violent protests and his reputation among prison officials and staff as a known 'troublemaker'. Thomas further suggested that Minogue and other prisoners in Unit 4 had successfully manipulated Sean Downie into participating in prisoner protests within the Unit. In making this suggestion Thomas created the implication that Unit 4 prisoners contributed to Downie's disciplinary transfer, and subsequent death, by encouraging him to engage in the militant pursuit of his rights. Minogue responded that such accusations were 'fanciful' and without any basis in fact (Inquest 1988-89b: 718). Thomas ended his line of questioning by suggesting it was Minogue's allegation that officers had murdered Sean Downie that was fanciful, and such allegations were evidently part of a 'campaign' by prisoners aimed at tarnishing the names and reputations of prison officers (Inquest 1988-89b: 720).

Minogue refused to give the name of the prisoner who alleged to him that Downie was murdered. He also strongly denied the claim by Thomas that he was engaged in a 'campaign' against prison officers:

> Rather than getting back at officers I have done myself a great disservice coming here today … The point is that I will now without a shadow of a doubt be subject to repercussion for my evidence here today. I will be gaining nothing out of this. I will only be losing. Quite frankly, I would have preferred not to be called. I stuck my head out in the Jika matter and we have a two man police task force investigating corruption, we have a two-bob judicial inquiry which is holding an inquest into the inquest and the ombudsman is investigating himself, so the point is if it

was something decent, I may be able to be more willing to come and stand up here. (Inquest 1988-89b: 699)

Coroner Dessau (1989: 7) acknowledged that in light of the 'hothouse atmosphere' apparent within Jika during this time she would accept Minogue's allegation that officers used foul language. However, she was unequivocal in her refusal to accept his allegations of officer impropriety, instead questioning Minogue's credibility as a witness: 'I was not impressed with Minogue as a witness of credit, particularly in his view of prison officers and I think it unsafe to accept his unsupported evidence'.

Other prisoners in Unit 4 – Richard Light, Olaf Dietrich and Rodney Minogue – also witnessed Downie's transfer to Unit 2 the afternoon that he died. They gave statements supporting Minogue's allegations that they could hear Downie being forcibly removed from his cell by officers. They further noted that the state of Downie's dishevelled bedding and mattress after the transfer suggested to them there had been a scuffle (Inquest 1988-89b: 'Statement Richard Light' 25/8/87; see also 'Statement Olaf Dietrich' 25/8/87). However, they refused to give evidence during the inquest proceedings due to their stated fear of reprisals in prison. Prisoner Richard Light specifically stated that due to the nature of his evidence and allegations made during the Jika fire inquest before Hallenstein, he had suffered repercussions (Inquest 1988-89b: 738-9). Rodney Minogue and Olaf Dietrich echoed such concerns and all prisoners noted they had been required to give evidence during the Downie inquest with little notice and no opportunity to seek legal advice and representation. Dietrich stated to Dessau, 'I just don't want my life being brought into public scrutiny again and I certainly don't want to be subject to the whims of certain prison staff with a sadistic mind' (Inquest 1988-89b: 743).

Unit 2 prisoner Mark 'Chopper' Read gave evidence that Dessau used to inform her findings. In alleging he often used the grilles in Jika cells to hang a washing line, he detailed how Downie could have hanged himself (Inquest 1988-89b: 664). He alleged Downie was visibly distressed after being transferred to Unit 2 and expressed this to him. He alleged he heard Downie destroying his cell and then fell asleep until the rescue operation. He found no delay in the prison officer emergency operations (Inquest 1988-89b: 673). Read's evidence largely supported statements put forward by prison officers involved in the emergency operations who reported they found Downie hanging from the sheet attached to the vent in his cell. Despite Read's notoriety and his lengthy criminal and prison histories, his reliability and credibility went unquestioned during his cross-examination. This it seems was due to the fact that his evidence supported the official version of events.

Coroner Dessau privileged Read's evidence with respect to the use of the grille over both Minogue's and the prison chaplain Father Peter Norden's evidence (Inquest 1988-89b: 89). As outlined previously, Minogue and Norden expressed their scepticism over the possibility of threading a sheet through the tiny perforated holes of a Jika cell grille. Norden stated during the inquest: 'I think any person who knows the layout of that cell would immediately say, "How on earth did he do it?"' (Inquest 1988-89b: 92). Minogue, who alleged he and other Unit 4 prisoners had attempted unsuccessfully to test the possibility, concluded it was an unachievable feat and would be particularly difficult for Downie, who was unable to see adequately without his glasses (Inquest 1988-89b: 683). After Downie's transfer to Unit 2, he was dressed in only his underwear and during this time had no access to his property, including his glasses (Inquest 1988-89b: 687). Despite such conflicting accounts, Dessau did not call for a grille to be brought in and tested during the inquest proceedings. Not only does this highlight a privileging of 'official' evidence to suit official versions of events, it demonstrates a troubling lack of rigour and inconsistency in testing the reliability of crucial evidence that suggested Downie may not have died by self-inflicted hanging.

Prisoner Allegations and the Matter of Dixon-Jenkins

Further evidence suggesting that Downie did not commit suicide were allegations put forward by prisoner John Dixon-Jenkins that Downie's death was a result of officer misconduct. Irrespective of the seriousness of Dixon-Jenkins' allegations, he was not at any stage of the Downie inquest called to give evidence. Nevertheless, his attempts to raise his concerns with the police and the authorities were ongoing. In the immediate aftermath of Downie's death, Dixon-Jenkins wrote statements regarding events leading to the death and letters complaining of his own treatment in Jika Jika. Office of Corrections investigators and Victorian Police interviewed Dixon-Jenkins several times regarding the matter during the years following the Jika inquests and the subsequent 1990 Murray Inquiry appointed to inquire into the conduct of the Office of Corrections during the Jika inquests. He alleged that in all such interviews he was advised he was mistaken in his allegations:

> I think the last thing ... in the world they ... want to find is that prison officers, including a prison governor, murdered a prisoner. If with similar evidence a prisoner was accused of murdering a prison officer that prisoner would have been convicted years ago. It is most suspicious that in five investigations into the death of Sean Downie not only was I not called, but my name was never even mentioned ... Additionally, one might wonder why there were five investigations if there were no serious doubts as to the cause of Downie's death. I smell a cover-up and a cover-up of the cover-up. (Inquest 1988-89b: 687)

Dixon-Jenkins insisted his allegations be treated seriously and continued to appeal for further investigations. He claimed that his persistence had led to his ongoing harassment by officers, alleging that he was threatened by a high-ranking officer who warned he would be the next to die. He stated at the time: 'I believe it is only a matter of time before great harm is done to me by, or on behalf of, prison authorities' (Inquest 1988-89b 'Statement John Dixon-Jenkins' 23/4/92).

While he was not formally called as a witness, Coroner Dessau considered Dixon-Jenkins' statements and allegations in his absence. In September 1989, just prior to final submissions by counsel, she made brief reference to the matter of his allegations, stating Dixon-Jenkins was out of the country and the Coroner's Office had been unable to contact him. During inquest proceedings Dixon-Jenkins was on parole, the implication being that while on parole he would be unable to leave the State, let alone the country, without permission (Inquest 1988-89b: 1990). This was not explained during the inquest proceedings but Dessau was not prepared to pursue the matter any further:

> It leaves me at the end of a very long inquest, after a great deal of evidence, with a copy document attributed to him. It has in it, in relation to these issues, self-admitted limitations and certainly against the thrust of an enormous amount of evidence that I have heard, so I do not propose to do anything further. (Inquest 1988-89b: 2053)

The Autopsy and Consideration of Forensic Evidence

In order to investigate Dixon-Jenkins' allegations that Downie was beaten and murdered, additional forensic and medical opinions were sought from Dr Ranson to ascertain if there was evidence of foul play. While Ranson on the whole concurred with the original autopsy performed by Dr Richard Byron Collins, it remains significant because he raised concerns and issues that were not addressed in Dr Collins' report.

As pathologist to the Coroner, Dr Collins was responsible for performing the original autopsy and presenting his report on the medical cause of Sean Downie's death. Overall his findings stated that the cause of death was consistent with hanging. However, he stated that there were no carbonaceous materials found in Downie's mouth, oesophagus or lungs (Inquest 1988-89b 'Statement by Dr Richard Byron Collins' 25/8/87). During the inquest this evidence raised the question as to whether the fire in Downie's cell was lit either after he had died or he had in some way been rendered unconscious prior to his death. The fundamental implication arising from such evidence was that there might have been additional parties present in the cell who were responsible for Downie's death. However, this possibility was largely discounted by Collins who reported he was unable to find any signs of trauma on Downie's body to suggest he had been subjected to a beating (Inquest 1988-89b: 437). During his cross-examination Collins made it clear that he could not state definitively either way as to whether the fire was lit before or after Downie had died. He was also unable to ascertain whether Downie was unconscious at the time the fire was lit. He responded to these issues by stating that his finding as to the cause of death was consistent with hanging and not fire (Inquest 1988-89b: 429). However, he did concur with the suggestion put forward by counsel for the authorities that it would have been possible for Downie to light the fire and then execute a suicide by hanging, particularly given the smallness of the cell (Inquest 1988-89b: 436).

The second opinion sought by Dr David Ranson to address the Dixon-Jenkins allegations, was made on the basis of Ranson's review of original autopsy reports, along with the available forensic photography. No independent investigations were made. Overall Ranson concurred with Collins in stating that, 'were violent force in the form of a beating to have been delivered to Sean Downie prior to his death, I would consider it inconceivable that no marks of this would be found following a thorough autopsy examination'. According to Ranson such a finding contradicted allegations put forward by Dixon-Jenkins that Downie had been involved in a physical confrontation with prison officers prior to his death (Inquest 1988-89b 'Victorian Institute of Forensic Pathology Medical Opinion Re: Sean Downie' p 3).

However, his findings did raise two further significant issues. First, he stated that the visible distribution of 'hypostatic lividity' over the body indicated to him that at the time the photographs were taken, 'the body had been lying in various positions on the floor for some time following death' (Inquest 1988-89b 'Victorian Institute of Forensic Pathology Medical Opinion Re: Sean Downie' p 3). Such an observation raised the question as to the length of time between Downie's death and the notification of police, forensics and other emergency services. While Ranson did not specifically state this as a concern, this observation accorded with the evidence put forward by the Metropolitan Fire Brigade (MFB) District Officer Peter Eagan who expressed concern that the MFB was not notified for up to an hour after the incident. While the incident was reported to have taken place at 4.55pm, they did not attend the scene until 6.21pm (Inquest 1988-89b: 1698).

Ranson also raised his concern at the concentration of burns located on Downie's face and on the upper part of his body, while the bottom part of his body was completely unscathed by heat damage. He stated:

If an individual was hanging in a room with a fire the seat of that fire being at floor level and some distance away, one would expect the heat damage distribution on the body to be more uniform and to involve the lower portions of the body equally or more so than the upper regions of the body, assuming the heat damage to be caused by direct radiant heat. (Inquest 1988-89b 'Victorian Institute of Forensic Pathology Medical Opinion Re: Sean Downie' p 3)

Ranson also stated that skin loss caused by the heat damage could have obscured underlying trauma to the body at the time of the autopsy and Collins may have overlooked this if he had not specifically tested for it. Collins had in fact made reference to this when giving evidence. Ranson concluded he could find no evidence to suggest injury or manipulation by third persons. Furthermore he stated that in his opinion it was unlikely given the build and size of Sean Downie that he could have been manoeuvred into a hanging position without any signs of injury left on his body, whether he was conscious or unconscious at the time (Inquest 1988-89b 'Victorian Institute of Forensic Pathology Medical Opinion Re: Sean Downie' p 4). Despite his stated concerns, Ranson was confident that Collins had conducted a thorough and sufficient autopsy the first time round. Dessau accepted Ranson's broader conclusions relating to the lack of physical injury apparent on the body and did not investigate Dixon-Jenkins' allegations further.

'Scientific Myths of Epistemology' and the Use of Expert Forensic Opinions

It is pertinent here to consider briefly some problems arising from the apparent privileging of forensic science opinions as 'expert', value-free evidence in judicial and coronial proceedings. Since the 19th century, scientific modes of inquiry have been privileged with an authoritative and 'commonsense' status. That is they have been traditionally regarded as 'the facts'; free from the 'impediments of value and subjectivity' and rather 'dictated by the logic of empiricism' (Freckleton 1997: 1144-5). Indeed, the popular confidence and authoritative weight allocated to scientific 'expert' evidence in criminal and civil proceedings demonstrate the lasting power behind such 'scientific myths of epistemology' (Freckleton

1997: 1144-5). As Ian Freckleton (1997: 1151-2) highlights, the taken-for-granted authority of 'expert' evidence is reinforced in the very manner by which it is presented. Thus the combination of impressive professional credentials, qualifications and demeanour on the part of expert witnesses provide the misleading impression that such reports comprise 'the facts' rather than constituting opinion or an interpretation of the available facts.

Contrary to the requirement of neutrality impressed upon forensic science professionals, Freckleton (1997: 1148) argues that certain circumstances may undermine such impartiality. He cites examples where police or government agencies have sought assistance from forensic scientists, who could potentially develop work relationships and come to view their primary function as 'helping' such agencies rather the providing an independent opinion on the available facts. For example, under such circumstances forensic scientists may feel obligated or influenced to provide 'pro-prosecution' evidence during criminal proceedings, or in the case of scientists employed by State-run laboratories, they may come to see their role as providing expert opinions favourable to the interests of government agencies. This is particularly pertinent to coronial inquests and post-death investigations in Victoria where the State Coroner's Office is amalgamated with the Institute of Forensic Science. An additional problem raised by Freckleton (1997: 1143) is the limited pool of forensic professionals available throughout Australian States. Freckleton notes that when a second opinion is sought during criminal or civil trials there is a tendency to opt for practitioners employed by a State-run forensic laboratory from another city rather than use the small number of independent practitioners within the jurisdiction.

Brown and Wilson (cited in Freckleton 1997: 1157) argue that well-publicised 'expert' forensic bungles in Australian cases, such as the criminal trial of the Chamberlains during the 1980s and 'Bomber' Barnes controversies, have resulted in an increasing level of cynicism directed towards forensic science and forensic scientists. The use of forensic evidence in the Chamberlain case constituted 'one of the more notorious examples of scientific malpractice' in the context of Australian criminal law (Freckleton

1997: 1162). In 1984 the Chamberlains were wrongly convicted of their daughter Azaria Chamberlain's murder on the basis of incorrect forensic scientific opinions. This related specifically to a substance found under the dashboard of the family vehicle reported by experts to be foetal blood. Later such opinions were found to be erroneous and the substance in question was reported as more likely Coca-Cola or blackcurrant juice than blood (1997: 1164).

While the use of botched evidence and opinion in the Chamberlain case raised concerns about human error in the laboratory, the Bomber Barnes controversy raised serious concerns regarding impartiality and accountability. Freckleton (1997: 1175) states that as a senior State-employed forensic scientist 'Barnes was shown to have had a disturbing history of giving biased, pro-prosecution evidence'. A key example of this was the 1996 inquest investigation into the death of Archie Butterly who had been shot dead while escaping from prison. Barnes gave evidence to the effect that a female prison officer who had aided Butterly's escape had been responsible for discharging the bullet that resulted in his death. During the inquest the coroner questioned Barnes' neutrality, based on evidence he had given at other trials. Ultimately a second opinion found a series of flaws in Barnes' evidence, arguing that there was no conclusive evidence to suggest who pulled the trigger (Freckleton 1997: 1171). Freckleton (1997: 1175) states that the Barnes controversy highlighted the dangers posed by an expert witness, 'whose opinions are not readily reviewable or are subtly skewed in favour of the side calling him'. Furthermore, Barnes as a senior scientist was known for his refusal to submit his findings to peer review processes and had an inclination to give evidence that was 'both overstated and ambiguous, but favouring the prosecution' (Freckleton 1997: 1175). The above cases thus raise critical questions in regards to the rigour and objectivity of forensic science and suggest that it is not in fact 'the wizardry it is often believed to be' (Dershowitz cited in Freckleton 1997: 1167).

The Role of Forensic Experts in Post-Death Investigations

The role of forensic experts and methods in post-death investigations are regarded as essential in determining the cause of death. In the RCIADIC National Report, Commissioner Johnson noted that the fundamental purpose of the autopsy is to 'discover and describe all the pathological processes, including injuries found on examination of the deceased. The object of the examination is to enable the pathologist to determine the cause of death, the identification of pathology contributing to death, and to correlate these to clinical observations made in life' (RCIADIC Report 1991: vol 1 s 4.4.1). Johnson further suggested that while it is the role of the pathologist to report exclusively on the medical cause of death, such findings should also yield some objective basis upon which to test evidence put forward by witnesses concerning the broader circumstances of death (RCIADIC Report 1991: vol 1 s 4.4.3). In regard to the Downie inquest this was not the case. This is due to the fact that the coroner's testing of evidence and allegations as to whether there was a third party involved in Downie's death focused solely on whether there was physical evidence of force in the form of bruising or injury. There were no questions raised as to whether the extensive burns to the upper regions of Downie's face and body were self-inflicted and no formal testing or evidence given, other than the word of Dr Collins, to suggest these burns were not instrumental in obscuring any deeper sign of injury or force.

Commissioner Johnson stated that it is essential that the pathologist responsible for the autopsy pay particular attention to any 'signs' consistent with ill treatment or foul play:

> It is desirable that there should be an extensive examination for the purpose of establishing whether the deceased had been bruised or manhandled. In cases of hanging, for example, such examinations may go a long way to eliminate any suggestion that the person was forcibly hanged or hanged after being killed in some other way to conceal the original cause of death. (RCIADIC Report 1991: vol 1 s 4.4.4)

In the case of Sean Downie, the idea that Downie's death may have been the product of a 'beating that got out of hand' or that a third party may have played some part in his death was dismissed on the basis of expert medical opinion rather than concrete evidence. In this context, the pathologists appeared more concerned with eliminating the possibility that foul play may have taken place, rather than exploring and testing the evidence objectively and thoroughly. Such evidence was not rigorously tested or weighed up against other evidence regarding the plausibility of threading a noose through the cell grille or the unreported 3.55pm cell visit by officers.

'The 3.55pm Cell Visit'

In her findings Dessau set aside a section titled 'the 3.55pm cell visit' where she dealt extensively with her concerns prompted by the cell visit by officers to Downie's cell, exactly one hour before the alarm was raised. Dessau (1989: 12) stated that she could not make 'definitive findings' about what occurred at the cell suffice to say that officers attended Downie's cell, spoke roughly to him about the mess he had made with his bedding, and then left the cell stating they would sort things out in the morning. According to Dessau, outside these observations there was no available 'credible' evidence to indicate what occurred during the exchange. SPO Jones, who had commenced duty in the control room, did not record the visit though it was his duty to record the comings and goings within the division. It was also evident he did not monitor from the control room what transpired throughout the exchange between Downie and the officers. 'Chopper' Read allegedly overheard the officers speaking to Downie through the trap door of the cell; they then left and he fell asleep (p 8). Prisoner Warburton reported that the officers had sworn at Downie calling him 'stupid cunt' for tearing up his mattress and stating he could sleep in it (p 9). Warburton could not recall whether the officers opened the cell door during the exchange. Dessau stated that while she heard second-hand evidence from prisoner Craig Minogue about what had transpired his evidence was essentially 'hearsay'. Interestingly, Dessau did not refer to the allegations and statements made by

Dixon-Jenkins in her findings. She only referred to the pathologists' 'extensive check for signs of trauma [that] revealed none' (p 9).

Nevertheless, Dessau still had concerns. First, she stated her disquiet that nobody seemed able to tell her 'with certainty' what prompted the visit; 'I would expect a simple answer to this issue. It was after all significant as a visit to a prisoner who was found dead very soon after' (p 9). Dessau also remained uncertain as to why three officers were required to go to Downie's cell when there was a shortage of manpower. She stated that while there was evidence to suggest this was 'fairly routine' she also noted it was a response described to her as 'unusual' (p 9). She further stated that she remained unconvinced that there was a sensible reason for three officers to venture into Unit 2, 'particularly for an incident over which they apparently had so little recall immediately thereafter' (p 9).

Dessau found it 'peculiar' that SPO Jones had not recorded the visit given that it would have proved 'logical and prudent' to do so given Downie had only been transferred that afternoon for 'management' problems (p 10). However, most troubling to Dessau was the fact that the visit was not for some time reported or recorded and the relevant OOC officials were not informed until King disclosed, in November 1987, that there was a visit. The other two officers did not report their involvement until the inquest investigation commenced under Dessau's direction during July in 1989. Overall, Dessau stated that:

> The curious and troubling aspects of the evidence that I have referred to leave me with a feeling of great unease about this visit. It is too exquisite a coincidence that the four relevant officers failed to recall this event as significant when they made their reports and police statements that night or the following morning and indeed for periods varying between months and years. I am convinced that the officers, at least for some months after Downie's death knowingly concealed that visit from this investigation. (p 11)

Dessau therefore recommended in her findings that the matter of the unreported cell visit and the unwillingness of the OOC to provide information during the initial proceedings of the inquest under Hallenstein be subjected to further investigation.

Sealing the Cracks: Further Internal and External Inquiries and the Ultimate Exoneration of the OOC

In the immediate aftermath of Sean Downie's death, a number of internal investigations were conducted. As stated above, initially these were not voluntarily released to the Coronial investigation. While such reports were exclusively 'internal' and protected from public scrutiny by the Privacy Act, they nonetheless constituted documents informed and structured by official discourse. Rather than representing authoritative texts supported by rationality, evidence and truth, they represent self-interested official submissions and assertions geared towards the exoneration of officials. Assistant Director of Security Norm Banner and Assistant Director of Programs Paul Delphine conducted an initial and general 'Enquiry into the Death of Prisoner Sean Downie' during October 1987. This report was compiled after interviews were conducted with the relevant prison officials and staff. The terms of reference addressed Downie's transfer to Jika, his behaviour and subsequent management while in Jika, his psychiatric state, and the response to and management of the emergency situation (Inquest 1988-89b: Exhibit AX). The report focused its concerns on the significant lack of supporting documentation regarding the various transfers of Downie between units in Jika and the failure of staff to deliver his civilian clothing prior to his death. Banner and Delphine took pains to establish thoroughly Downie's increasing aggression and threatening behaviour while in Jika. They documented his deteriorating attitude and instability yet concluded, 'Although Sean Downie's behaviour had warranted three independent referrals for psychiatric assessment within seven months, there was no evidence that he suffered from a psychiatric condition' (Inquest 1988-89b: Exhibit AX). Such a finding highlights the paradox faced by authorities. While they had to justify the transfer of a remand prisoner to Jika Jika on the basis of the risk they posed to security and their demonstrated 'dangerousness', to avoid facing liability they also had to discount the possibility that the prisoner suffered from a psychiatric condition.

Banner and Delphine also referred to the emergency response by prison staff. They wholly rejected the 'adverse publicity' initiated by the MFB, who raised their concern at what they believed was an unreasonable delay in their notification by prison staff. Banner and Delphine defended staff actions in stating that they were 'acting in accordance with the Unit's Standing Orders, which require that the OIC [officer in charge] assess the fire risk and then act accordingly' (Inquest 1988-89b: Exhibit AX). Banner and Delphine concluded they found no fault in the emergency response by officers involved. Conversely, prison officer Iain Macdonald, who was involved in the emergency response, alleged that during his interview with Banner and Delphine he had raised his own concerns regarding the lack of emergency equipment in the unit and the fact that there were no ventilation or smoke extraction systems in an airtight division (Inquest 1988-89b: 503). After broaching these concerns, Macdonald alleged that Banner turned to inform the stenographer to delete that section of the notes. When Banner and Delphine were asked about this incident during the Downie inquest they both denied the allegation (Inquest 1988-89b: 1593; see also 1772). During the course of the inquest it became clear that the notes compiled by the stenographer for Banner and Delphine's report were missing or destroyed. While Delphine stated he could not specifically remember destroying them, he admitted he did have a 'habit of destroying things' he no longer had any need for (Inquest 1988-89b: 1594).

Due to the issues raised, Banner and Delphine's report prompted three further reports. The OOC Director of the Criminal Justice Unit, John Van Gronigan, conducted a report in response to Banner and Delphine's findings in December 1987 to be forwarded to the Attorney General. He stated his concerns that the entire incident would most definitely attract criticism of the OOC. He commented, 'the entire matter indicates a serious lack of accountability and professionalism as well as possible insubordination' (Inquest 1988-89b 'Memorandum Addressed to Attorney-General's Department, Re: Death of Sean Downie' 23/12/87). He also recommended that the OOC should address such issues and investigate the matter further. A further 'suicide audit report' was compiled by Stephen Kerr on behalf of the Corrections Health Service and this comprised a report specifically related to Downie's personal history and his circumstances in prison (Inquest 1988-89b 'Suicide Audit Report: Sean Downie' 11/87).

Deputy Director-General Michael Ryan conducted a further confidential and internal inquiry into Downie's death in March 1988, where he drew the unexpected conclusion that the real cause of Downie's death was:

> the physical design of 'K' Division and the managerial policies and procedures that were practised at the time. All this contributed to an environment that fostered aggression, hostility and non-conformity from prisoners and probably regular examples of mismanagement by prison staff, including bastardisation. (Inquest 1988-89b Ryan 'Inquiry' 3/3/88)

Such a statement constituted an extraordinary admission and was only released to the coroner after counsel for the families had made a Freedom of Information (FOI) request for the document, which was at first rejected and was only successful after they appealed to the Administrative Appeals Tribunal. Ryan's statement was significant in that it represented official acknowledgement that conditions in Jika Jika were a contributing factor in the culmination of crisis and death during 1987.

The 1990 Murray Inquiry

In 1990, the Murray Board of Inquiry investigated and reported on the matters referred to by Coroner Dessau in her investigations and findings pertaining to Sean Downie's death. The inquiry, chaired by Tony Murray QC, was established to investigate unresolved allegations and issues that extended beyond the jurisdiction of coroners. These allegations related to both the Downie inquest and Jika fire inquest investigated by Hallenstein. The Murray Inquiry was established as part of a series of investigations appointed by the Cain Government to inquire into a range of matters that will be addressed in further detail in Chapter Seven. The Murray Inquiry did not provide scrutiny or accountability over Downie's death and rather served to protect the interests and legitimacy of the OOC, its officials and staff. While this is subject to detailed examination in

Chapter Seven, the ineffectiveness of the Murray Inquiry lay with its narrow terms of reference (Murray Report 1990: 6-7).

With respect to the Downie case, Murray reported the OOC had breached its obligations through its failure to cooperate with the coroner in providing information. However, Murray attributed such shortcomings to mere carelessness, 'a mistake' or failure by department officials to check upcoming dates. Murray could not find such inaction by the department to be 'wilful', which is 'a necessary ingredient for an offence', and so consequently no action was prescribed (Murray Report 1990: 45).

In addressing the intimation by Coroner Dessau that the prison officers who made the final visit to Downie's cell had colluded with one another and were not frank in giving evidence during the inquest, Murray was unable to comment. He stated that these allegations were not encompassed by the terms of reference and as far as he was concerned, 'the matter was fully explored at the inquest and the evidence of each relevant prison officer was thoroughly tested' (Murray Report 1990: 45).

A further inquiry into the Victorian Prison System by Peter Lynn in 1993 reported that certain actions had been taken in response to circumstances surrounding the death of 'prisoner "X"', Sean Downie (Lynn Report 1993: 182-3). He stated that after the closure of Jika, there was ministerial action and 'a substantial corporate effort to be seen as less secretive and to be less concerned about exposure to the risk of criticism from sources outside the Department' (Lynn Report 1993: 182). Lynn reported the OOC had placed the officers responsible for failing to report the visit to Downie's cell on misconduct charges and these were heard in 1991. All four Officers charged were subsequently acquitted (Lynn Report 1993: 183). To clarify, the officers were charged only for failing to report the cell visit. The actual purpose of the cell visit and what transpired during the exchange between CPO King and Downie was never brought to public attention beyond what emerged through the Downie inquest.

Coroner Dessau neglected to adequately address a host of troubling issues and inconsistencies in evidence throughout the inquest proceedings. It is palpable from the transcripts and evidence that despite the unexplained and unreported cell visit to Downie's cell by officers, Dessau did not adequately investigate any suggestions pointing to – or prisoner allegations of – prison officer misconduct. In a subsection of Dessau's findings titled 'The 3.55pm Cell Visit', no mention was made of Dixon-Jenkins' absence from the witness list, or his allegations made from within Unit 2 at the time of Downie's death. Instead, during the inquest a great deal of time was spent ascertaining prisoner officer levels of emergency training, while clarifying Jika emergency procedures and standing orders. Much time was also spent ascertaining why it had taken so long to process Downie's request for his civilian clothing. Extensive questions were asked to ascertain who was to blame for this and why he had not been given his property or some of his clothing after he had been transferred to Unit 2 during the afternoon of his death.

This chapter is not intended to build a case to argue that Sean Downie's death can be attributed to foul play or misconduct by officers. Given the lack of available evidence and information it is impossible to do this. However, it can be stated that the omissions regarding this matter in the official reports speak more loudly than the inclusions privileged as 'authoritative' and 'truth'. Much has been made of the independence enjoyed by coroners and subsequent powers of investigation. The purpose of this chapter has been to draw attention to the inadequacies of this process and the consequences. These inadequacies can be traced directly to the entrenched ideologies and official discourses prevalent within official responses to deaths in custody, which privilege state interests. The result is to circumvent state scrutiny, accountability and justice for the friends and families of the deceased.

The Downie inquest signified ongoing tension between state and prisoner accounts. In the case of Sean Downie and the death of the Jika five, the OOC defended against, and most vehemently rejected, prisoner allegations of staff misconduct and mismanagement, prisoner brutality and abuse. On a grander scale the conflict between official accounts and prisoner allegations represented a battle over the legitimacy of hi-tech high-security prisons such as Jika and whether such institutions served as an acceptable or indeed humane means of containing the systems' high-risk and long-term prisoners. While such a debate received comprehensive public attention and interest throughout the proceedings of the Jika fire inquest, this saturation coverage overshadowed the proceedings and outcomes of the Downie inquest and the host of inadequacies and troubling issues raised above.

CHAPTER SEVEN

Imprisoning Crises: Official Responses to the Jika Fire as Strategies of Damage Control and Concealment[37]

Late in the afternoon of 29 October 1987, Prison officer Desmond Sinfield was in the records office checking warrants when he heard the Pentridge alarm sound. Another officer ran in and announced frantically that Jika was on fire. Sinfield was in the Pentridge Security Squad and as he ran 400 metres to the burning division, he met seven or eight security members along the way. By the time they reached the scene the door to Side 2 had been breached, prisoners removed and work had begun on Side 1. Sinfield was struck by the chaos, 'blokes were yelling and running everywhere. You could smell it, and see the black smoke coming out of Unit 4. No one seemed to be in charge'.

Access to the area was uncontrolled and as the emergency operation progressed the call for Pentridge officers to assist was met with more and more officers pouring into the foyer area. Senior District Officer Wayne Garrard of the Metropolitan Fire Brigade (MFB) likened the scene to a 'Myer's bargain basement sale at nine in the morning', and stated that if the MFB firemen had attempted to take control they would have been 'lynched'. Despite the apparent urgency of the situation and Garrard's advice that the

---

[37] The following italicised account is based on State Coroner Hal R Hallenstein, *Finding of Inquisition upon the Bodies of James Loughnan, David McGauley, Arthur Gallagher, Robert Wright and Richard Morris*, 28/7/89, Victorian Department of Justice Resource Centre (Hallenstein 1989) pp 60-76; Andrew Rule, 'One man's truth was a shock to the prison system', *Sunday Age* 25/10/98; Alex Messina, 'Fire Chief tells of confusion at Jika fire', *Age* 13/4/89; Alex Messina, 'Fireman tells of chaos and frenzy at Jika fire' *Age* 15/4/89.

foyer be cleared of excess prison officers to allow better MFB access, Governor Donovan emphasised that for safety reasons the MFB should wait outside while Pentridge staff got the Side 1 prisoners out. He stressed the risk of possible 'booby traps' and that prisoners may attempt to take hostages as part of their protest; 'we have five killers in there. We'll look after them, we'll get them out'.

Sinfield assumed control of attempts to breach the Side 1 corridor doors. He and prison officer Stillman were the two main officers at the forefront of these operations. Sinfield with a firemen's axe and Stillman with a sledgehammer forcefully inflicted alternate blows to smash the bulletproof glass in the door. However, the congestion created by numerous officers in the foyer was so great that Sinfield and Stillman were impeded. Sinfield was pushed forward into the path of Stillman's sledgehammer and was consequently struck on the head and injured. Nonetheless, he continued to work at the doors in spite of his injuries. When a hole was finally smashed through the glass, toxic smoke spilled out and many officers were overwhelmed by fumes.

At this point Governor Penter directed all officers not wearing breathing apparatus to leave the Unit. Sinfield and Stillman ignored the order and kept working. When the Side 1 door was eventually breached it was 5.10pm, approximately one hour after the fire had reportedly been lit. A sound resembling a thunder rumble resonated before black smoke cascaded into the foyer area. Many officers were badly affected by the smoke and were treated outside the complex by ambulance staff. A total of 14 officers were hospitalised. According to Garrard, in the chaos that ensued there was no apparent strategy or leadership amongst the attending officers. Some men were working beyond their capacity, others who had received treatment for smoke inhalation posed a threat to themselves by continually returning to the smoke filled foyer; 'some men were panic-stricken and disorientated, running backwards and forwards; wearing breathing apparatus with face masks off, sweating, red in the face. Some with shirts on, some with shirts off, some disorientated, irrational and yelling'.

After the door was first breached, Sinfield squeezed through the door into the Unit. He recalled that it was blacker than being blind; 'I put a hanky over my mouth, wet it and felt my way along the walls, yelling as much as I could for the prisoners to lie down on the floor until we could rescue them. I went into three cells feeling for bodies with my feet. I felt one body, the first one we pulled out'. He returned with breathing apparatus and a light to locate the other prisoners and realised at this point that the intensity of the heat had caused his nylon pants to melt and stick to his legs and the wax on the top of his boots bubbled. Gradually all the bodies were removed from Unit 4 and after fruitless attempts at resuscitation, Arthur Gallagher, James Loughnan, David McGauley, Richard Morris and Robert Wright were pronounced dead.

Like many prison officers involved in the emergency response to the Jika fire, Desmond Sinfield's injuries were far-reaching both physically and emotionally. He had burned his legs, hands, eyes and nose. He coughed up black mucous for weeks. He developed asthma and a mysterious bowel complaint requiring surgery, and long after the inquest he continued to carry a heavy burden of emotional stress.

At the inquest, Sinfield told the truth, as he saw it, about Jika's 'fatal flaws', and the mishandling of the emergency response that led to the deaths. Sinfield's evidence reflected negatively on the way that the government and the prison administration had run Jika Jika and the prison system generally. He gave his account despite intimidating and aggressive threats by Office of Corrections (OOC) officials who made it clear staff were to convey a uniform account of events that worked in the interests of the prison authorities. Because he defected from this line, Sinfield was publicly discredited, humiliated and vilified by the OOC during the inquest. Despite his treatment, Sinfield's willingness to tell the truth led to a number of other officers submitting evidence that diverged from the official line. Most important, Sinfield's accounts of the fire and his allegations that officials attempted to threaten and intimidate him ultimately thrust the OOC into damage control. Officials were thereafter forced to publicly defend

allegations of corruption and the institutional and organisational
legitimacy of the prison administration.

This chapter returns to the starting point of the book in order to address official responses to allegations of organisational corruption, staff misconduct and mismanagement that arose from the 1987 Jika fire and inquest investigation that followed. After the fire, the OOC faced investigation and critical scrutiny over numerous issues including alleged misconduct and abuse of prisoners; staff mismanagement and malaise; and a demonstrated lack of leadership and staff incompetence during the emergency responses to the Jika barricade and fire. Officials also faced considerable criticism over their apparent failure to address the urgent need for a review of emergency procedures and staff training for fire in Jika after the deaths of prisoners Barry Quinn in 1984 and Sean Downie in August 1987. Moreover, the very design of Jika had been subject to censure and the use of remotely operated electronic pneumatic doors came under attack after Attorney General Jim Kennan closed the complex in the immediate aftermath of the fire.

After Jika's closure the OOC spun into damage control as it faced ensuing liability in what was the most significant 'crisis of legitimacy' for the prison authorities since Jika opened in 1980. This crisis was magnified by three additional factors. First, the authorities were confronted with the possible publicity and controversy that could arise from a coroner's investigation into the unusual and contested circumstances surrounding the death of Sean Downie. However, due to the delays outlined in Chapter Six, it turned out that the Downie inquest coincided directly with the fire inquest and was thus overshadowed by the dramatic events that unfolded during the latter. Second, the situation was further compounded for authorities by general public and parliamentary debates about the need for greater organisational accountability and reform within the Victorian prison system (Goldie 1987).[38] Finally,

---

[38]   David Goldie's documentary *Out of Sight, Out of Mind* was aired on the ABC
       program *Four Corners* only a few months before the Jika fire and provided an
       extensive and controversial look inside Australia's most notorious prisons. It

such debates were fuelled by publicised prisoner allegations of abuse during the emergency response in conjunction with embarrassing anonymous allegations of mismanagement and corruption that emerged from internal official sources. Despite these allegations and the apparent crisis at hand the State Government rejected calls for an independent inquiry or Royal Commission. In this context, the inquest served as the only avenue for scrutiny in the wake of the institutional crisis surrounding Jika. For officials, the inquest signalled an opportunity to clear the OOC of any liability.

The inquest that followed the Jika fire during 1988 and 1989 marked one of the most lengthy and expensive post-death investigations in Victorian history. Initially expected to last three weeks, the inquest proceedings spanned seven months. The sheer length and expense of the fire inquest can be directly attributed to the obstructive measures taken by the OOC to deflect public scrutiny, independent appraisal and criticism. This chapter critically presents and analyses these strategies. It is argued that officials did not see their role as providing open cooperation and assistance to the coronial process. Rather, officials viewed the inquest as an exercise in damage limitation and an opportunity to build a case to avoid liability and essentially protect the interests and public image of the OOC. During the inquest the OOC attempted to suppress evidence, silence witnesses, attack and discredit its critics. Most notably the OOC sought to challenge and effectively curtail the powers of the coroner and when such attempts were unsuccessful it desperately resorted to publicly questioning the State Coroner's credibility.

Hallenstein's response was unequivocally reflected in his findings, which levelled a double-barrelled blow at the OOC. He handed down adverse criticisms with respect to the OOC's

---

highlighted concerns about conditions within prison systems throughout all Australian States and sparked renewed debates about prison reform. It was noted in the documentary that in comparison to other Australian States, the makers were granted limited access to Victorian prisons. The filmmakers provided inside footage of Jika and interviewed one prisoner who aired critical views about Jika but the coverage was very brief.

handling of the fire as well as attacking and questioning the conduct of the OOC during the inquest proceedings. He stated that during the inquest:

> The Office of Corrections has sought to be unaccountable. When pushed by Coroner's investigation, it has treated the Coroner as an adversary, both in the courts and by way of personal and public attack. It has objected, protested and litigated, rather than provide information exclusively within its possession. It has used public resources to protect itself, its interests and its image. It has been prepared to bully, apply pressure and deceive, rather than to face the truth. It has placed itself in priority to the community it serves. (Hallenstein 1989: 116)

Significantly, Hallenstein recommended an independent inquiry or Royal Commission to further investigate such matters, stating the manner in which the OOC attempted to thwart investigation, conceal and manipulate information to gain a position of advantage could be described as 'corrupt'. The OOC's attempts to stifle and effectively shut down the fire inquest are illustrative of the willingness of officials to shield and conceal important truths from public knowledge. As will be demonstrated, the growing blatancy of the OOC's strategies rendered them counter-productive as they became increasingly visible to the public.

This chapter documents the various tactics employed by the OOC to avoid scrutiny and organisational accountability in the face of ensuing liability stemming from investigations into the Jika fire and deaths of five prisoners. In particular it considers the official use of negative imagery associated with violence, dangerousness and social inadequacy within 'official' accounts and explanations for the protest fire and deaths. It also examines how such imagery was deployed to discredit accounts and evidence that contradicted the OOC version of events. Overall, this chapter considers the OOC's defensive and obstructive strategies to exert control over and at times attempt to stifle the coroner's investigations. Brief consideration is also afforded to the outcomes of the fire inquest, State Coroner Hallenstein's findings and official responses, particularly the 1990 Murray Report. However, to begin, this chapter examines the immediate events and allegations surrounding the protest fire and Robert Wright's unsuccessful application for reclassification.

Wright's Re-Classification and Events Preceding the October Fire

In October 1987, Robert Wright had, with the exception of a six-month period during his 1983 escape, been confined in Jika for seven years. He was the longest serving prisoner in Jika. In 1986 he detailed his experience in Jika in a series of letters that appealed to public figures to take action over conditions. His grievances mirrored those of many other Jika prisoners during this time. He spoke of the alleged taunts by officers, his isolation and the unreality of life in an 'echo chamber' where there was no fresh air and a desperate need for drug-induced sleep (R Wright cited in *Age* 15/7/89 p 2). He wrote:

> I would like to bring to your attention the incredible long list of violence that has plagued Jika since it was opened in 1980. There have been murders, stabbings, bashings and mutilations. Nearly all have stemmed from the atmosphere created in units, or by prison staff who have manipulated the environmental pressures to suit their own ends. (R Wright cited in Inquest 1988-89a: 611)

It was suggested during the inquest that officials had been so angered and embarrassed by the 1983 escape that Wright had allegedly been told by the then Chairman of Classification Michael Ryan that he could 'rot' in Jika Jika (Inquest 1988-89a: 630). During the inquest proceedings Michael Ryan denied the allegation and stated Wright's continuing classification to Jika had nothing to do with security. Rather, he maintained Wright was classified as 'management' because he was the 'worst behaved' prisoner in the division over a three-year period (Inquest 1988-89a: 614-15). Ryan also stressed that in 1985 classification officials told Wright that if he 'behaved' for the next two years he would get reclassified (Inquest 1988-89a: 626). Wright instead ran a spirited campaign against the Jika regime and classification. He engaged in frequent nuisance protests including wiping toothpaste on windows, shaving cream on cameras and salad on windows. He was also identified by officials to be the ringleader behind the recurrent bronze-up campaign in Jika between 1986 and 1987 (Inquest 1988-89a: 624). Nonetheless, officials had suggested during an R&A meeting in May 1986 that after the upgrade of security in Pentridge Wright should be able to move to mainstream by 1987 (Inquest 1988-89a: 627-8). During this time the other three 1983 Jika escapees had been reclassified to the mainstream, but Wright remained in Jika.

On 6 October 1987, Wright's reclassification was once again considered and recommended by R&A. It was then taken to the DCC who upheld the approval and then referred recommendations to the Director of Prisons who had the final decision. The day before the fire the Director of Prisons refused Wright's transfer (Hallenstein 1989: 2). In an unusual move this news was communicated to Wright personally in the Unit 4 foyer by the Assistant Director of Prisons Paul Delphine, Supervisor of Classification Michael Ryan and Governors Herron and Penter. Ryan informed Wright of the unfavourable decision and Herron encouraged him to make a life for himself in Jika. Wright responded angrily stating, 'this is not the last you'll hear of it … it's on and it's on soon' (Hallenstein 1989: 3). Delphine or Ryan allegedly responded by laughing and commenting, 'I don't think he's a happy boy' (Inquest 1988-89a: 99). Afterwards Wright told one of the Governors, 'They don't care, I heard them laughing … I had nothing in 1981. I've got nothing now. I'll rot in here … if that's what they want to do with us, they can expect a blood bath' (Inquest 1988-89a: 100-1). Wright immediately informed prisoners on both sides 1 and 2 the planned protest would be on for the next day. Craig Minogue later stated that he knew Wright would not accept the decision, particularly after he had been given the impression a month earlier that his reclassification would go ahead (Inquest 1988-89a: 1092).

While Wright's reclassification was a prominent trigger for the fire, Unit 4 prisoners participated as part of a broader protest against conditions in Jika. One of the survivors of the fire stated anonymously that immediately prior to the fire the nature of the situation for prisoners in Jika was desperate and that it was felt that the planned protest was a last resort action designed to 'help things along the path to a Royal Commission' (PRG 1988: 21). Up to this point some prisoners had held bronze-ups and participated in publicised hunger strikes while others had written numerous letters to journalists, complained to the Ombudsman and even written to parliamentary ministers and the Attorney General Jim Kennan directly, in order to push for urgent remedial action.

Representations put forward by prisoners during this time projected a sense of fear, desperation and foreboding about the prospect of violence, crisis and possible death. In this context the fire served as a desperate last resort by a specific group of prisoners concerned with their rights. This is a crucial point that must be emphasised. In the immediate aftermath of the fire and during the inquest that followed, the OOC and its staff attempted to misrepresent and use the protest to suit particular interests and agendas.

A primary example of this occurred in the immediate aftermath of the fire when a group of anonymous prison officers leaked allegations to the media that the protest was in response to the controversial transfer of AIDS prisoners to the division (Inquest 1988-89a 'OOC Memorandum from Superintendent of Inspections Michael Ryan to Director-General Peter Harmsworth' 11/4/88; see also *Herald* 30/10/87 p 4). Immediately prior to the fire, Jika staff were engaged in a dispute with officials over understaffing and the transfer of such prisoners. The leaked allegations sparked a series of newspaper headlines that linked the protest exclusively to AIDS prisoners who had been transferred during the afternoon on the day of the protest. Attorney General Jim Kennan denied the claims, stating the prisoners involved had not in the past demonstrated any concerns over this issue (*Australian* 30/10/87 p 5). During the inquest prisoners rejected the allegations, and accused staff of having actively encouraged the protest in order to exploit it and advance the agendas of a staff industrial campaign against the transfer of AIDS prisoners to the division (Inquest 1988-89a: 1334-5; see also *Sun* 30/10/87 p 1; *Age* 30/10/87 p 1). Prisoner Richard Light heatedly responded to such misrepresentations:

> If you're not going to listen to people who were involved in the protest, who are you going to listen to? There were many forms

of protest down there, hunger strikes, people mutilating themselves, people wiping shit all over the walls. I mean people had had enough ... officers considered this as a normal occurrence in Jika, for people to live like this. (Inquest 1988-89a: 1334-5)

Craig Minogue summarised the reasoning behind Unit 4 prisoner involvement in the protest:

The reasons are long but I feel they should be listed. They were:- 1. Long-term placement in Jika; 2. The R&A Classification Committees; 3. Constant intimidation and standover tactics; 4. Threats of violence and death from prison officers; 5. The dehumanising conditions and mind games in the Division; 6. The double standards that existed between what the protection prisoners received and what we received; 7. Deaths of inmates in Jika under suspicious circumstances; 8. And to a much lesser extent, the transfer of AIDS inmates to Jika. (Inquest 1988-89a: 1082)

The surviving Unit 4 prisoners alleged that the protest had been planned eight weeks in advance and both Sides had managed to stockpile flammables, including eight weeks of newspapers and magazines (Inquest 1988-89a: 1776-7). This was managed despite the fact that the accumulation of potentially flammable materials was prohibited by Jika regulations, which allowed a maximum of six books and one magazine to each Unit. Rodney Minogue believed the authorities were well aware of the threat of fire and he cited the specific occasion where Wright informed Governor Penter that he was sick of Jika and there were not many protests left but to 'torch the joint' (Inquest 1988-89a: 1776). Moreover, he alleged that Wright took great pains to frequently mention the protest in the presence of officers while Gallagher recorded the details of each exchange in his diary including the times, which prison officers and prisoners were present, what was said and who overheard (Inquest 1988-89a: 1774-6). Rodney Minogue stated the objective of the protest was to completely destroy Side 1, and prisoners then hoped to claim compensation. They would do this by arguing the case that prison staff and senior officials knew about the protest but had failed to take adequate action to prevent it. Rodney Minogue believed that staff went as far as to even encourage the protest, alleging that after the threats of fire had been made Side 1 prisoners were given access to a storage area that had a bookcase stocked with 150 books (Inquest 1988-89a: 1776-7).

Numerous representations made to the media by the family members of the deceased alleged that just days before the fire prisoners disclosed plans for the protest to visiting loved ones in the presence of prison staff (*Age* 30/10/87; see also *Sun* 30/10/87 p 3). The OOC maintained during the inquest that while it was common knowledge there was trouble brewing in Jika in Unit 4, staff and officials remained unaware that the protest action would consist of fire (Inquest 1988-89a 'OOC Memorandum from Superintendent of Inspections Michael Ryan to Director-General Peter Harmsworth' 11/4/88). Despite this, relatives, church representatives and prisoners alleged Governor Penter had been told directly there would be fire. An internal and confidential report that emerged later stated that the lack of available evidence to support such allegations would make it impossible for families and prisoners to make a case at the inquest (Inquest 1988-89a 'OOC Memorandum from Superintendent of Inspections Michael Ryan to Director-General Peter Harmsworth' 11/4/88).

It emerged at the inquest that despite staff being on alert due to potential for trouble in Unit 4, the division as a whole was under-resourced and understaffed. There were also other problems, such as the malfunctioning of the Unit 4 foyer doors. Visiting Stafford engineer technicians had been told on the day of the fire that the doors had to be fixed due to the anticipation that there 'was going to be trouble in Unit 4' (Hallenstein 1989: 15). The doors were disconnected from the pneumatic system and a faulty mechanism was removed pending placement. In the meantime engineers had offered to replace the mechanism from a functioning door in another Unit. However, Penter instructed the doors should be left as they were. Meanwhile at approximately 3.00pm, the AIDS prisoners were transferred to Unit 2. Almost immediately, all senior staff were subsequently called to Unit 2 due to the fact that prisoner Danny James had climbed up the inside of the exercise yard cage in a protest against the AIDS prisoners in the Unit (Hallenstein 1989: 15-16). It was at this moment that the Unit 4 protest was launched into action.

After Wright gave the go-ahead, prisoners placed chairs in all the cells so the doors could not be closed and piled their bedding and cell property in preparation for the barricades. At approximately 3.30pm Unit 4 prisoners were interrupted by a surprise cell check by prison officer Tate. Governor Herron had ordered the cell check as a cautionary measure. When Tate entered to conduct the check, towels and bedding were scattered across the floors, beds were unmade and the day room furniture was stacked in a pile. In Side 1 piping had been cut from the washing machines and the air vents and plumbing fixtures had been tampered with (Hallenstein 1989: 18-20). Prisoner Light recalled that even though the Unit was in complete disarray, Tate took no action (Inquest 1988-89a: 1272). Whatever concerns she may have had, Tate did not rate such irregularities as urgent and took no action beyond referring the matter on to senior staff. The nature of staff hierarchies and divisional bureaucracy dictated it was not her role to deal with such matters beyond conducting the cell check and reporting anything unusual to her seniors on paper (Hallenstein 1989: 20). As Tate left the Unit she reportedly turned to see prisoners barricading the doors by tying sheets, stacking furniture and Side 1 prisoners using a broken tennis net to tie theirs (Hallenstein 1989: 25). Once the alarm was raised, Side 2 prisoners reported on the whole little was done by staff to intervene and diffuse the situation while some prison officers aggravated matters by yelling abuse and threats (Inquest 1988-89a: 2049).

Craig Minogue stated during the inquest that he believed the fire had been lit so that the MFB would be called and if firemen were there it would prevent the prison officers 'bashing' or 'killing' prisoners (Inquest 1988-89a: 1090). Richard Light also told the inquest that Side 2 prisoners participated in the protest for the purpose of bearing witness to any prison officer beatings that might take place. He stated prisoner fears stemmed from:

> the general treatment and conditions down there and after what I'd seen of the treatment which led to the death of Sean Downie, it left me very edgy and I think a few other prisoners as well … We had prior to this … been threatened down there, had our lives threatened by the same officer who was in on the beating

of Sean Downie and this made us very wary. (Inquest 1988-89a: 1285)

It must be emphasised that the 1987 Jika fire effectively triggered a sequence of public controversies and feverish debates about the need for accountability and reform in the Victorian prison system. Official responses to the Jika fire must be understood in the broader context of emerging allegations that the Victorian prison administration was moribund and riddled with corruption. While claims of abuse and corruption had always been prevalent within prisoner testimony, after the fire allegations also began to emerge from prison officer ranks. Such allegations were sensationalised in newspaper reports and aired on national commercial television programs. In August 1988 a critical Uniting Church report by Alan Austin made a series of serious allegations against prison authorities and staff. The report was released three months prior to the beginning of the Jika fire inquest, yet it echoed and indeed fortified many of the concerns and grievances raised by prisoners throughout the 1980s. Most significantly, the report levelled the allegation that corruption was rife throughout the prison system in areas including:

> supply of drugs, trading of contraband; criminal bashings of prisoners; (as distinct from the 'normal' prison bashings as a means of punishment and control); murder of prisoners; payment of prisoners to commit assaults and murders, usually with privileges, transfers or early parole; and elaborate cover-ups of these things to thwart apprehension of the real offenders. (Austin Report 1988: 20)

The report claimed that there was 'more than enough validated testimony presently in the hands of the Attorney General, the OOC and the State Ombudsman to warrant a full Royal Commission' into such serious matters (Austin Report 1988: 20). Noteworthy were allegations that prison officer brutality remained central to the H Division disciplinary regime nine years after Jika Jika's opening. In addition, it was alleged that considerable evidence, along with the direct testimony of prisoners, existed to implicate prison officers in the deaths of the prisoners who died in the fire (Austin Report 1988: 20). Quite markedly, Austin's report claimed that:

Unofficial reports emanating from employees within Pentridge allege that prison officers appear divided evenly on the question of whether the Jika Jika prison officers could or would have contributed by their inaction to the deaths of the five prisoners. Not all workers within the prison by any means accept the official Government position that prison officer complicity in the deaths is an outrageous baseless slander. (Austin Report 1988: 20)

Austin (1988: 20) concluded with respect to these allegations that legitimate questions should be raised as to 'the conduct of officers in Jika Jika at that time'.

Austin's report was not happily received by the authorities, who immediately moved to impose a ban on Austin and two prominent chaplains from visiting Pentridge. The ban was quickly lifted for the chaplains after conditional amendments were made to the publication two weeks later (*Sunday Press* 30/7/89). However, the ban remained for Austin, who stood by the report and maintained his view that there was substantial evidence that abuses of power were rife throughout the Victorian prison system. The report was particularly significant in that this evidence came not only from prisoners but also from concerned prison officers and officials working within the system.

Discrediting Resistance as Dangerousness and Violence: Official Images of the Jika Five

After the deaths of the Jika five, Melbourne's daily newspapers were flooded with an unprecedented amount of coverage of events.[39] In the tabloids much of this coverage prioritised an emphasis on the criminal records, violence and dangerousness of the deceased. The same grainy photograph reproduced in all media reports showed four of the deceased, Wright, Loughnan, Gallagher and McGauley appearing animated, joking and smiling together in a group shot taken in prison only two weeks before the fire. In stark contrast to this image of humanness were the accompanying

---

[39] Courtesy Victorian Department of Justice Resource Centre, 'K Division Fire and Aftermath: Newspaper Clippings, October 1987'.

PART TWO : CONCEALING CRISIS

sensationalised headlines, 'Gruesome death for cold-blooded murderers', 'Five were convicted of violent crimes' (for these and other examples see *Australian* 31/10/87; see also *Australian* 30/10/87; *Age* 30/10/87 p 8). The *Herald* published photographs of the deceased prisoners next to comprehensive summaries of their criminal records: Richard Morris: 'a vicious killer'; David McGauley: 'a vicious and callous killer'; James Loughnan: 'certified insane'; Robert Wright: 'Victoria's most hated killer'; Arthur Gallagher: 'Probably the least dangerous of the five. Claimed he feared for his life in K Division. Came close to death in a hunger strike' (*Herald* 30/10/87 p 22). In another article, Chief Inspector of Police Graham Sinclair, who had led previous investigations into the murders committed by Wright, was interviewed by the *Sun*. He stated that Wright 'had a lot of mongrel in him ... his death has done everybody a favour' (*Sun* 31/10/87).

A report in the *Sun* made offensive, sarcastic reference to the obituaries and tributes by aggrieved friends and family members two days after the men had died. The report by Susan Bamber commented, 'Few among the general public would mourn the death of men described as ruthless and brutal criminals. But the tributes revealed the prisoners were well-loved by some' (*Sun* 31/10/87). Bamber incongruously contrasted loving tributes by friends and family with the violent reputations of the deceased:

> "God loves the pure at heart", was another tribute to Gallagher, imprisoned for armed robbery ... "Your humour, your laugh, your infectious smile reflected your love and purity of heart" ... read one tribute to Robert Lindsay Wright, one of Australia's most hated criminals ... "You had a smile for everyone and a heart of gold", wrote the family of David McGauley, who was jailed for life for the callous murder of a one legged man at Bundoora in 1979. (*Sun* 31/10/87)

Incidentally, this reporting presented a marked contrast to the representation of prison officers who had been 'drawn into the most violent of all protests' and who 'courageously' and selflessly risked their lives to breach the doors and save the prisoners (*Sun* 31/10/87). While partly designed to satisfy a public thirst for the sensational, the use of such negative and violent imagery demonstrates the apparent reliance placed on official sources of information by media outlets reporting on stories associated with crime and the criminal justice system.[40] Furthermore, with respect to the fire and deaths of the Jika five, such reporting reflected the primacy of the official account, which self-interestedly sought to direct attention away from the institutional failings that led to the protest fire and deaths by instead focusing on the criminal histories of the deceased. Scraton, Sim and Skidmore (1991: 118) argue that the use of negative imagery within media coverage of prison disturbances and protests is instrumental in that it not only legitimates direct responses by the prison authorities in such situations but also promotes the view that 'behind all prison protest lies a minority hard core of violent men, whose objectives are to disrupt the regime, intimidate other prisoners and injure prison officers'. Such an observation is applicable to representations by OOC who attempted to represent the fire as a violent disturbance by a specific minority group of 'troublemakers' who were well known for their views on Jika Jika and of prison officers who worked there.

As demonstrated with the Sean Downie case, the use of violent imagery was strategic. It served to divert attention away from the actions of the OOC and the conditions in Jika that prisoners protested against by focusing on the character of protesting prisoners and in the case of the fire, the deceased prisoners, as unmanageable, non-compliant and in particular violent. A further implication is that the construction of 'reputations', grounded in imagery associated with criminality, social inadequacy and violence, have the implicit effect of legitimating and justifying deaths in custody, as though there is somehow an 'acceptable' death in custody (Scraton & Chadwick 1987: 220). It is thus emphasised that the most powerful tool state agencies have at their disposal after the occurrence of a death in custody is the criminal and prison record of the deceased.

When asked to respond to Wright's letters regarding the detrimental impact of his lengthy confinement in Jika during the

---

[40] For a more comprehensive discussion about the media construction of crime and prison protest see Scraton et al 1991: 112-13; see also Hall et al 1978.

inquest proceedings, Manager of Special Projects Michael Ryan was dismissive. He believed Wright's complaints were unremarkable and not uncommon from the many other prisoner complaints, which he argued could be characterised as the 'lament of the high-security prisoner' (Inquest 1988-89a: 611-12). However, out of all prisoners, Ryan was adamant in submitting that in Jika Wright posed 'the worst' management problem for the authorities (Inquest 1988-89a: 661). The time spent establishing the lengthy criminal and prison records of the deceased was unprecedented during Ryan's testimony. Ryan detailed every incident report and minor infraction relating to each of the prison records of the deceased and the surviving Unit 4 prisoners (Inquest 1988-89a: 447-501, 652-70). While these profiles were extensive, James Loughnan, Arthur Gallagher and Robert Wright's records are referred to as examples.

Ryan produced James Loughnan's criminal and prison record in detail during the inquest. Loughnan was depicted as psychiatrically unstable and posing a number of security risks due to his frequent attempts to escape. Prior to his classification to Jika, Loughnan had escaped from Pentridge in 1974 by clinging to the axle of a police van and in 1977 during an attempted escape from B Division he had allegedly jumped from a prison wall, breaking both his ankles (Inquest 1988-89a: 491). Loughnan had in addition escaped 'at least five times' from various mental institutions and according to Ryan, had during 1985 been 'suspected' of plotting an escape involving firearms and a 'possible' hostage situation. Ryan also made reference to the fact that Loughnan had ultimately been classified to Jika due to his 'suspected' involvement with some 'serious' bashings and the alleged 'burning' of a particular prisoner in B Division (Inquest 1988-89a: 490). Overall, much was made of Loughnan's 'demonstrated' psychiatric instability, his disturbed violent tendencies and frequent risk posed to prison security. Whether Loughnan may have been more appropriately housed in a secure psychiatric care unit, rather than a high-security facility, was not discussed.

In contrast to Wright, who was serving time for multiple murders, Arthur Gallagher was serving his prison sentence for an armed robbery conviction. His classification in and out of Jika

231

stemmed from a number of incidents that appeared to be largely related to non-compliance. Overall, Gallagher was depicted as a rebellious prisoner who refused to conform to the prison routine, refused to shave or wear prison regulation clothing or sleep in his bed and 'spent much time huddled under the bench of his cell' (Inquest 1988-89a: 495-6). However, Ryan stated that information disclosed to the authorities suggested Gallagher was planning an armed escape and had enough cash outside prison to finance such a plan and it was this 'suspicion' that ultimately led to his classification. During the inquest there was a strong emphasis on official concerns regarding ongoing threats to prison security posed by Gallagher's 'activities'. Ryan stated Gallagher had been 'suspected' of plotting a serious conspiracy to firebomb B Division prison officer quarters and was charged when stocks of Molotov cocktails were found in prisoner cells (Inquest 1988-89a: 496). Gallagher was later cleared of these charges but he was classified to Jika regardless. Gallagher believed his classification to Jika stemmed from his political affiliations with prisoner rights organisations and his involvement in protests inside (Inquest 1988-89a: 498). Ryan rejected this, stating that Gallagher rated a high enough risk to the security of the prison for the Director of Prisons to be concerned with his case (Inquest 1988-89a: 497-8).

Wright's notorious criminal history and prison record comprised a central focus during the inquest due to the fact that his classification case was perceived as the precipitating event leading to the protest fire. According to Ryan, Wright was 'disruptive', 'threatening', 'dangerous', 'violent' and posed a significant 'security risk' to the prison generally (Inquest 1988-89a: 477-85; see also 'K Division Incident Reports, March-September 1987'). Wright had been convicted of multiple murders, two of which occurred during his escape and the circumstances of these were detailed. Comprehensive reference was made to Wright's 'influence' over prisoners, his past hatching of multiple and elaborate escape plans, his destruction of cells and government property, his alleged standover tactics and threats to staff safety and his continual involvement in the Jika bronze-up campaigns. It was concluded overall that Wright's prison record demonstrated he was not to any degree 'conforming with acceptable and required standards of application and behaviour' (Inquest 1988-89a: 660). Therefore, on the basis of Wright's lengthy prison record, Ryan made the statement that out of the 50 plus prisoners coming through Jika during this time Wright posed the absolute 'worst' management and security problems (Inquest 1988-89a: 661). State Coroner Hallenstein refused to accept Ryan's assertions and told him that there was no evidence to support such a claim and that it would be impossible for him to accept such a generalisation based on Ryan's word only (Inquest 1988-89a: 661).

Objections were also raised over Ryan's unsubstantiated claims regarding several incidents allegedly involving Wright, some of which included threats to kill officers, and Wright being 'suspected' of having assaulted prisoners based on his being 'one of a number of prisoners' in a yard where the incident occurred (Inquest 1988-89a: 659). Ryan also raised allegations that Wright had shot at police with a firearm during his recapture, even though he had been acquitted of these charges in a criminal court (Inquest 1988-89a: 631). Nonetheless, Ryan admitted that such allegations continued to influence the decisions of the Divisional Classification Committee, particularly when incidents involved breaches of prison security. He admitted that in the interests of prison security it was often necessary for the DCC to disregard acquittals and 'operate outside the rules of natural justice' (Inquest 1988-89a: 633).

Whether or not Wright had been acquitted of such charges was ultimately inconsequential to the OOC. Central to the purpose of detailing them was the fact that they enhanced the 'official' profile of Wright as a non-compliant, unpredictable, dangerous and violent criminal, thus deflecting attention away from the circumstances in which he died in the Jika fire. Such was the implication with respect to the construction of the 'official' profiles of the other deceased prisoners, Loughnan, Gallagher, McGauley and Morris. As Scraton and Chadwick (1987: 220) have pointed out, the official establishment and development of negative reputations ultimately suggests that '*They* – the people who have died – are the problem', that their criminal and prison records somehow justify their deaths.

Defending the OOC: The Official Discrediting of Prisoner Evidence and the Desmond Sinfield Affair

Initially the OOC moved to present the inquest with a uniform account of the fire and the emergency response. Such a move reflects a long tradition of state institutions in which accused professionals have defensively attempted to 'close ranks' in order to successfully avert independent scrutiny and accountability (Scraton et al 1991: 65). This was reflected within an official internal memorandum addressed to the Director-General by Michael Ryan in April 1988. It should be clarified that after this memorandum was circulated Ryan became responsible for the daily management of the OOC's affairs at the inquest. In the document Ryan emphasised the need for the OOC to adopt a 'policy' in terms of its 'understanding' of the fire, which would need to 'be put consistently and uniformly to the Coroner'. Ryan went on to state:

> It is obviously important that the Office of Corrections quickly settles its stance in regard to the cause of the fire, and brief representation so that as strong a case as possible may be made out in preparation for the concerted criticism which is sure to come from counsel representing the families of the deceased persons. (Inquest 1988-89a 'OOC Memorandum from Superintendent of Inspections Michael Ryan to Director-General Peter Harmsworth' 11/4/88)

The annual OOC report to Parliament in June 1988 was subsequently prefaced by a letter from Harmsworth addressed to the minister. It specifically mirrored the 'official understanding' earlier suggested in Ryan's memorandum:

> The tragic loss of life of prisoners on the 29th October, 1987, when prisoners in Unit 4 in 'K Division' ... erected and set fire to barricades despite strenuous rescue efforts by staff, five prisoners died. In both the hostage and fire incidents, staff involved applied themselves in a thoroughly dedicated and professional and courageous manner. A number of staff have since received awards for the exemplary and commendable bravery. (Director-General Peter Harmsworth cited in Hallenstein 1989: 107)

Counsel acting for the families of the deceased, Mr Brind Woinarski QC, later stated that Ryan's memorandum was at best 'an outline of a whitewash ... an invitation to lie, and a deliberate and

234

mischievous attempt to remove all suggestion of fault and blame' (*Age* 14/7/89 p 2).

Ryan's memorandum also anticipated the additional concern that prisoners would want to attend the coroner's inquest in order to 'condemn and criticise the policies and practices as they were in K Division [Jika Jika]. An attempt will be made to paint K Division [Jika Jika] in such dark colours that the result was literally to drive prisoners mad, make men crazed with bitterness and hatred to the point that violent protest had to result'. It was further acknowledged that such representations could impact adversely on the interests of the OOC in paving the way for future compensation claims by prisoners and the families of the deceased (Inquest 1988-89a 'OOC Memorandum from Superintendent of Inspections Michael Ryan to Director-General Peter Harmsworth' 11/4/88).

Just as the OOC anticipated, surviving Jika prisoners did give evidence during the inquest and made a series of allegations relating to their treatment during the fire emergency response. Much to the distaste of the OOC, Hallenstein allowed prisoner evidence about conditions, prisoner grievances and the impact of the restrictive environment in Jika. Within such evidence a number of serious allegations about prison officer abuses of power and misconduct were made. Prisoner evidence depicted a troubling picture of institutional dysfunction and mismanagement within Jika and many of the allegations and complaints about life in Jika that emerged during the inquest have been raised in previous chapters. Prisoners were aware that there were considerable risks associated with providing such evidence and a number of prisoners specifically cited instances where they had been intimidated and threatened to 'keep quiet' (Inquest 1988-89b: 738-43). However, prisoners came forward with the hope that the inquest would provide an avenue for a Royal Commission or independent inquiry into the prison system.

Prisoners reported that prison staff did little to prevent the protest fire and that some prison officers actively baited and threatened prisoners (Inquest 1988-89a: 2029). It was also alleged by all surviving prisoners that after the fire had been lit they were able to hear prison officers calling from the foyer, 'die you bastards' and 'hope you all choke' (Inquest 1988-89a: 1080, 1259, 2030). Prisoner Wayne King stated, 'They hated us and wanted us to die because they think of us as troublemakers' (Inquest 1988-89a: 2031).

Light and Minogue claimed that after they emerged from the breached Unit doors they staggered unassisted before a line of prison officers holding batons and shouting abuse (Inquest 1988-89a: 1080, 1260). Minogue reported he was brutalised by one prison officer and Light, who had been overcome with asthma, alleged he was roughly dragged across the floor. Olaf Dietrich gave evidence that he witnessed one prison officer beating Wayne King with a baton while he was being carried out (Inquest 1988-89a: 2115). Dietrich's account was confirmed by MFB officer Peter Rees who told the inquest he witnessed one prison officer beating a prisoner who appeared 'ungrateful' for his rescue (*Sun* 28/4/89). Prison staff denied the allegations.

Prisoner evidence was subject to aggressive lines of cross-examination and the credibility of prisoner witnesses was vigorously challenged and questioned by counsel for the authorities, Jeremy Rapke. As for the deceased, comprehensive criminal and prison records were detailed in order to cast doubt over the reliability of witnesses while dismissing prisoner allegations as vexatious and dishonest. This is briefly illustrated with respect to Craig Minogue, Richard Light and Olaf Dietrich.

Craig Minogue told the inquest that he believed his transfer to Jika Jika was political. He stated that due to the nature of his wrongful conviction over the Russell Street bombing, the government and the police had more say in his classification than the prison authorities (Inquest 1988-89a: 1178). However, counsel for the OOC Jeremy Rapke questioned Craig Minogue extensively about his criminal convictions and the prison record that, he argued, led to his ongoing classification in high-security. He also questioned him about incidents involving his throwing of milk, food and crockery, threats and attacks on staff, alleged attacks on other prisoners, his frequent involvement in prison protest and his general attitude of non-compliance (Inquest 1988-89a: 1178-89). Similar to the treatment of his evidence during the Downie inquest, Minogue was questioned about these matters in order to discredit his evidence and draw attention away from his complaints while instead focusing on his apparent 'dangerousness'.

Richard Light alleged that prison officers had run him into a concrete pillar after his rescue from the fire (Inquest 1988-89a: 1318). Due to inconsistencies in his statements, Rapke attempted to discredit Light by questioning his honesty while also raising Light's theft and burglary convictions as 'crimes of dishonesty' (Inquest 1988-89a: 1344). He also drew attention to Light's history of violence and questioned him extensively in regards to his criminal record and convictions. Light appealed to Hallenstein that he was not on trial and should not have to answer the questions. However, the coroner upheld Rapke's line of questioning stating: 'Mr. Rapke says you have made allegations against people in the prison system. His clients say you are a liar, and he is now testing whether or not you are a liar' (Inquest 1988-89a: 1351). Rapke also drew attention to Light's record of non-compliance in prison, including escape charges, allegations he had cracked a window and a high number of black book entries (Inquest 1988-89a: 1361-7).

Rapke also claimed that prisoner Olaf Dietrich was dishonest. He questioned him comprehensively over inconsistencies detected in his statements and his evidence given at the inquest (Inquest 1988-89a: 2210-18). To further this case, Rapke also raised Dietrich's 'crimes of dishonesty' including theft, deception and forgery (Inquest 1988-89a: 2228). He depicted Dietrich as a 'violent person', with a 'violent disposition', who had frequent 'violent outbursts', resulting in charges stemming from his destruction of prison cells and property (Inquest 1988-89a: 2222-4). Reference was also made to his involvement in numerous protests and barricades. Rapke's questioning was lengthy due to the fact that Dietrich refused to answer many of the questions and continued to appeal to the Coroner. At one point Dietrich responded angrily:

> He's saying now I'm totally dishonest. I'm not totally dishonest. I'm being truthful about what happened down there. Nobody will ever bring out what happened down there 100 per cent, because the brick wall just won't let it, and I take objection to the way this man's asking me questions about incidents that may have happened, or didn't happen [sic]. (Inquest 1988-89a: 2230)

As discussed previously, when state agencies are faced with allegations of institutional abuse, the most pervasive and powerful device they have for deflecting those allegations are the criminal and prison records of prisoners. These records are instrumental in the official construction of reputations and dehumanising stereotypes associated with criminality and dangerousness. They function to both discredit and stigmatise prisoner evidence as 'untruth', while privileging and vindicating official accounts as 'truth'. The treatment of prisoner evidence during the fire inquest remains significant due to the fact that it ultimately deterred prisoners from giving evidence at the Sean Downie inquest as prisoners feared having their entire criminal histories and prison records once again dredged up (Inquest 1988-89b: 738-43).

Hallenstein (1989: 110) noted in his findings that up until prison officer Desmond Sinfield gave evidence at the inquest, 'the inquest proceeded … as routine and prison officers gave evidence which could at least in part be described as consistent and uniform' or in accordance with the 'official understanding' of the fire prescribed by Ryan. In February 1989 Sinfield addressed his concerns and analysis of 'problems, failures, conduct and performance of prison officers responding to the fire' (Hallenstein 1989: 110). Sinfield told the inquest that at the time of the fire prison officers were 'so incompetently trained they did not know how to handcuff or search prisoners or use prison rescue equipment' (*Sun* 30/5/89). He also alleged that during the emergency response he had called for pneumatic bags that could be used to force open barricaded doors but none of the officers knew where they were (*Sunday Press* 28/5/89). Due to his criticisms, Sinfield was subjected to a gruelling cross-examination by counsel for the OOC, Jeremy Rapke, who questioned Sinfield's reliability and credibility as a witness by bringing up confidential information relating to pending firearms charges and his medical history (*Sunday Press* 28/5/89). Hallenstein (1989: 110) forestalled this line of cross-examination, later stating in his findings:

> In cross-examination of Sinfield by counsel for the OOC, there was material thrown at him of a personal, private and

embarrassing nature, being private and confidential material held by the OOC as Sinfield's employer.

It later emerged other prison officers who had been identified by the OOC as potentially 'hostile witnesses' were present during Sinfield's cross-examination. One of these officers, Eric Leeburn had allegedly been told by Ryan afterwards, 'We had to do that. We didn't like doing it, but it was necessary and we'll do it again' (Hallenstein 1989: 110). As Sinfield left the inquest after his cross-examination he alleged that there was a heated exchange between himself and Michael Ryan, who allegedly told him, 'You've fucked everything ... you've ruined the whole case ... you've let down the whole system, all your mates' (Hallenstein 1989: 111). Ryan later denied that such an exchange had taken place (*Age* 8/6/89 p 1). Sinfield was subsequently suspended from duty by the OOC due to the pending firearm charges that had been earlier raised during the inquest.

After Sinfield's evidence an additional five prison officers came forward with evidence that reflected adversely upon the OOC. Hallenstein referred to their accounts as reflecting a 'new understanding, an analysis not previously available', during the inquest proceedings (*Age* 8/6/89 p 1). The inability to suppress critical witnesses thus led the OOC to switch its attention to Coroner Hallenstein.

Re-defining the Coroner's Powers: Harmsworth Versus Hallenstein

In March 1989, Director-General Peter Harmsworth attempted to stifle and ultimately prevent aspects of Hallenstein's investigation by making a formal submission to the Supreme Court arguing in his investigations he had admitted into evidence testimony that exceeded his jurisdiction as set out in the Coroner's Act 1985 (*Harmsworth v The State Coroner* SCV 9/3/89 at 991 per Nathan J). Harmsworth's submission raised specific concerns that Hallenstein had admitted into evidence testimony:

> (i) Relating to the policy of permitting remand and convicted prisoners to be housed together, (ii) the reasons for and functioning of the administrative and physical division of the

prisons located in the Coburg complex, (iii) the functioning of the security unit operated from the Pentridge Division of the Coburg Complex, (iv) aspects of the budgetary arrangements of the prisons in the Coburg Complex, and (v) finally input by the Metropolitan Reception Prisons Tactical Response Group into prison design. (*Harmsworth v The State Coroner* at 991 per Nathan J)

Harmsworth further submitted that Hallenstein had exceeded his powers by 'inquiring into the theory of and attitude to maximum-security detention within K Division [Jika Jika] and the prison system generally from the late 1970s to the present day'. It was also argued that Hallenstein's call for all Unit 4 prisoner correspondence to both the Ombudsman and OOC and the details of all fires occurring within Pentridge over the last decade was outside the ambit of the inquest (*Harmsworth v The State Coroner* at 991 per Nathan J).

Such concerns also arose in response to Hallenstein's willingness to admit into evidence prisoner allegations of staff misconduct, abuse and the harsh impact of the Jika high-security environment. Harmsworth (1989a: 1) stated:

> Counsel for the OOC and myself became increasingly concerned at the length, breadth and scope of the inquest. We had real difficulty in grasping the relevance of various issues which had been raised ... The impact on staff of giving evidence was also beginning to take its toll. Allegations of prisoner witnesses implicating various officers, which received widespread publicity, together with sessions of fairly intensive cross-examination proved distressing to a number of staff.

It was these factors and the belief that the coroner's powers needed to be 'better defined', that informed Harmsworth's decision to lodge a submission with the Supreme Court (Harmsworth 1989a: 1).

While Justice Nathan declined to make declarations in favour of the OOC, he did concede there were grounds on which he could have justified restraining the focus of the Jika inquest. Justice Nathan cautioned that while the coroner was obliged to inquire into prison deaths, 'an inquest into particular deaths in a prison is not and should not be permitted to become an investigation into prisons in which deaths may occur' (*Harmsworth v The State Coroner* at 996). Justice Nathan (at 995) stated:

The enquiry must be relevant, in the legal sense to the death or fire, this brings into focus the concept of 'remoteness'. Of course the prisoners would not have died if they had not been in prison. The sociological factors which related to the causes of their imprisonment could not be remotely relevant.

Justice Nathan also stated (at 996) inquest investigations must be directed to specific ends and that an inquiry into personalities would never end and would never arrive 'at the coherent, let alone concise, findings required by the Act, which are the causes of death ... Such discursive investigations are not envisaged nor empowered by the Act. They are not within jurisdictional power'. Despite such cautioning, Justice Nathan concluded (at 999) with the disclaimer, 'it is inconceivable that a State Coroner would proceed in any way in conflict with the law as I have defined it'.

Both Harmsworth and Hallenstein claimed they were vindicated by Justice Nathan's judgment. Hallenstein argued his powers had not been curtailed in any way and the ruling would have little bearing on the future proceedings of the inquest, while Harmsworth believed the finding successfully clarified the coroner's powers, which vindicated the OOC's concerns about proceedings (*Age* 10/3/89).

While Justice Nathan had refrained from finding in favour of the OOC's submission, his comments again highlight inadequacies associated with the issue of narrow focus in inquest investigations. In Victoria, State Coroner Hallenstein played a role in investigating all seven Jika prisoner deaths throughout 1987. Given that an essential role of the coroner is to make recommendations in the interests of preventing future similar deaths (see Johnstone 1988: 143; see also Hallenstein 1989: 105), it seems reasonable Hallenstein broadened his investigations to consider some general aspects of the disciplinary and managerial high-security regime in Jika. Hallenstein's scope was further justified by the fact that the fatal fire constituted a general protest against conditions in a high-security institution. There is much research emphasising the detrimental impacts and harms associated with long-term confinement in high-security conditions (Funnell 2006: 70-4; Rhodes 2004; Haney 2003: 124-56; Fellner & Mariner 1997; Haney & Lynch 1997). Moreover, in the case of Jika Jika, there is a documented relationship between such conditions and death. In 1987, a broader relationship between high-security conditions and deaths in custody was reflected in the Australian Institute of Criminology national statistical survey of deaths in custody (Brown 1988a: 56). However, there has been no qualitative acknowledgement and assessment of these statistics and no further studies to document the relationship between high-security environments and death. Nonetheless, despite the broader relevance of conditions in Jika to the deaths, Hallenstein remained restricted under the Act to investigate and make findings in relation to the immediate causes and circumstances of death.

Two months after Justice Nathan's Supreme Court ruling it was revealed, during inquest proceedings, that Michael Ryan had allegedly sought to pressure prison officers into changing sections of their evidence so that their statements accorded with the uniform line on the fire. Allegations emerged that during an OOC inquest brief in November 1988 Sinfield had raised his concerns about the emergency response with Ryan and had subsequently been threatened that if he did not change his evidence material would be thrown at him in court. In a dramatic turn of events Sinfield had handed a tape-recording of this conversation to counsel assisting the coroner and parts of this were reproduced within Hallenstein's findings (Hallenstein 1989: 109-10). The conversation suggested that Ryan had spent time procuring material to use 'against' Sinfield if he gave a critical assessment of the fire during the inquest. It was also suggested by other prison officer witnesses that Sinfield's aggressive cross-examination during February in 1989 led them to believe the department had material to use against them (Hallenstein 1989: 114).

The Ryan and Sinfield affair thereafter became a focus for the coroner's investigations. It was alleged that Ryan had sought to suppress evidence, had perhaps destroyed evidence, procured perjury, intimidated witnesses and sought to actively mislead the inquest (*Age* 13/7/89 p 2). More specifically it was suggested that some officers could have been pressured to 'change small but crucial' parts of their statements that were tendered as evidence during the inquest proceedings (*Sun* 28/4/89). It was admitted by

Ryan that one of these officers had alleged he had heard Robert Wright threaten to 'burn the place down' if his reclassification application was unsuccessful. However, the officer in question disowned the allegation during inquest proceedings. Despite this, Ryan denied there had been any impropriety in the OOC inquest-briefing conferences, or that officers had been directly pressured to change their statements (*Sun* 28/4/89). During Hallenstein's questioning of Ryan, counsel for the OOC Jeremy Rapke, interrupted to accuse Hallenstein of treating Ryan like a 'common criminal' and stated, 'There is a reasonable apprehension that your worship is biased'. He called for Hallenstein to disqualify himself from making any finding, comment or recommendation about the evidence (*Sun* 8/6/89 p 2). Once again, inquest proceedings were adjourned so that Hallenstein could examine the transcripts to consider Rapke's submission. On recommencement of proceedings Hallenstein rejected Rapke's claims stating:

> The mere fact that a party may or may not like the coroner's process does not lead to a conclusion adverse to the coroner ... Bias is not constituted simply because one party in the proceedings is unhappy with a decision. (*Sun* 8/6/89 p 2)

Hallenstein further contended the bias claims were 'grossly distorted, untenable, misleading, of little assistance, unsustained by facts, and wrong'. The OOC immediately considered an application to have Hallenstein's ruling tested in the Supreme Court, but decided to wait until the final findings were delivered (*Age* 9/6/89 p 1).

Prior to adjournment of the inquest proceedings, the OOC counsel Jeremy Rapke attempted in his submission to redirect Hallenstein's attention to the immediate cause of death, arguing that the prisoners were well aware of the risks associated with fire and had brought about their own deaths by building the barricade and lighting the fire. Rapke further submitted it would be impossible to design a prison that would prevent a determined prisoner from harming themselves or others (*Age* 11/7/89 p 2; 13/7/89 p 2). Moreover, he asserted that in housing prisoners in Jika Jika since 1980, the OOC had fulfilled its duty of taking 'reasonable care' for prisoner safety (*Age* 11/7/89 p 2; 13/7/89 p 2).

As stated, throughout the inquest much was made of the comprehensive prison records and violent criminal histories of the deceased prisoners. It was the OOC view that the Jika fire constituted a disturbance executed by a minority group of 'troublemakers' and 'desperados' willing to try anything to get out of Jika. It was also argued protest ringleaders were all well known for their frequent involvement in violent disturbances and protests, their general distaste for authority and ongoing campaign against Jika officers.

In stark contrast, counsel for the deceased Brind Woinarski QC, characterised the fire as a desperate protest against the dehumanising conditions inside Jika. It was the submission of Woinarski that the five prisoners would not have died but for the 'multiple and monumental' failings of the OOC. Arguing that Wright's classification case signified the ultimate trigger for the protest, Woinarski stated that the actions of senior officials who had taken the unusual step of personally informing Wright of his classification had broken the news in a manner not dissimilar to 'rubbing a dog's nose in its own excrement' (*Age* 5/7/89 p 2; see also *Sun* 15/7/89 p 1). Overall Woinarski submitted that immediately before and after the fire had been lit, the apparent inaction, inadequate training of prison officers, lack of leadership and wasted time contributed to the ultimate deaths of the prisoners. Woinarksi further argued that the most damning evidence against the department was the possibility that the prisoners were already dead by the time prison staff notified the MFB (*Age* 5/7/89 p 2; see also *Sun* 15/7/89 p 1). He concluded his submission with an appeal for a Royal Commission.

Counsel assisting the Coroner Ross Ray also emphasised that the inquest should find that the OOC did little to prevent or respond to the threat of serious protest (*Sun* 22/7/89). In criticising Rapke's submission that had appealed for a finding that would clear the OOC of civil liability and moral culpability, Ray stated there were numerous issues regarding the OOC's handling of the fire emergency response that warranted criticism (*Sun* 22/7/89). Ray pointed to an 'extraordinary' piece of evidence heard during the inquest that was illustrative of the amount of time it took for staff to breach the Unit 4 doors. On the day of the fire, a prison officer, Colin Thompson, who was on duty at the Supreme Court in Williams Street, Melbourne, had found out about the fire over the phone while having a conversation with another prison officer from Pentridge. He thereafter obtained permission from his senior to go off duty, got into his car at the court, and drove to Coburg, which would take approximately 30 minutes in peak hour traffic. Once at Pentridge he parked the car and walked to Jika where he became involved with the final stages of the rescue operation (*Sun* 22/7/89).

Hallenstein's Findings

In late July 1989, Hallenstein handed down his findings wherein he criticised the OOC. Hallenstein found that Side 1 prisoners including Wright, Loughnan, Gallagher, McGauley and Morris died of asphyxia that resulted from carbon monoxide poisoning following smoke inhalation (Hallenstein 1989: 80). The estimated times of death for each prisoner varied between 4.15pm to 4.25pm. According to Hallenstein, prisoners therefore died just prior to the arrival of the MFB and 45 minutes to an hour before the doors to Side 1 were breached.

Hallenstein found that while Wright was directly responsible for lighting the fire and causing the death of himself and others in Side 1, he stated that Loughnan, Gallagher, McGauley and Morris also contributed to Wright's and their own deaths through their engagement in preparations for the barricade and fire. Prisoners Minogue, Light, King and Dimitrovski in the smoke affected Side 2 were also found to have contributed to the deaths of Side 1 prisoners by panicking and diverting the attention of rescue efforts from Side 1 (p 82).

Above all, Hallenstein found that the OOC by its employees, servants and agents contributed to the deaths of Wright, Loughnan, Gallagher, McGauley and Morris. He stated that:

> [The OOC had] failed to account for, and respond to: the warnings of barricade and fire; the barricade of Side 1 corridor door; the fire which required breach, immediately, of the barricaded Side 1 door; the risk of injury to, and death of Side 1

prisoners from reasonably foreseeable smoke inhalation. The OOC also failed to have available a planned, swift practised, and certain method of breaching a barricaded door in circumstances where the events of barricade and fire had been reasonably foreseeable and warned of. The ultimate failure of the OOC in this case lies in its own hierarchical, ineffectual and moribund administration. (pp 97-8)

Hallenstein observed that in the bluestone sections of Pentridge there was a well-practised response to barricades, whereas in Jika Jika, 'there was no plan, consideration, or practicality to forcibly breach any barricaded door' (p 92). In Jika this was made further impracticable if not impossible by the electronically operated pneumatic sliding doors. Hallenstein thus recommended the fundamental need for the manual operation of prison doors without reliance on any 'mechanical, electrical, pneumatic, hydraulic or other system' (pp 102-3).

Hallenstein characterised the fire fighting response by Jika prison officers as 'no response at all' (p 94). He also pointed to the fact that no fire alarm or fire equipment was used and no attempts were made in the early stages after the fire had been lit to contact the MFB. Hallenstein reported that it was not until several minutes after the fire had been lit that the 'unplanned and totally fortuitous' call by prison officer Wall was made to the MFB (p 95). He also questioned the inability of the MFB officers to take control once they had arrived at the emergency scene and he dismissed the rationale behind this that MFB officers feared for their safety. He asked, 'what was the threat when the prisoners were behind doors which could not be opened?' (p 79).

Hallenstein also condemned the futile entrapment of CPO Thorpe within the Unit 4 spine, which had redirected the efforts of the emergency response. This had caused the fatal delay that ended all hope of saving Side 1 prisoners:

> By the time of Thorpe's release at 4.27pm, all the Side 1 prisoners were dead. They had all died in circumstances where not one prison officer had effected any realistic activity at all to either breach the Side 1 door, or extinguish the fire, or remove the prisoners from the smoke-logged unit. (p 97)

According to Hallenstein Desmond Sinfield was one of the few officers who had made a real attempt to free the prisoners (p 71). Despite this he was critical of the lack of leadership demonstrated at the emergency scene and the fact that prison officers were running about in frenzied, panicked states and showing no discipline. Due to the fact that the emergency scene remained unsecured, Hallenstein stated that the large number of prison officers congregating at the scene 'constituted no more than an uncontrolled crowd' (p 100). Overall, Hallenstein observed:

> If one looks at the prison administration, by looking at the performance of prison administration with respect to this fire, one finds ineptitude, failure and non-performance in almost every aspect of the events examined. In this case, the prison administration is seen to be in a state of general collapse. (p 101)

Hallenstein made a brief reference to prisoner allegations of prison officer mind games and the exercise of abusive power in Jika. While stating the inquest was not in a position to comment on such matters, Hallenstein did warn that 'a lack of sound administrative procedures in K Division [Jika Jika] and a lack of command control and discipline ... provided fertile ground for the spring of abuse' (p 102).

Amongst numerous recommendations pertaining to the implementation of emergency response plans, equipment, procedures and staff training, Hallenstein recommended that there be an appointment of a Royal Commission, Board of Enquiry or Judicial Inquiry (p 106). The obstructive conduct and behaviour of the OOC during the inquest constituted a large part of Hallenstein's findings, and in this context his final comments are worth citing in full:

> The conduct of the OOC in this case raised deep and fundamental concern for our community's free institutions and its democratic style. Like any public institution, the OOC is accountable to the community it serves. Unlike many public institutions, the affairs of the OOC are behind closed walls and are not easily subject to public scrutiny. The OOC has misinterpreted this position of advantage as a license for secrecy, rather than as requiring the maximum of openness and accountability. This OOC has used this position of advantage to try and manipulate the facts to try and prevent their proper

investigation, and in a manner which could be described as corrupt. (p 115)

It was reported that during the delivery of the findings, the family and friends of the deceased 'audibly gasped and then cheered and applauded Hallenstein's comments and call for an inquiry' (*Sun* 29/7/89 pp 3-5). David McGauley's mother Ella McGauley tearfully told reporters that she was happy with the outcome and that her son could now rest in peace and that the finding Hallenstein delivered 'is what we came for. He [David] did not die for nothing' (*Age* 29/7/89 p 1). Robert Wright's sister Colleen Hunter told reporters that everything the families had wanted to come out, had come out, 'The reason we wanted this out in the open was for other prisoners. You cannot help our boys, but you can help the others' (*Age* 29/7/89 p 1). One of the founding members of the Prisoners Action Group (PAG), Paul Brand, had stated that PAG had been concerned in the beginning that the inquest would prove to be a whitewash but they were satisfied with the outcome. Brand also stated PAG would be calling for a full Royal Commission into the Victorian prison system, 'The five guys who died in the fire can rest in peace. Mr Hallenstein's decision was a very good ... the man has done his job properly under a lot of adversity and we commend him for it' (*Age* 29/7/89 p 26).

In contrast to the families, prison officers publicly expressed their anger towards the findings delivered by Hallenstein in which he ignored the rescue efforts and instead 'chose to paint a black picture of the officers' failings' (*Sunday Press* 30/7/89 p 4). It was pointed out that five of the prison officers who made rescue attempts were still yet to return to work and were suffering from medical and psychological repercussions. One prison officer called for the government to 'flick off' the coroner's findings; 'The coroner went overboard spraying us, then almost in a footnote he said the five contributed by building a barricade and lighting a fire. Commonsense declares the men brought it on themselves' (*Sunday Press* 30/7/89 p 4).

After considering the judgments, Minister for Corrections Steve Crabb announced the appointment of three separate inquiries to investigate the issues arising from Hallenstein's findings. These included an independent board of inquiry established to inquire into the conduct of the OOC during the Jika fire inquest; the undertaking of an independent review of the OOC's fire and emergency services capability; and a review of the adequacy of the present procedures for public accountability undertaken by the Ombudsman Norman Geschke (OOC 1989; see also Harmsworth 1989b). The government also announced that allegations of corruption levelled against various sections of the Victorian prison system and not just Jika Jika would be subject to investigation by a special police task force headed by the former head of the Police Prison Liaison Unit, Chief Inspector Terry Mulgrew.[41]

Director-General Peter Harmsworth (1989b: 2) acknowledged the OOC would be facing some 'trying times ahead ... The OOC has many achievements to be proud of and we ought not forget these as we get on with the job. The OOC has nothing to fear from the various reviews and in fact only good can come from their findings'. In reality the OOC had nothing to fear from the government's response, as each investigation proved a far cry from the independent scrutiny, appraisal and accountability prescribed by Hallenstein. The Cain Government's response draws attention to the vast gulf that exists between a coroner's findings and recommendations and their subsequent practical implementation. Hallenstein called for a Royal Commission or a general independent judicial inquiry in the prison system. Yet the four-pronged approach announced by the Victorian State Government was not independent, nor did any of the terms of reference provide for the type of generalised inquiry necessitated by the seriousness of the allegations levelled at the OOC, particularly claims that the prison system was riddled with corruption.

---

[41] These allegations emerged during the week preceding the conclusion of the Jika fire inquest and were reported on Channel 10 News and in the *Herald* Melbourne daily newspaper. Among the numerous claims, were allegations that management and staff were involved with drug deals, embezzlement, theft, assisting escapes, standover tactics and security breaches, to name some (see Harmsworth 1989b).

Investigating the Inquest: The 1990 Murray Report and the Government Response as Official Whitewash

There is insufficient space in this book to extensively document the events surrounding each of the separate inquiries appointed by the Victorian Government. However, some general observations regarding their adequacy are raised before considering the 1990 Murray Report in further detail. The review of the adequacy of public accountability measures within the OOC was anything but independent. It required the Ombudsman Norman Geschke to investigate and review the adequacy and effectiveness of his own office (Geschke 1990). In this context, the Ombudsman was effectively investigating himself.

The police taskforce appointed to investigate allegations of corruption publicised through the media lacked independence and rigour (Mulgrew 1989). Chief Inspector Terry Mulgrew led the taskforce, yet he could not be considered independent due to his past relationship to the OOC that extended between 12 and 14 years and included a period where he served as the Head of the Police Prison Liaison Unit (*Herald* 3/8/89 p 1). Moreover, the taskforce essentially provided a bandaid solution in its investigation of specific allegations. Such investigations would not in any way address the systemic occurrence of corruption, because while police are able to investigate specific incidents and allegations, they do not have the power or ability to investigate a whole system (*Age* 2/8/89 p 2).

OOC official John Griffin was nominated to conduct the review of emergency management arrangements adopted by the OOC since the Jika fire (Griffin 1989). While the review focused on the sufficiency of changes in the physical environment and security procedures since the fire, the terms of reference did not include an examination of the relationship between prison staff and prisoners.

In each of the inquiries not one term of reference addressed the issues raised by prisoners or the families and friends of the deceased about what had led to the Jika barricade and fatal fire. There was no scope for inquiring into the relationship between prisoners and prison officers or the impact of high-security conditions, and no avenue for investigating the reasons for the high rate of deaths in the Jika Jika High-Security Unit. The above inquiries once again illustrate the powerful functions of official discourse in official inquiries, which ultimately operate to protect state agencies under scrutiny over discreditable episodes. As Phil Scraton (2002: 112) argues:

> The political purpose of official discourse is never a full and open inquiry. Rather it is intended to reaffirm public confidence in a deeply flawed and much criticised criminal justice system, reconstruct new forms of operational legitimacy and secure strategies ostensibly which demonstrate a willingness to respond to public concern.

Scraton's observations are well illustrated through the 1990 Murray Report, appointed to investigate the conduct of the OOC during the Jika fire inquest. Retired Supreme Court Judge Tony Murray QC was appointed to head the report on the behaviour of the OOC as part of the government response to Hallenstein's findings. Overall the Murray Inquiry was strategically devised to downplay and reverse many of Hallenstein's trenchant criticisms and more specifically aimed to reduce the potential damage caused by his use of the term 'corrupt'. The Murray Inquiry served as a legitimising tool for the OOC, which faced a significant crisis of legitimacy on numerous fronts. If it were possible to water down or indeed overturn Hallenstein's findings, the families of the deceased would be unable to make compensation claims.

As with many independent inquiries, a key shortcoming with the Murray Inquiry was its restrictive terms of reference. Each term focused on the behaviour of the OOC during the Jika fire inquest. The terms included, to investigate whether the OOC impeded or attempted to impede the preparation and conduct of the inquest; whether the OOC extended its full cooperation to the coroner during the inquest; whether there was any 'dishonesty, impropriety or breach of duty', on the part of any officer or employee or former officer or employee; and whether any persons should be subject to disciplinary action for their conduct (Murray Report 1990: 64). If there was evidence to suggest dishonesty, impropriety or a breach of duty by any person associated with the OOC, a further term of reference allowed for recommendations for any action that might avoid the future repetition of such conduct (p 64). During Murray's proceedings these terms of reference were expanded to consider the same issues with respect to the conduct of the OOC during the Sean Downie inquest (p 65).

The narrowness of such terms lay in the fact that they provided little scope for investigation beyond matters already subject to scrutiny during the fire inquest. The purpose of a 'general and independent inquiry' was so that issues located outside the ambit of the inquest could be adequately investigated and appropriate action taken. Hallenstein had already investigated and found that the OOC did act improperly in pursuit of its own interests; that it was obstructive in its refusal to cooperate fully; and that it did attempt to impede the coroner's investigations. The question thus arises: Why would these matters require re-investigation? In this context the Murray Inquiry constituted nothing more than an investigation into the inquest and was structured to rehash many of the issues already investigated by Hallenstein. The inquiry as a whole created the impression that the State Coroner was subject to review rather than the OOC (*Age* 7/8/89 p 2). On this basis alone the Murray Report provided nothing more than an opportunity for the OOC to re-write Hallenstein's findings, and this is exactly what happened.

Overall the Murray Report reads as an OOC investigation into the shortcomings or indeed 'misunderstandings' that informed Hallenstein's findings. In the introductory sections of the report, Murray likened the proceedings of the fire inquest to a situation where the OOC and its officials were subject to 'criminal trial' (Murray Report 1990: 5). In response to each of Hallenstein's findings with respect to the conduct of the OOC during the inquest, Murray gave an extensive explanation that favoured the OOC. The Supreme Court application, the failure to cooperate fully in the provision of evidence, the Ryan and Sinfield affair, the alleged intimidation of prison officers and the accusations of bias levelled against Hallenstein were all downplayed by Murray as either unintentional or over-zealous attempts to protect the interests of the OOC and certainly not part 'of a chain of events as the Coroner has described it' (p 25; see also pp 10-29).

Throughout the inquest the OOC had demonstrated an ongoing failure to meet Hallenstein's requests for information. The official reasons given for these failures were that the evidence was 'unavailable', 'unknown' to the authorities or simply 'lost' (Hallenstein 1989: 113, see also 116; Inquest 1988-89a). Murray dealt with these allegations as part of the inquiry. In his findings, Hallenstein raised the issue of an internal investigation, referred to as the 'Tyne Report' and conducted in November 1987, that outlined 'facts, failures, issues, analysis, problems, concerns and recommendations about the fire and death' but which had not been freely provided to the coroner by the OOC (Hallenstein 1989: 113). Murray addressed this allegation in his report under the heading, 'The late production of the Tyne Report' and was defensive of the OOC (Murray Report 1990: 22-4). He believed that many staff remained unaware of the existence of the report. He also stated that all the information available in the Tyne Report had been duly provided to Hallenstein in the form of witness statements. Murray did recognise the fact that the collation of all this material within one document with findings and recommendations would have made things easier for Hallenstein. However, he concluded that he could find no evidence to suggest the report was deliberately withheld or constituted a 'sinister omission' (p 24). Despite this he found the OOC was at fault for not initially providing it to the coroner.

Aside from the Tyne Report, the OOC also failed to provide other evidence to the inquest. A prison officer alleged an unknown person deliberately destroyed the Jika Jika black books in order to conceal information from the inquest (p 35). It was also alleged that two days before the fire, a tape-recording taken of a conversation between Unit 4 prisoners had suggested there would be trouble. However this tape had, during the course of investigations, disappeared with no explanation (p 33).

Another issue was the 'lost' videotapes and photographs of the fire emergency response. The authorities maintained that the videotapes were not provided to Hallenstein because they were 'lost'. However, it was alleged by staff that the videotapes had not recorded properly because the camera was defective. Prison staff also claimed photographs taken at the scene had been developed but did not 'come out' and so they were thrown out (pp 32-4). While attempts by staff to record events at the scene were criticised during the inquest, Murray defended the actions: 'I am unable to arrive at a sinister conclusion in relation to the video taken or not taken ... It appears to me that a film of the events may have been a useful record for the future' (p 33). He also stated he felt it would be extremely unlikely photographs would have contained evidence that would be 'damaging' to the OOC and on this basis he found it difficult to believe the photographs were disposed of for the purpose of concealing evidence (p 34). Despite Murray's suggestion that none of the above examples constituted 'sinister omissions' on the part of the OOC, the 'loss' of evidence or the failure to provide information constitute typical responses by state agencies to maintain institutional secrecy.

During the inquiry prison officer Teresa Tate raised other allegations with respect to the conduct of prison officers at the emergency response. Perhaps the most serious allegation, which was supported by other prison officer witnesses, was that Gallagher had been alive when he was brought out of the fire (p 31). Hallenstein had heard such evidence during the inquest but dismissed it. However, Tate further alleged during the Murray Inquiry that a senior officer had stated he did not want Gallagher brought out alive (pp 30-1; Sun 21/9/89 p 27). She also claimed that officers had run Gallagher against concrete walls after he was brought out of the fire. Murray did not detail such specific allegations in his report. However, he did question Tate's reliability as a witness and dismissed her and other prison officer evidence with respect to signs of life in Gallagher. Murray expressed concern about the apparent readiness amongst certain prison officers to give evidence 'contrary to the interests of their employer, the OOC'. This statement was particularly directed to prison officers such as Desmond Sinfield whom Murray characterised as a 'biased witness' against the OOC (Murray Report 1990: 22).

Despite the dramatic events that unfolded during the Jika inquest, Murray found that there was no need for disciplinary proceedings to be taken but he added a disclaimer, 'this is not to say that the OOC has been completely absolved of all criticism or that none of the employees or officers, past and present, were guilty of any impropriety, dishonesty or breach of duty' (p 54). Murray observed that during the inquest the OOC displayed an 'exaggerated determinism' in displaying a favourable version of events. He further stated:

> This is not to suggest this determinism extended to the deliberate suppression or subversion of the truth. It is only to be expected that in times of trouble an organisation will and in my view should, within the bounds of truth and honesty, try to present a brave face. I think in this case the OOC probably went too far. (p 54)

Murray went on to comment that the cross-examination of Sinfield during the inquest signified a 'monumental error of judgement' on the part of the OOC as it fostered a sense of 'mistrust' and 'suspicion' amongst prison officers while reinforcing existing divisions between officials and prison staff (pp 54-5).

With respect to Hallenstein's use of the term 'corrupt' in his findings, Murray considered that the use of such a term was:

> Most unfortunate and I do not think for a moment that the Coroner intended to use that word in the sense in which it seems to be presently commonly used, namely in the sense of improper financial gain or bribery ... I should say emphatically that in the course of my Inquiry and, so far as I am aware, in the course of the Inquest, there has been no suggestion of any kind of corruption in the sense that that word is commonly used today. (p 55)

Murray was subsequently unable to recommend any action that might avoid a future repetition of events. He stated, quite incredibly:

> I am afraid that if another similar disaster should occur the events of the Inquest and of my Inquiry will have done nothing to lessen the suspicion, mistrust of the prison officers. (p 55)

He went on to state that he hoped the OOC would endeavour to apply a more 'orderly' and 'structured' approach to providing information to coroners, but 'this is not to say that it should not in future be prepared to protect itself if it is legally advised to do so' (p 55).

Despite the extent of crisis in Jika and Hallenstein's trenchant criticisms and recommendations, the OOC was able, through the use of strategic ideological mechanisms and official discourse, to reverse the coroner's findings and avoid full scrutiny and accountability. The complex events and allegations surrounding the Jika fire inquest, the Murray Inquiry and the other official investigations that followed are little documented and critiqued and for this reason they require further attention.

After the fire, Jika Jika was closed; the electronic doors and controls were removed and the Units were refurbished. The division was subsequently reopened as a medium security section with double the accommodation capacity and a new staff unit management program that provided specialist therapy based programs for HIV and drug addicted prisoners (OOC nd). As part of the new program, some Units were once again used to house women prisoners. Officials and senior staff acknowledged with respect to the division, as they did with H Division that:

> In hindsight, Jika had an appalling history. Between 1980 and 1987 incidents, which were to include escapes, serious assaults, murder and suicide, plagued the unit's operations. (OOC nd: 7)

These observations represent hollow acknowledgements. As a result of the decision by prison authorities to privatise the Victorian prison system in the 1990s, the Port Phillip Prison that opened to replace Pentridge experienced a considerable number of management problems, riots and a record number of deaths in custody (*Time* 6/4/98). In addition, Jika's successor, the Barwon Acacia High-Security Unit, has experienced significant problems associated with prisoner allegations of abuse and the prioritisation of security above all other considerations (P Reed Interview 15/5/04; see also Derkely 1995: 751-2). More recently, renewed concerns that the current system is ill-equipped to cater for prisoners convicted for terrorist-related or gangland offences has led to multi-million dollar security upgrades across Barwon Prison as a whole. Part of this upgrade is the $6.8 million Melaleuca High-Security Unit, touted by Victorian officials as a 'super prison within a prison' (*Herald Sun* 12/9/06). In this context it can be seen that Jika Jika's fatal outcomes failed to enliven any real reform or change. Rather, as the above case studies suggest, there has been a re-emphasis on security and efficiency, which has ultimately resulted in the transportation of unresolved issues and crises to other new prisons, though with equally fatal consequences.

EPILOGUE

The landscape that once comprised the various divisions of Pentridge has now been incongruously reclaimed, remoulded and redeveloped as a residential and commercial precinct renamed 'Pentridge Village'. Driving down the hill along Murray Road from West Preston towards Coburg, it is still possible to see the surrounding bluestone walls and watchtowers. Yet these have ceased to mark and guard the perimeters of a prison complex and instead secure a new and exclusive, walled housing estate.

Entering the residential precinct of Pentridge Village is a surreal and unsettling experience. Bluestone walls border the front gates and a tan facade has been attached with a fountain and the gold letters 'Pentridge Village'. There is a series of neatly manicured garden beds and the streetlights in the entrance are decorated with a chain of black and green advertising banners. These are spattered with a number of idyllic images of young professionals and families enjoying the lush green parklands and cosmopolitan lifestyle of an inner city housing estate. One banner bearing a close-up image of a father holding his child's hand proclaims, 'It's here!' The images on the banners are advertisements devised to attract the right 'type' of buyers and occupants to Pentridge Village. A particularly large billboard situated next to the Pentridge Village 'reception office' depicts a young family of four, joyously strolling together through parklands on a bright sunny day. The parents are visibly professional; the father is piggybacking his child and the mother carries a picnic basket. They are sharing a joke together. The image is accompanied by the advertising slogan, 'So close ... So friendly ... So individual'. As part of the promotional push, a brochure invites prospective buyers to 'escape' to Pentridge Village.

*All of this newness is visibly juxtaposed with the fragmented yet
stubborn reminders of a prison past. Even now, old leftover scraps
of razor wire cling defiantly and symbolically to the surrounding
tops of the walls. The residential dwellings back directly on to the
preserved heritage sections of Pentridge that will be used for the
forthcoming museum and commercial precinct of 'Q.M. Pentridge
Piazza'. At the front gates the emblematic 'H.M. Pentridge Prison
Est. 1851' sign sits uncomfortably beside a bannered image of a
cafe latte promoting the forthcoming commercial developments.
The gutted remnants of the prison are cordoned off by more
bluestone and loom over the fence lines of the neighbouring
suburban blocks of the Pentridge Village Housing Estate.*

*Every road, avenue, court and street has been given a name to pay
tribute to the particular historical significance of each site: Stockade
Street, Quarry Court, Governors Street, and Watchtower Street.
Perpendicular to the outer boundary fence of the estate is Jika
Street. This marks the perimeter of the decommissioned Jika Jika
High-Security Complex. People now live there. The actual site of
the complex itself is a pile of asphalt stumps and concrete rubble. A
five-star motel is destined for this place in the not too distant
future.*

The physical eradication of the Jika Jika High-Security Unit is in
many ways deeply symbolic of official attempts, during the late
1980s and early 1990s, to deflect attention from a series of
discreditable episodes resulting in crisis and death. Processes of
denial and 'forgetting' characterise predominant responses in
Australia to traumatic histories of violence and injustice. Yet the
erasure and neutralisation of physical reminders and the onset of
collective amnesia impede all hope for healing and redressing
injustice. Traumatic histories are not so easily buried and forgotten.
Inevitably, the powerful force of human lived experience imposes
indelible reminders and marks 'in documents, in bodies, in
communities and places, in buildings, streets and landscapes'
(Gibson 2002: 179). Despite Jika Jika's demolition, an entrenched
unacknowledged and unresolved legacy remains. This legacy
continues to weigh heavily on the prisoners who experienced and

survived Jika and the friends and families who lost loved ones. The memories and personal repercussions stemming from his time in Jika remain fresh for Peter Reed:

> I'll never forget, never. I'm not an animal but I was treated like one … My father visited me once in Jika and he nearly had tears in his eyes. And he said to me I can't come and see you in this place, I can't visit you here. It reminded him of the war and that's what it was a war. No I won't forget. (P Reed Interview 15/5/04)

There have also been little documented and long lasting adverse repercussions for prison officers, particularly those involved in the fire. Aside from the much-publicised impact on ex-officer Desmond Sinfield it has been reported that many officers 'later left the service. Some suffered breakdowns others became alcoholics. One became uncontrollably violent and later shot himself' (*Sunday Age* 25/10/98 p 5).

This book has endeavoured to unearth, excavate and reconstruct experiential accounts of life and death in high-security, an institution very rarely subject to public scrutiny. The result is an unauthorised, unresolved institutional account of abuse, desperation, resistance and death concealed by official responses that have served only to circumvent accountability, justice and secure organisational impunity.

Officially advocated as a necessary solution to house the system's 'worst' prisoners, Jika Jika was devised as an escape and resistance-proof panopticon that would maximise order and instil total disciplinary control. Jika's development cannot be viewed in isolation from the challenges posed by the ascendancy of prisoner rights movements in Victoria and other Australian States during this time. The development of modern high-security units generally must be situated in the international context of official responses to prisoner rights movements and the corresponding development of strategies aimed at curbing such resistance through coercive control (Ryan 1992: 84). Spokesperson for the Victorian Prisoners Action Group summed this up in stating the core official objective informing Jika's development mirrors original intentions for constructing the maximum-security H Division and the construction of the infamous punishment cages before that:

> And that reason is, quite simply, fear – the deep-seated fear which authoritarian regimes always exhibit when they sense even the slightest erosion of their ability to effectively crush those who in any way challenge their authority. (*Age* 1/8/89 p 5)

While Jika's blueprints comprised an official response to threats of prisoner resistance, in practice the regime was subject to rigorous transgression and challenge. As previous chapters have discussed, the unaccountable power structures, abusive excesses and pressures created by conditions in Jika only served to intensify prisoner frustrations, feelings of injustice and therefore exacerbate extreme acts of desperation and violent resistance. Thus during the 1980s, Jika's walls concealed an internal struggle between officials and prisoners that ended in crisis.

For the many uncomfortable and troubling questions arising from the fire and the long list of deaths occurring throughout 1987, the authorities and government remain unaccountable. There has been no acknowledgement or recognition of prisoner experiences and little or no justice for the families and friends who lost their loved ones. The authorities eluded numerous allegations of prison officer abuse, misconduct and official corruption and refused to address the warning signs and serious problems experienced in Jika from the very moment the institution opened in 1980 through to the fatal crisis in 1987. Subsequent official responses, during the Sean Downie and fire inquests, signalled a marked prioritisation of the OOC's interests and a simplistic disregard for accounts alleging negligence, misconduct or complicity by the OOC and their staff in the deaths. Overall, official responses to the Jika deaths point to the fundamental political dynamics and ideologies that underpin the broader conduct of official inquiries and investigations into deaths in custody (Scraton 2002: 112). Moreover, the behaviour of the OOC in these cases illustrates an official over-reliance on individual prisoner violence, dangerousness and social inadequacy as simplistic explanations and excuses for institutional malfunctions, crisis and deaths. As the legacy of Jika suggests, the recycling of official denial has contributed to repetitious processes of 'rationalising the unthinkable' (Pilger 1992: 4). This involves the development and sophistication of technologies, which John Pilger believes to be 'the function of the experts, and mainstream media, to normalise the unthinkable for the general public' (Pilger 1992: 4).

The Jika Jika High-Security Unit is a localised case-study with international relevance. It must be firmly grounded in the body of case studies and research documenting links between high-security regimes and harm. As discussed, there is much evidence confirming the detrimental psychological pressures and long-term impacts of lengthy periods spent idle in conditions of total lockdown and sensory deprivation (see e.g. Funnell 2006: 70-4; Rhodes 2004; Haney 2003; Fellner & Mariner 1997; Haney & Lynch 1997). Moreover, increased official secrecy and the dehumanising stigmatisation of prisoner populations as 'worst of the worst' and 'high-risk' has a polarising effect, giving rise to frustrations, abuses of power, violent cultures, self-harm, disorder and in some cases death (Rhodes 2004; see also Fellner & Mariner 1997). Official responses to problems in high-security are always retributive, involving the escalation of security and discipline. It is paradoxical that such responses serve to exacerbate rather than address in any real terms institutional problems.

In the United States where high-security and supermax are steadily becoming the norm, officials dismiss the credibility of critical studies, arguing such research is not systematic and is overly informed by prisoner accounts, advocacy and litigation (King 2005: 124-9). Official studies also argue gains associated with the deterrence value of high-security far outweigh possible negative effects (see Ward & Werlich 2003; ABC *Four Corners* 7/11/05). These studies measure the impacts of high-security units on the basis of individual statistics and the 'effectiveness' of such institutions in terms of the broader prevention of prison violence (Ward & Werlich 2003; see also King 2005). Haney and Lynch (1997: 495) argue such research is geared towards the minimisation of concerns over high-security and its harmful impacts and has implicitly served to authorise its increased use. Moreover, Sim (1994: 105) points out that official solutions focused on identifying and segregating the system's 'worst' prisoners do not in practice reduce the occurrence of violence in other parts of prison nor beyond its walls, primarily because such violence is treated as an individual problem rather than the complex creation of institutional conditions and violent masculine cultures.

The Scottish Barlinnie experiment in the 1970s demonstrated profound successes associated with therapeutic and rehabilitative alternatives in managing difficult prisoners. However, its optimism and gains were overshadowed by a growing preoccupation with security and control seen by prison authorities as the only viable approach to housing high-risk and serious offenders. The officially propagated relationship between individual propensities for violence and the correlative development of criminal justice policy is not isolated to Jika Jika. It is a perennial official concern, continually repackaged and simplistically promulgated to satisfy the implementation of increasingly draconian methods of institutional control. In particular, the official generation of moral panics surrounding 'risk' are closely related to the correlative reproduction of security-based regimes as a preventive and retributive response. This discussion is particularly relevant to recent concerns raised over the practice of holding unconvicted 'terror suspects' in austere and brutal conditions for indefinite periods as a preventative measure in the 'war on terror'. Moreover, it is central to the continuing uncritical reproduction and proliferation of 'new and improved' high-security units throughout Australian States and internationally.

The prevailing impacts and predominance of official discourses of 'risk' present difficult challenges to those interested in reform. Sim refers specifically to the dangers that stem directly from the official mobilisation of such discourses against the powerless. He argues:

> Criminologists (and indeed so-called 'practitioners') need to develop a more comprehensive definition of what the concept [of risk] means if it is to have any analytical viability. This would involve shifting their professional gaze away from an overwhelming concern with, and concentration on, the behaviour of the powerless and the risks they pose, to considering how the powerful have utilised and continue to

utilise their self-referential propensity for being at risk to justify and legitimate political and policy clampdowns. (Sim 2004: 128)

Critical scholars clearly have a role to play in maintaining open dialogue and debate, developing critical research agendas, and perhaps most importantly opening up uncomfortable silences around abusive power and human suffering. Henry Giroux (2005: 190) contends that the primary role of the 'oppositional academic' should be to uncover impunity, to make power accountable, 'to make clear ... the moral and political stakes about what it might mean to contribute to a culture and social order in which human suffering goes unnoticed and actually becomes normalised'. Phil Scraton concurs, recognising the transformative power of critical research agendas in providing agency and voice to those who have been silenced. He observes that critical social analysis sets an oppositional agenda in that it 'seeks out, records and champions the view from below ensuring that the voices and experiences of those marginalised by institutionalised state practices are heard and represented' (Scraton 2004). Individual experiences of injustice and suffering are a central starting point in the process of igniting rational and informed debate about how we imprison those considered beyond rehabilitation and redemption.

Prisons, particularly high-security institutions, do not present solutions. As Angela Davis argues, they 'do not disappear problems, they disappear human beings. And the practice of disappearing vast numbers of people from poor, immigrant, and racially marginalised communities has literally become big business' (Cunneen & Davis 2000: 4-7). Nonetheless, populist law and order campaigns remain effective in drumming up fears and retributive prejudice through the use of imagery associated with racial otherness, social inadequacy and above all, 'dangerousness'. The recycling of official denial only contributes to the erasure of a collective depth of knowledge and critical understanding about the past. Likewise, an unwillingness to honestly and openly confront traumatic episodes can only give rise to the resurfacing of past problems.

Edward Said states that the role of contemporary scholars is dependent upon their ability to 'uncover the contest, to challenge and defeat both an imposed silence and the normalised quiet of unseen power, wherever and whenever possible'. He has also appealed for us to 'protect against and forestall the disappearance of the past' (*Age* 21/5/01 p 11). This book has sought to write against the official obfuscation of accounts firmly situated within ongoing concerns located in the contemporary national and international context of large-scale imprisonment, human rights abuses and increased scrutiny and public accountability for state agencies. It presents a beginning in a local body of knowledge but is also grounded in broader concerns associated with the human costs of high-security imprisonment. From the deeply painful and unresolved history of one institution, the Jika Jika High-Security Unit, greater responsibilities flow.

BIBLIOGRAPHY

Coronial Inquest Files, Transcripts and Findings

Inquest 1982, Coroner's investigation into Glen Joseph Davies, 1982, State Coroner's Office, VPRS P/0002, Unit 000777

Inquest 1985, Coroner's investigation into the death of Barry Robert Quinn, 1985, State Coroner's Office, Case No. 1996/84 CR

Inquest 1988, Coroner's investigation into the death of John James Williams, 1988, State Coroner's Office, VPRS 8166/SR/0003, Unit 85

Inquest 1988-89a, Coroner's investigation into the deaths of James Richard Loughnan, David McGauley, Arthur Bernard Gallagher, Robert Lindsay Wright and Richard John Morris, 1988-1989, Public Records Office Victoria, file number 1989/680, VPRS 24/P7

Unit 74:

Complaint by prisoners Ian Murdon, Peter Reid, Craig Minogue, Gareth Thornton and Rodney Minogue 29/3/87, Exhibit 42

K Division Incident Reports: March-September 1987

Letters to the Ombudsman by Olaf Dietrich, Richard Light and Rodney Minogue 1987, Exhibit 79

Notes and letter to the Ombudsman by Richard Morris 6/87

Office of Corrections Memorandum from Superintendent of Inspections Michael Ryan to Director-General Peter Harmsworth 11/4/88, Exhibit 87

Photographs of bronze-up, vandalism and graffiti Undated, Exhibit 18

Prison Officer Thorp, Prisoner Incident Report Form 15/6/87

Statement and further notes by Craig Minogue 7/7/88

Statement by prisoner Olaf Dietrich 12/8/88

Statement by prisoner Wayne King 3/11/87

Statement by Rodney Minogue 24/3/88

Undated notes and complaints by prisoner Richard Light, Exhibit 32

Various prisoner complaint letters, Exhibit 80

Unit 75:

Letter from James Bazley to State Coroner Hallenstein 6/3/88

Photograph Unit 4 corridor, Metropolitan Fire Brigade 1987 Exhibit 109

Police Commander P. H. Bennett, Report to Chief Commissioner of Police Re: 30/7/83 Jika Breakout 19/10/83, Exhibit 183

Unit 76:

Security Planning Committee Minutes and Brief 16/8/77, Exhibit 154

Social Welfare Department Prisons Division, Security Planning Committee Minutes 29/12/76, Exhibit 153

Inquest 1988-89b, Coroner's investigation into the death of Sean Fitzgerald Downie, 1988-1989, Public Records Office Victoria, file number 1989/664, VPRS 24/P7

Unit 64:

C.I.B. Arson Job Sheet Case No. 3696: Current Position of Inquiry 24/8/87

Statement by Governor Alan Davis 24/8/87

Statement by Governor Edgar Penter 24/8/87

Statement by Olaf Dietrich 24/8/87

Statement by Prison Officer Noel Gough 4/8/89

Statement by Prison Officer Reading 24/8/87

Statement by Rodney Minogue 24/8/87

Unit 66:

Office of Corrections Incident Report 21/8/87, Exhibit AK

Office of Corrections Incident Report 24/8/87, Exhibit T

Office of Corrections Memorandum 12/8/87

Unit 67:

David Ranson, Victorian Institute of Forensic Pathology Medical Opinion Re: Sean Downie

Deputy Director-General M B Ryan, Inquiry into the Death of 'K' Division Prisoner Sean Fitzgerald Downie 3/3/88, Exhibit BH

Director of Criminal Justice Unit John Van Gronigan, Memorandum Addressed to Attorney-General's Department, Re: Death of Sean Downie 23/12/87

Manager Corrections Health Service Stephen Kerr, Suicide Audit Report: Sean Downie 11/87, Exhibit BJ

Paul Delphine and Norm Banner, Enquiry into the Death of Sean Downie, Exhibit AX

Forensic Photographs 24/8/87

Statement by Dr Richard Byron Collins 25/8/87

Statement by John Dixon-Jenkins 23/4/92

Dessau LM 1989, Coroner, Finding of Inquisition upon the Body of Sean Fitzgerald Downie, 21/9/89, Public Records Office Victoria, VPRS 24/P7

Hallenstein HR 1989, Coroner, Finding of Inquisition upon the Bodies of James Richard Loughnan, David McGauley, Arthur Bernard Gallagher, Robert Lindsay Wright and Richard John Morris, 28/7/89, Public Records Office Victoria, VPRS 24/P7, Unit 79

Reports, Inquiries and Official Documents

Allom Lovell & Associates 1996 *HM Pentridge and HM Metropolitan Prison (Coburg Prisons Complex) Conservation Management Plan* Prepared for the Department of Treasury and Finance and the City of Moreland Melbourne August 1996

Austin Report 1988, Austin, Alan *'I was In Prison' ... A Report on Prisons in Victoria* Division of Social Justice Uniting Church Melbourne August 1988

Challinger Report 1982, Challinger, Dennis *Jika Jika: A Review of Victoria's Maximum-security Prison* A Report to the Director General of Community Welfare Services August 1982

DCWS 1980, Department of Community Welfare Services Division of Correctional Services *Jika-Jika High-Security Unit H.M Prison Pentridge* Government of Victoria July

DCWS 1980, Department of Community Welfare Services 'Jika Jika' in *Community Welfare Services Newsletter* No 2 June p 5

Dillon Report 1978, Dillon, JV, Ombudsman of Victoria *Report of the Ombudsman on Investigation into Cause of Unrest in 'H' Division, Pentridge, during the weekend commencing 15 April 1978* Government Printer Melbourne

DPW 1979, Department of Public Works *The Jika Jika Security Unit*, Concrete Institute of Australia Awards for Excellence

DSW/PWD 1978, Dixon, Brian, Minister for Social Welfare, and Tom Austin, Minister of Public Works *Jika Jika Security Unit Commemoration Plaque* A joint publication by the Department of Social Welfare and The Public Works Department September

Geschke, Norman 1990, Ombudsman of Victoria *Report on the Accountability of the Office of Corrections* July

Griffin, John 1989 *Inquiry into the Adequacy of Emergency Arrangements adopted by the Office of Corrections since the Jika Jika Fire On 29 October 1987* 19 September

Harmsworth, Peter 1989a, Director-General of the Office of Corrections 'K Division Coronial Inquest – Supreme Court Ruling on Coroner's Role and Powers' *Newsbreak* Vol 4 No 2 Office of Corrections March

Harmsworth, Peter 1989b 'K Division Inquest and Allegations of Corruption' *Newsbreak* Vol 4 No 7 Office of Corrections August

Holding, Tim 2006, Minister for Corrections Victoria 'Media Release: Holding unveils Melaleuca High-Security Unit' 11 September

Jenkinson Report 1973-74, Jenkinson, KJ *Report of the Board of Inquiry into Allegations of Brutality and Ill Treatment at H.M. Prison Pentridge* Government Printer Melbourne

Lynn Report 1993, Lynn, Peter *Report on Allegations of Maladministration, Corruption and Drug Trafficking within the Victorian Prison System* Government Printer Melbourne August

Mountbatten, Earl of Burma 1966 *Report of the Inquiry into Prison Escapes and Security* UK Home Office

Mulgrew, Terry 1989, Detective Chief Inspector *Victoria Police Task Force Report on Allegations of Corruption within the Office of Corrections* December

Murray Report 1990, Murray, BL *Report on the Behaviour of the Office of Corrections in relation to the Conduct of the Inquest by the State Coroner, upon the bodies of James Richard Loughnan, David McGauley, Arthur Bernard Gallagher, Robert Lindsay Wright, Richard John Morris and in relation to the Inquest conducted by the Deputy State Coroner, Ms. Linda Dessau, upon the body of Sean Fitzgerald Downie* Tabled by the Minister for Corrections in State Parliament Victoria 7 March

Nagle Report 1978, Nagle, JF, Commissioner *Report of the Royal Commission into NSW Prisons* Vol III Parliament of New South Wales

Office of the Inspector of Custodial Services 2001 *Report of an unannounced inspection of the Induction and Orientation Unit and the Special Handling Unit at Casurina Prison* Report No 1 March

OOC 1989, Office of Corrections Victoria 'Media Release: Government Responds to Jika Inquest Findings' 31 July

OOC nd, Office of Corrections Victoria *Unit Management in Victorian Prisons: K Division Staff Manual* Government Printer Melbourne

RCIADIC Report 1991, Johnson, Elliott QC, Commissioner *National Report of the Royal Commission into Aboriginal Deaths in Custody* Volume 1 & Overview and Recommendations Australian Government Publishing Service Canberra

Swan, John F 1977-78, Chief Architect *Pentridge High-Security Unit* A planning brief prepared by Project Group General Public Works Department for the client Correctional Services Division of the Social Welfare Department

Ombudsman Victoria 2004, Victorian Office of the Ombudsman 'The history and functions of the Ombudsman', www.ombudsman.vic.gov.au/amb1.html, accessed 18 September 2004

Prisoner Writings

Abbot, Jack Henry 1981 *In the Belly of the Beast* Random House New York

Boyle, Jimmy 1979 *A Sense of Freedom* Macmillan London

Davison, Remy 1996 'An interview with Ray Mooney' *Australasian Drama Studies* No 28 April pp 52-62

Justice Action 2003 'Goulburn High Risk Management Unit Prisoner Offer of Hope' Justice Action Sydney July

Matthews, Bernie 1978 'Katingal, the concrete coffin' written from inside Katingal

Matthews, Bernie 2006 *Intractable: Hell Has a Name, Katingal: Life Inside Australia's First Supermax Prison* Pan Macmillan Sydney

Minogue, Craig 1994 'Isolation' *Eureka St* Vol 4 No 8 October p 23

Minogue, Craig 2002 'Prisoners' rights: human rights and excursions from the flat lands' in Brown and Wilkie (eds) *Prisoners as Citizens, Human Rights in Australian Prisons* Federation Press Sydney pp 196-212

Minogue, Craig nd 'A Collection of Essays by Craig Minogue,1993-2000' personal collection of essays written from inside prison

Mooney, Ray 1985 *Every Night! Every Night!* Yackandandah Play Scripts Montmorency

PAG 1985a, Prisoners Action Group *Jail Notes* Vol 1 No 1 March

PAG 1985b, Prisoners Action Group *Jail Notes* Vol 1 No 2 November

PAG 1986, Prisoners Action Group *Jail Notes* Vol 1 No 3 November

PAR 1999, Prison Action and Reform 'A documented report: abuse in Risdon Prison' Prison Action and Reform Hobart

PAR 2005, Prison Action and Reform 'Tasmania: a system to die for' Prison Action and Reform Hobart

PRG 1988, Prison Reform Group *Jika Jika Revisited* first edition of *The Doing Time Magazine* Prison Reform Group Melbourne

PRG 1989, Prison Reform Group *The Prison Record* Prison Reform Group Melbourne

Read, Mark ('Chopper') 1991 *From the Inside: The Confessions of Mark Brandon Read* Sly Ink Smithfield

Roberts, Gregory David 2003 *Shantaram* Scribe Publications Melbourne

Vaux, Janet 1978 'The last screw violence at Katingal' *Jail News* Prisoners Action Group Vol 1 No 1 10 June pp 3-6

Books, Articles and Other Sources

ABC *Four Corners* 7/11/05, Masterson, Chris 'Supermax' Australian Broadcasting Commission

ANZJC 1972, *Australian and New Zealand Journal of Criminology* 'Editorial' Vol 5 No 2 pp 67-9

Architecture Australia 1982 'Architect Awards – New Buildings: The Jika Jika High-Security Unit Coburg' Vol 71 No 6 December pp 74-5

Armstrong, Jim and Peter Lynn 1996 *From Pentonville to Pentridge: A history of prisons in Victoria* State Library of Victoria Melbourne

Becker, Howard 1967 'Whose side are we on?' *Social Problems* Vol 14 No 3 pp 234-47

Bosworth, Mary and Eamonn Carrabine 2001 'Reassessing resistance: race, gender and sexuality' *Punishment and Society* Vol 3 No 4 pp 501-15

Brown, David 1988a 'Deaths in Australian prisons: a review' in Hogan et al *Death at the Hands of the State* Redfern Legal Centre Publishing Sydney pp 51-60

Brown, David 1988b 'In the course of duty? Kenny Evans: A postscript' in Hogan et al *Death in the Hands of the State* Redfern Legal Centre Publishing Sydney

Brown, David and Meredith Wilkie (eds) 2002 *Prisoners as Citizens, Human Rights in Australian Prisons* Federation Press Sydney

Campbell, Brian, Laurence McKeown and Felim O'Hagan (eds) 1994 *Nor Meekly Serve My Time: The H Block Struggle 1976-1981* Beyond the Pale Publications London

Carlen, Pat and Frank Burton 1979 *Official Discourse: On Discourse Analysis, Government Publications, Ideology and the State* Routledge and Kegan Paul London

Carlton, Bree 2001 'Researching secrecy: state power and prisoner resistance in the Australian high-security prison' *Melbourne Historical Journal Special Issue*, Proceedings of the Mass Historia Postgraduate Conference University of Melbourne pp 50-6

Carter, Keith 2000 'The Casuarina prison riot: official discourse or appreciative inquiry' *Current Issues in Criminal Justice* Vol 12 No 3 pp 363-75

Churchill, Ward and Jim Vanderwall (eds) 1992 *Cages of Steel: The Politics of Imprisonment in the United States* Maissoneuve Press Washington

Cohen, Stanley and Laurie Taylor 1972 *Psychological Survival: The Experience of Long-Term Imprisonment* Penguin Books Middlesex

Connell, Bob 1987 *Gender and Power: Society, the Person and Sexual Politics* Stanford University Press California

Corcoran, Mary 2006 *Out of Order: The Political Imprisonment of Women in Northern Ireland 1972-1998* Willan Cullompton

Cresswell, Tim 1996 *In Place/ Out of Place: Geography, Ideology and Resistance* University of Minnesota Press Minnesota

Cunneen, Chris 1996 'Detention, Torture, Terror and the Australian State: Aboriginal People, Criminal Justice and Neo-colonialism' in Bird et al (eds) *Majah: Indigenous Peoples and the Law* Federation Press Sydney pp 13-37

Cunneen, Chris 1997 'Hysteria and Hate: The Vilification of Aboriginal and Torres Strait Islander People' in Cunneen et al (eds) *Faces of Hate: Hate Crime in Australia* Hawkins Press Sydney pp 137-61

Cunneen, Chris 2001 *Conflict, Politics and Crime: Aboriginal Communities and the Police* Allen and Unwin Sydney

Cunneen, Chris and Angela Davis 2000 'Masked racism: reflections on the prison industrial complex' *Indigenous Law Bulletin* Vol 4 No 27 pp 4-7

Danaher, Geoff, Tony Schirato and Jen Webb 2000 *Understanding Foucault* Allen and Unwin Sydney

Davis, Angela 2003 *Are Prisons Obsolete* Seven Stories Press New York

Davis, Angela 2005 *Abolition Democracy: Beyond Empire, Prisons and Torture* Seven Stories Press New York

Dayan, Joan 2002 'Cruel and unusual: parsing the meaning of punishment' *Law-Text-Culture* Vol 5 No 2 pp 7-43

De Certeau, Michel 1984 *The Practice of Everyday Life* Trans. Steven Rendall University of California Press Los Angeles

Derkely, Karin 1995 'Leg irons: return to the nineteenth-century? Challenge to the use of leg irons on two prisoners in the maximum-security unit at Barwon Prison' *Law Institute Journal* Vol 69 No 8 pp 751-2

Donnison, David 1978 'Special unit' *New Society* January pp 80-1

Dunne, Bill 1992 'The U.S. prison at Marion, Illinois: an instrument of oppression' in Churchill and Vanderwall (eds) *Cages of Steel: The Politics of Imprisonment in the United States* Maissoneuve Press Washington pp 38-82

Edney, Richard 1997 'Prison officers and violence' *Alternative Law Journal* Vol 22 No 8 pp 289-97

Fellner, Jamie and Joanne Mariner 1997 'Cold-storage: super-maximum security confinement in Indiana' Human Rights Watch New York

Finanne, Mark 1997 *Punishment in Australian Society* Oxford University Press Oxford

Findlay, Mark 1982 *The State of the Prison: A Critique of Reform* Mitchellsearch Bathurst

Fitzgerald, Mike 1975 *Control Units and the Shape of Things to Come* Radical Alternatives to Prison Publications London

Fitzgerald, Mike 1977 *Prisoners in Revolt* Penguin Books Middlesex

Fletcher, Karen 1999 'The myth of the "Supermax Solution"' *Alternative Law Journal* Vol 24 No 6 pp 274-8

Foucault, Michel 1991a *Discipline and Punish: The Birth of the Prison* Penguin Books Middlesex

Foucault, Michel 1991b 'Questions of method' in Burchell et al (eds) *The Foucault Effect: Studies in Governmentality: With Two Lectures and an Interview with Michel Foucault* University of Chicago Press Chicago

Freckleton, Ian 1997 'Judicial attitudes toward scientific evidence: the Antipodean experience' Symposium of International Perspectives on Scientific Evidence *UC Davis Law Review* Vol 30 No 4 pp 1137-227

Freckleton, Ian and David Ranson 2006 *Death Investigation and the Coroner's Inquest* Oxford University Press Melbourne

Funnell, Neal 2006 'Where the norm is not the norm: The Department of Corrective Services and the Harm-U' *Alternative Law Journal* Vol 31 No 2 pp 70-4

George, Amanda 2002 'Tales of a private women's prison: writ in women's lives' *Hecate* Vol 28 No 1 pp 145-53

Gibson, Ross 2002 *Seven Versions of Australian Badland* University of Queensland Press Brisbane

Giroux, Henry 2005 *Against the New Authoritarianism, Politics After Abu Ghraib* Arbeiter Ring Publishing Manitoba

Goffman, Erving 1961 *Asylums: essays on the social situation of mental patients and other inmates* Anchor Books New York

Goldie, David 1987 'Out of Sight, Out of Mind' *Four Corners* Australian Broadcasting Commission

Gordon, Avery 2006 'Abu Ghraib, Imprisonment and the War on Terror' *Race and Class* Vol 48 No 1

Green, Penny and Tony Ward 2004 *State Crime, Governments, Violence and Corruption* Pluto Press London

Hall, Stuart, Chas Critcher, Tony Jefferson, John Clarke and Brian Roberts 1978 *Policing the Crisis: Mugging, the State, and Law and Order* Macmillan Press London

Haney, Craig 2003 'Mental health issues in long-term solitary and "supermax" confinement' *Crime and Delinquency* Vol 49 No 1 pp 124-56

Haney, Craig and Mona Lynch 1997 'Regulating prisons of the future: a psychological analysis of Supermax and solitary confinement' *New York University Review of Law and Social Change* Vol XXIII No 4

Haney, Craig and Phillip Zimbardo 1998 'The past and future of US prison policy: twenty-five years after the Stanford Prison Experiment' *American Psychologist* Vol 53 No 7 pp 709-24

Hillyard, Paddy, Christine Pantazis, Steve Tombs and Dave Gordon (eds) 2004 *Beyond Criminology: Taking Harm Seriously* Pluto Press London

Hogan, Michael 1988 'Let sleeping watchdogs lie: The NSW Coronial Inquest system and deaths involving state agencies' in Hogan et al *Death in the Hands of the State* pp 115-90

Hogan, Michael, David Brown and Russell Hogg (eds) 1988 *Death in the Hands of the State* An 'Inquest' and Alternative Law Journal Publication Redfern Legal Centre Publishing Sydney

Hogg, Russell and David Brown 1998 *Rethinking Law and Order* Pluto Press Sydney

Human Rights Law Resource Centre 2006 'Submission to UN High Commissioner for Human Rights Regarding conditions of detention of unconvicted remand prisoners in Victoria, Australia'

Human Rights Watch 1999 'Red Onion State Prison: super-maximum security confinement in Virgina' Human Rights Watch New York

Ignatieff, Michel 1978 *A Just Measure of Pain: The Penitentiary in the Industrial Revolution* Columbia University Press Columbia

Jackson, Michael 1983 *Prisoners of Isolation: Solitary Confinement in Canada* Toronto University Press Toronto

Johnstone, Graeme 1988 'An avenue for death and injury prevention' in Hugh Selby (ed) *The Aftermath of Death* Federation Press Sydney pp 140-84

Kilroy, Debbie and Anne Warner 2002 'Deprivation of liberty – deprivation of rights' in Brown and Wilkie (eds) *Prisoners as Citizens: Human Rights in Australian Prisons* Federation Press Sydney pp 40-6

Kimmett, Edgar, Ian O'Donnell and Carol Martin 2003 *Prison Violence: The Dynamics of Conflict, Fear and Power* Willan Cullompton

King, Roy 2005 'The effects of supermax confinement' in Liebling and Maruna (eds) *The Effects of Imprisonment* Willan Publishing Cullompton pp 124-9

Liebling, Alison 2001 'Whose side are we on? Theory, practice and allegiances in prisons research' *British Journal of Criminology Special Issue: Methodological Dilemmas of Research* Vol 41 No 3 pp 472-84

Liebling, Alison and Shadd Maruna (eds) 2005 *The Effects of Imprisonment* Willan Publishing Cullompton

Lucas, WE 1976 'Solitary confinement: isolation as coercion to conform' *Australian and New Zealand Journal of Criminology* No 9 September pp 153-7

McCoy, Alfred 2006 *A Question of Torture: CIA Interrogation From the Cold War to the War on Terror* Metropolitan Books New York

McCulloch, Jude 2001 *Blue Army: Paramilitary Policing in Australia* Melbourne University Press Melbourne

McKeown, Laurence 2001 *Out of Time: Irish Republican Prisoners Long Kesh 1972-2000* Beyond the Pale Publications Belfast

Minc, Ariane 2006 'Interview with Charandev Singh' *Jailbreak* Community Radio 2SER Sydney 9 May

Morgan, Steve 1999 'Prison lives: critical issues in reading prisoner autobiography' *The Howard Journal* Vol 38 No 3 pp 328-40

Newburn, Tim and Elizabeth Stanko (eds) 1994 *Just Boys Doing Business? Men, Masculinities and Crime* Routledge London

O'Melveny, Mary 1992 'Portrait of a U.S. political prison: the Lexington High-Security Unit for women' in Churchill and Vanderwall (eds) *Cages of Steel: The Politics of Imprisonment in the United States* Maissoneuve Press Washington pp 112-22

Oikawa, Mona 2000 'Cartographies of violence: women, memory, and the subjects of "internment"' *Canadian Journal of Law and Society* Vol 15 No 2 pp 39-69

Parenti, Christian 2000 *Lockdown America* Verso London

Perera, Suvendrini 2002 'What is a camp … ?' *Borderlands e-journal* Vol 1 No 1, www.borderlandsejounal.adelaide.edu.au/vol1no1_2002/perera_camp.html, accessed 14 January 2003

Physicians for Human Rights 2005 *Break Them Down: Systematic Use of Torture by US Forces* Physicians for Human Rights Washington

Pickering, Sharon 2001 'Undermining the sanitised account: violence and emotionality in the field of Northern Ireland' *British Journal of Criminology* Vol 41 No 3 pp 485-501

Pilger, John 1992 *Distant Voices* Vintage London

Pugliese, Joseph 2002 'Penal asylum: refugees, ethics, hospitality' *Borderlands e-journal* Vol 1 No 1, www.borderlandsejournal.adelaide.edu.au/vol1no1_2002/pugliese.html, accessed 14 January 2003

Rhodes, Lorna 1998 'Panoptical intimacies' *Public Culture* Vol 10 No 2 pp 285-311

Rhodes, Lorna 2004 *Total Confinement: Madness and Reason in the Maximum Security Prison* University of California Press Berkeley

Rinaldi, Fiori 1977 *Australian Prisons* F&M Publishing Canberra

Rodriguez, Dylan 2003 'State Terror and the Reproduction of Imprisoned Dissent' *Social Identities* Vol 9 No 2 pp 183-203

Rodriguez, Dylan 2006 *Forced Passages: Imprisoned Intellectuals and the US Prison Regime* University of Minnesota Press Minneapolis

Ross, Jeffrey 2003 *The Dynamics of Political Crime* Sage California

Russell, Emma 1998 *Fairlea: The History of a Women's Prison in Australia 1956-1996* The Public Correctional Enterprise CORE Melbourne

Ryan, Mike 1992 'Solitude as counter-insurgency: The U.S. isolation model of political incarceration' in Churchill and Vanderwall (eds) *Cages of Steel: The Politics of Imprisonment in the United States* Maissoneuve Press Washington pp 83-109

Sabo, Don, Terry Kupers and Willie London (eds) 2001 *Prison Masculinities* Temple University Press Philadelphia

Santos, Michael 2006 *Inside: Life Behind bars in America* St Martin's Press New York

Scott, James 1985 *Weapons of the Weak: Everyday Forms of Peasant Resistance* Yale University Press New Haven

Scraton, Phil 1999 'Policing with contempt: the degrading of truth and denial of justice in the aftermath of the Hillsborough disaster' *Journal of Law and Society* Vol 26 No 3 pp 273-97

Scraton, Phil 2002 'Lost lives, hidden voices: "truth" and controversial deaths' *Race and Class* Vol 44 No 1 pp 107-18

Scraton, Phil 2004 'Speaking truth to power: experiencing critical research' in Smyth and Williamson (eds) *Researchers and their Subjects: Ethics, Power, Knowledge and Consent* The Policy Press Bristol pp 175-94

Scraton, Phil and Kathryn Chadwick 1987a *In the Arms of the Law: Coroner's Inquests and Deaths in Custody* Pluto Press London

Scraton, Phil and Kathryn Chadwick 1987b 'Speaking ill of the dead: official responses to deaths in custody' in Scraton (ed) *Law, Order and the Authoritarian State: Readings in Critical Criminology* Open University Press Philadelphia pp 212-36

Scraton, Phil, Joe Sim and Paula Skidmore 1991 *Prisons Under Protest* Crime, Justice and Social Policy Series Open University Press Milton Keynes

Semple-Kerr, James 1988 *Out of Sight, Out of Mind: Australia's Places of Confinement, 1788-1988* S.H. Ervin Gallery in Association with the Australian Bicentennial Authority Canberra

Shaylor, Cassandra 1998 '"It's like living in a black hole": women of colour and solitary confinement in the prison industrial complex' *New England Journal of Criminal and Civil Confinement* Vol 24 No 2 pp 385-416

Sim, Joe 1990 *Medical Power in Prison: The Prison Medical Service in England 1774-1989* Open University Press Milton Keynes

Sim, Joe 1994 'Tougher than the rest? Men in Prison' in Newburn and Stanko (eds) *Just Boys Doing Business? Men, Masculinities and Crime* Routledge London pp 100-17

Sim, Joe 2003 'Whose side are we not on? Researching medical power in prisons' in Tombs and Whyte (eds) *Unmasking the Crimes of the Powerful: Scrutinising States and Corporations* Lang New York pp 239-57

Sim, Joe 2004 'The victimised state and the mystification of social harm' in Hillyard et al (eds) *Beyond Criminology: Taking Harm Seriously* Pluto Press London pp 113-32

Tombs, Steve and Dave Whyte (eds) 2003 *Unmasking the Crimes of the Powerful: Scrutinising States and Corporations* Lang New York

Vinson, Tony 1982 *Wilful Obstruction: The Frustration of Prison Reform* Methuen Sydney

Waller, Kevin 1998 'The modern approach to Coronial Hearings in Australasia' in Selby (ed) *The Aftermath of Death* Federation Press Sydney pp 2-10

Ward, David and Thomas Werlich 2003 'Evaluating super-maximum custody' *Punishment and Society* Vol 5 No 1 pp 53-75

Wicker, Tom 1975 *A Time to Die* Quadrangle New York Times Book Company New York

Wright, Paul 2000 'The cultural commodification of prisons' *Social Justice* Vol 27 No 3 pp 15-21

Zdenkowski, George 1979 'Katingal: to be or not to be?' *Legal Service Bulletin* Vol 4 pp 220-1

Zdenkowski, George and David Brown 1982 *The Prison Struggle: Changing Australia's Penal System* Penguin Books Ringwood

Newspaper Articles

Newspaper articles sourced from: Coburg Historical Society Collection, Coburg Library: HM Pentridge Prison Newspaper Clippings File (undated); Victorian Department of Justice Resource Centre: 'K Division Fire and Aftermath: Newspaper Clippings, October 1987'; 'Newspaper Clippings: K Division Inquest, November 1988 to July 1989'; and 'Newspaper Clippings: Inquiries into Office of Corrections Arising from the Findings into the K Division Inquest'.

Advertiser
> 21/3/89 'Ex-Warder tells of Jika "mind games"'

Age
> 3/10/72 Kevin Childs 'Objector tells of five days in riot torn gaol'
> 20/7/73 Kevin Childs 'Pentridge is "unfit for zoo animals"'
> 26/9/73a 'Editorial: Guided tour of Pentridge'
> 26/9/73b 'Report names officers'
> 23/11/73 'Pentridge report "one-eyed"'
> 25/7/80 Bill Birnbauer 'Now concrete cages the incorrigibles'
> 30/10/87 Tom Noble and Paul Conroy 'Five die in prison fire, Jika protesters set alight their barricade'
> 30/10/87 p 1 'Protest not linked to AIDS carriers, says prison chief'
> 30/10/87 p 8 Leith Young 'Five were convicted of violent crimes'
> 10/3/89 Alex Messina 'Jika Jika Fire Death Request Dismissed'
> 13/4/89 Alex Messina 'Fire Chief tells of confusion at Jika fire'
> 15/4/89 Alex Messina 'Fireman tells of chaos and frenzy at Jika fire'
> 30/5/89 Alex Messina 'Coroner accused of bias at Jika inquest'
> 8/6/89 Alex Messina 'Jika coroner refuses to disqualify himself: Hallenstein dismisses grounds for bias claim'
> 9/6/89 Alex Messina 'Prison office drops Jika inquest complaint'
> 5/7/89 Alex Messina 'Jika Jika QC seeks royal commission'
> 11/7/89 Alex Messina 'Prisoners died by their own hand, inquest told'
> 13/7/89 Alex Messina 'Bureaucrat was unfairly accused, jail inquest told'
> 14/7/89 Alex Messina 'Bureaucracy shares death blame, Jika inquest told'
> 15/7/89 Alex Messina 'Jika Jika QC seeks royal commission'
> 29/7/89 p 1 Fiona Athersmith 'For kin, the end was worth the waiting'
> 29/7/89 p 26 Fiona Athersmith 'Inquiry would be a shocker, says Maclellan'
> 29/7/89 p 27 'The Coroner takes the pragmatic approach to death; quotes from the Inquest'

1/8/89 Mark Brolly 'A "great step forward" that tripped up on hard reality'

2/8/89 Alex Messina 'Broader inquiry into prisons urged'

7/8/89 Alex Messina 'Comment: not quite what the coroner ordered'

17/8/84 Andrew Rule 'Jika Jika gets new name'

18/11/00 David Reardon 'Torture bed used in WA Jails: Report'

21/5/01 Edward Said 'The case for intellectuals'

Age Good Weekend Magazine

9/8/03 Andrew Rule 'Back from the Badlands'

Australian

17/2/87 Peter Lowe 'Jika Jika prison an experiment gone wrong'

30/10/87 Glenn Mitchell and Gerard Brown 'Five prisoners killed in AIDS protest fire'

31/10/87 'Gruesome death for cold-blooded murderers'

16/7/05 Elizabeth Wynhausen 'Penal prescription a poor cure'

Bendigo Advertiser

31/10/87 'Letters warn of growing violence'

Border Morning Mail

21/3/89 'Young wardens stirred inmates, inquest is told'

Courier-Mail

7/4/86 'Prisoner's brother starts hunger strike outside jail'

Herald

15/2/72 'Show H Division lawful'

17/5/72 Ian Hamilton 'Restriction on jail inquiry, Pentridge will get "bash" probe'

1/8/83 John Lyons 'Escape – and anger breaks out'

21/1/87 'Jails fail on UN test – Kennan'

30/1/87 Sharon Krum 'Pentridge Division must go – group'

13/2/87 Trent Bouts 'How Hell came to Pentridge'

30/10/87 p 1 Penelope Debelle, Greg Kerr and Barbara Sharp 'Govt. shuts Jika Jika, too risky after fire – Kennan'

30/10/87 p 4 Jo McKenna 'Guard tells of prison fire threat'

30/10/87 p 22 Sandra Lee 'Bans, strikes, riots'

5/12/88 J Hall 'Prisoners told to die during fire, court told'

3/8/89 Louise Talbot 'Jail taskforce chief blames officials'

Herald-Sun

31/5/06 Michael Warner 'Court, Jails win boost in security'

12/9/06 Paul Anderson 'A home for our most dangerous'

Moreland Courier

7/2/00 'Jika Jika, the final days: residents can choose to stay for life – grey walls come tumbling down'

National Times

> 3-8/5/76 Anne Summers 'Life at Supermac's: is the new Grafton just one more prison problem?'

Sun

> 4/10/72 'Jail wardens boo governor: Pentridge at a standstill'
>
> 31/8/73 'Jail warders in the clear'
>
> 17/4/78 Geoff Wilkinson 'Prisoners go wild'
>
> 22/8/79 Patricia Wilson 'Garden view and security'
>
> 29/9/82 Michael Wilkinson 'Jika – it's a winner!'
>
> 25/8/87 'Jika Hanging, cabbie case man second prison death'
>
> 30/10/87 'Prisoners made pact of death'
>
> 30/10/87 p 3 'They were ready to die'
>
> 30/10/87 p 1 'Five die in jail "hell", Fear of AIDS "the spark"'
>
> 31/10/87 Craig Johnstone 'Jika cell death plea'
>
> 31/10/87 p 10 Tom Prior 'Jika is jinxed'
>
> 28/4/89 Kelly Ryan 'Warders hit Jika survivor'
>
> 30/5/89 Kelly Ryan 'Jika Fire "pressure": jail officer "given gruelling quiz"'
>
> 8/6/89 Kelly Ryan 'Coroner rejects Jika inquest bias claims'
>
> 15/7/89 Kelly Ryan 'QC calls for probe into penal system'
>
> 22/7/89 Kelly Ryan 'Office failed to act on threats: counsel'
>
> 29/7/89 Kelly Ryan and Ian Jackson 'Coroner blasts "lies": call for probe into prison system'
>
> 21/9/89 Alison Sloan 'Pentridge officer "wanted man dead"'

Sunday Age

> 25/10/98 Andrew Rule 'One man's truth was a shock to the prison system'

Sunday Press

> 30/9/73 Kevin Childs 'H for Hell: a chilling look at a prisoner's life in Pentridge Prison's feared H Division'
>
> 28/5/89 Kevin Norbury 'Jail Fire Hero Suspended'
>
> 30/7/89 Sue Hewitt 'Corruption report "was right"'
>
> 30/7/89 p 4 Sue Hewitt 'Not worth it – warders'

Sunday Review

> 3/9/71 Ian Baker 'Articulate prisoners disturb Pentridge'

Telegraph

> 24/11/87 'Jika Jika, terrible electronic zoo'

Time

> 6/4/98 Susan Horsburgh 'System under siege'

Truth

> 24/4/76 Governor Ian Grindlay 'The Governor's Pentridge papers – The dirty dozen'

INDEX

Abbott, Jack Henry 191

Aboriginal prisoners 57
  see also Royal Commission into
    Aboriginal Deaths in
    Custody

adjustment principles 15

Administrative Appeals Tribunal
  211

AIDS prisoners 223, 225

Allen, Neil 51

Anderson, Paul 150

Architecture Institute Award for
  New Buildings 79

assaults 6, 25, 65, 80

asylum seekers 24–5

attempted escapes 6

attempted suicides 6, 17, 80, 144

Attica siege (US) 20

Austin, Alan 227–8

Australian Institute of Criminology
  186, 242

autopsies, purpose of 206

'banging up' 129

Banner, Norman 50, 157, 176, 209–
  10

Barlinnie Special Unit (Scotland)
  66–7, 263

barricades 6, 132, 147, 148

Barwon Prison Acacia High-
  Security Unit (Vic) 18, 19, 256

Bathurst Gaol (NSW) 20, 67

Bazley, James 101, 104, 110, 140

Becker, Howard 29, 50–1, 190

behaviour modification 15, 61, 68–
  9, 112–13, 114

Bentham, Jeremy 24

Bezanovic, - (Prison Officer) 155

bodily resistance 130, 132–3, 137–9

Bogard, William 23

'Bomber' Barnes controversy 204,
  205

'the bottom' 45

Boyle, Jimmy vi, 67

Brand, Paul 248

Britain
  Barlinnie Special Unit (Scotland)
    66–7, 263
  behaviour modification
    techniques for prisoner
    control 61, 112–13
  Mountbatten Report into
    security in prisons 66, 67
  prisoner protest actions 20, 41
  prisoner protests at Peterhead
    Prison (Scotland) v–vii

'bronze-up' 128–9, 137–8

Brown, David 29

Builders Labourers Federation 76

Butterly, Archi 205

Cain Government 211, 249

Cain, - (Senior Prison Officer) 155,
  159, 160, 161, 163, 177

Carrolan, - (Chief Prison Officer)
  48

Carter, Keith 129, 148

Casuarina High-Security Unit
  (WA) 18

cell assault mattress 159

Certeau, Michel de 22–3

Challinger, Dennis 62, 81

Challinger Report
  commissioning of 62, 80–1
  findings 81
  institutional, structural and
    operational flaws 81

official reception of findings 94, 95

physical impact of high-security 85–6

prisoner classification procedures 82–5

prisoner management, placement and privileges 87–91

programs and useful work for prisoners 91–3

Chamberlain murder trial 173, 204–5

Chanter, Raymond 48

chemical gases 17

CIB Arson Squad 156

citizenship, confiscation of 24

civil death 24

Close Katingal Campaign 76

Cohen, Stanley 40, 102, 130

Collins, Richard Byron (Dr) 201–3

Concrete Institute of Australia Award for Excellence 79

Connell, Bob 27

Coroner's Act 1985 (Vic) 177, 180, 186–8, 242

coronial inquests
coroner's power to make recommendations 188, 241–2

into deaths in high-security institutions 185–6

findings of contribution 184

investigations of deaths in custody 179, 180–9, 183, 184

official discrediting of prisoner evidence 194–9, 234–8

powers of investigation 180, 181, 182, 184–5, 239–45

into prison suicides 182, 183, 185

and public accountability 180–1, 188–94

role and purpose 180, 182–4, 188–9

treatment of evidence 183, 190–4

Victorian legislation 177, 180, 186–8

Crabb, Steve 248

criminal justice, history 8

Cuneeen, Chris 57–8

D Division (Pentridge Prison) 41, 48

Davies, Glen 80, 89–90, 95

Davis, Angela 264

Davis, - (Prison Governor) 149, 158, 159

deaths in custody
'acceptable' deaths 194

in high-security prisons 14, 18, 185–6, 241–2

insufficiency of coronial inquest 179, 180–9

national review 186

official discourse and responses to 28–30

post-death investigations 190

primacy acceded to official accounts 179

role of coronial inquest 189–94

role of forensic experts in post-death investigations 206–7

statistics 14, 242, 256

treatment of 'non-official' evidence vi, viii, 191–4

see also Downie, Sean; Jika five; Royal Commission into Aboriginal Deaths in Custody (RCIADIC); Williams, John

Delphine, Paul 157, 176, 209–10, 222

Department of Public Prosecutions (DPP) 184, 187

deprivation theory of prison suicide 185

Dessau, Linda (Coroner)

findings of Downie Inquest 178

recommendations of Downie Inquest 178

recommendation that visit to Downie's cell be further investigated 177, 207-8, 212

representations of Downie's character and mental state 186, 192-3, 195

treatment of evidence in Downie Inquest 198, 199, 200-1, 203, 212-13

Dietrich, Olaf (prisoner)

allegations against CPO King 164

allegations against prison officers 4, 122-3, 236

barricade protest 147

discrediting of his evidence at Jika fire Inquest 237

fear of giving evidence at Downie Inquest 167, 198

on foreign objects in food in Jika 108

hunger strike 144

on 'Jika talk' 136

protest over visiting procedures 158

theft of documents used in his trial 146

transfer to Jika 116, 122

'troublemaker' tag 155

Dillon, JV (Victorian Ombudsman) 36, 54

Dillon Report 36, 54-6

Dimitrovski, Michael 2-3, 106-7, 136, 245

disciplinary crackdowns 6

disciplinary power and resistance, in high-security 22-5, 100, 124, 126-30, 148

disciplinary strategies, psychologically geared 15, 61, 63-9

Divisional Classification Committee (DCC)

composition and role of 83, 84-5

operations of 114-20, 154

Dixon, Brian (Minister for Social Welfare) 69

Dixon-Jenkins, John (prisoner)

allegations of officer brutality and abuse 123, 144-5, 167-9

documenting the abuse 140, 144-5

Downie Inquest 167, 169, 199, 200-1, 208, 213

experiences in Jika 101, 123, 140

suspicions regarding death of Sean Downie 140, 153, 167-9, 200-1

transfer to Jika 167

Dockies Gang (H Division, Pentridge Prison) 64

Doing Time Magazine 119

'Doing Time Show' (radio) 141

Donovan, - (Prison Governor) 216

Dowdle, Maurie 105-6

Downie, Sally 108, 110-11, 173-4

Downie, Sean (prisoner)

the 3.55pm cell visit prior to his death 207-8, 212-13

autopsy and forensic evidence 201-3, 206-7

death in custody viii, 6-7, 109, 137, 140, 141, 144, 148, 152, 152-3, 218

emergency response to his death 156-7, 162, 172, 178, 202, 210

experiences in Jika 108, 111, 135, 147, 186

external and internal inquiries into death 209-10

family's account of his time in Jika 173-4

imprisonment on remand and
transfer to Jika 153–4
inconsistencies in reports of his
death 166–7, 168–9, 170–1,
172–3, 179, 199
Inquest into his death 167, 169,
176–8, 179–80, 191–4, 207–8
Lynn Report 212
Murray Inquiry 200, 211–12
noncompliance and resistence in
Jika 154–6, 157–8, 193
OOC investigation of his death
157, 176–7, 209–10
Prison Chaplain's comments
174–5
prison officers' accounts of his
behaviour 157–64, 191–2
prisoner accounts of events
leading to his death 164–73,
195–7, 199–201
drug aversion therapies 68
Eagan, Peter 156, 202
Eastwood, Edwin 80, 89–90
Edney, Richard 26–7
'electronic zoos', viii 6, 17
escapes 6, 17, 66, 125–6, 132
Europe, prisoner protest actions 41
Everynight! Everynight! (play) 38,
39–40

Fairlea Women's Prison (Vic) 83
Findlay, Mark 63
Finnane, Mark 19
fires 6, 17, 41, 83, 132
see also Jika fire
Fitzgerald, Mike 66, 113
Fitzsimmons, - (Prison Officer)
155, 159, 160, 161–2, 164
forensic evidence
in Azaria Chamberlain murder
case 204–5
in Bomber Barnes case 204, 205

relationship between experts
and government agencies
204
role of experts in post-death
investigations 206–7
use of expert forensic opinions
203–5
forgetting, ideologies of 8
Foucault, Michel 22, 23, 37
Freckleton, Ian 204

Gallagher, Arthur
classification dispute 118–19,
140, 143, 146
death in custody viii, 4, 194, 217,
245, 254
Gallagher, Billy 143
gaols see prisons
Garrard, Wayne 215, 216
Geschke, Norman 249
Giroux, Henry 264
Godfrey, Michael 48, 51
Goffman, Erving 24
Gough, Noel (Prison Officer) 152,
161, 162–4
Goulburn High-Risk Management
Unit (NSW) 18
Grafton Intractables Unit (NSW)
53
green bans 76
Griffin, John 250
Grindlay, Ian 33, 47
Gronigan, John Van 210

H Division (high security unit,
Pentridge Prison)
1978 riots 36, 53–6
disciplinary charges 44, 49
Dockies Gang 64
escapes 37
induction of prisoners 43–4
industry yard prisoners 44

inquiry into viii–ix
labour yard prisoners 44
legacy of 56–8
myth-making 34, 47
official representations of 77
Ombudsman's Report 53–6
Overcoat Gang 64
politicisation of prisoners 35
prison officers responses to
    prisoner allegations 46–7
prisoner allegations of abuse 35,
    45, 46, 54–6, 57, 104
prisoner campaigns to expose
    brutal regime 34, 35
prisoner classification
    procedures 39, 42–3, 55–6,
    83
prisoner representations of
    violence and resistance 37–
    40
prisoner resistance in 1970s 20,
    33, 33–4, 35
purpose and function 35, 56
racialised violence and terror
    57–8
self-mutilation 46
standing orders 38, 42, 43, 44
transfers to 39, 42, 49
see also Dillon Report; Jenkinson
    Inquiry; Jenkinson Report
Hallenstein, Hal (State Coroner)
    accused of exceeding his powers
    239–45
    Jika fire Inquest 3, 4, 7, 140, 211,
    235, 237, 238, 239–43, 245–9,
    251
    objectives of Victorian coronial
    service 187
    Sean Downie Inquest 176–7
    Williams Inquest 151, 215–18,
    219–20
Hamer, Rupert James 41, 60
Hamilton, Paul 192

Haney, Craig 63
Harmsworth, Peter 177, 234, 239–
    41, 249
Hebb, Donald 102
hegemonic masculinity 27
heritage significance 7–8
Herron, - (Prison Governor) 112,
    222, 226
hierarchies of credibility 29, 50–1,
    190
    and official discrediting of
    prisoner evidence 194–9
'high-risk' criminals 18–19
high-security confinement
    and deaths in custody 186, 241–
    2
    hallmarks of 16
    human costs 17–18
    increasing overuse and
    normalisation of 14
    physical and psychological
    harms associated with 15,
    74, 78, 102–3, 241–2, 262
high-security prisons
    in Australia 16–19
    and cultures of violence 25–8
    disciplinary power and
    resistance 22–5, 100, 103–4,
    124, 148
    hi-tech security and design 15–
    16, 59–60
    institutional dysfunction and
    violence 21–2, 61–2
    and the magnification of
    disorder 23
    for new category of high-risk
    inmates 13, 18–19, 20, 22, 63
    politics of 14, 19–22
    psychological control and
    coercion 63–9
    purpose and design 13
    relations between staff and
    prisoners vii–viii, 6, 61

see also supermax prisons
Hill, - (Prison Officer) 162
Hilton bombing (Sydney) 64
historical selectivity 8
Hogan, Michael 180, 188, 193
Hogg, Russell 29
human rights violations 10, 18, 128
hunger strikes 6, 87, 132, 143–4
Hunter, Colleen 248

Ignatieff, Michel 23
importation theory of prison
    suicide 185
Indigenous prisoners 57
    see also Royal Commission into
        Aboriginal Deaths in
        Custody
informers 38
inquest investigations 4–5
inquests *see* coronial inquests;
    Downie, Sean; Jika fire Inquest;
    Williams, John
Institute of Forensic Pathology 187
Institute of Forensic Science 204
institutional concealment 28
institutional crisis, official
    discourse and responses to 28–
    30
international terrorist activity 18,
    64

jails *see* prisons
James, Danny 172–3, 174, 225
Jenkinson Inquiry
    events leading to 41
    findings 48–52
    focus on H Division 42–3
    investigatory powers 41, 42
    official version vs prisoner
        allegations regarding H
        Division regime 37, 43–48,
        50–2

and the politics of maximum-
    security classification 40–3
and power of 'official truth-
    making' ix, 48–52
reason for 36
terms of reference 41, 45, 49
Jenkinson, Kenneth Joseph 34, 40
Jenkinson Report 34, 48–52
Jika fire
    deaths viii
    emergency response by prison
        staff 3–4, 215–17, 238, 244–5,
        246–7, 248, 254
    events preceding 221–8
    Jim Kennan views aftermath of
        fire xii
    official images of Jika five 228–
        33
    protest action by prisoners 1–2
    reactions of prison officers to
        protest 1–2, 235–6
Jika fire Inquest 211, 215–18
    Desmond Sinfield affair 238–9
    findings 219–20, 245–9
    government response 250–7
    Hallenstein's findings 215–17,
        245–9, 251
    inquiries to investigate issues
        arising from findings 248–
        50
    'lost' evidence 253–4
    Murray Report 250–7
    obstructive measures by OOC
        219–20, 247–8, 252, 253–4
    official discrediting of prisoner
        evidence 234–9
    official responses to 261
    prison officer evidence critical of
        management in Jika 238–9
    prisoner evidence of
        mismanagement and abuse
        in Jika 235–8, 240

re-defining the Coroner's powers 239–45

recommendations 247

Jika five *see* Gallagher, Arthur; Loughnan, James; McGauley, David; Morris, Richard; Wright, Robert

Jika Jika High-Security Unit (Pentridge Prison)

barricades 147, 148

beginnings of 59–63

'black book' 134–5, 253

closure 4, 218, 256

communication between prisoners 129, 136–7

conceptualising resistance in 130–4

cost of design, construction and operation 79, 80

cultures of violence and prisoner allegations 120–4, 144, 223

drug use 149–50

'electronic zoo' viii, 6

escaping the 'escape-proof' complex 125–7

exercise yards ('the cage') 86

heritage assessment 77–8

hi-tech security 70–3, 77, 78

hunger strikes 143–4, 223

institutional history 13–14

institutional structural and operational flaws 81

leadership problems 163

legacy of H Division 56–8

loss of privileges 134–5, 146

'mind games' by prison officers 106–14, 120, 145–6, 174

mismanagement 211

official channels for lodging complaints or grievances 142–3

official opening 5, 75–80

official responses to prisoner allegations 112, 119, 144

philosophy, design and structure 5, 20–1, 22, 69–75, 79–80, 218, 260–1

physical eradication of 8, 259

physical impact of high-security 74, 77, 78, 85–6

physical layout 69–73, 70, 71, 211

power meets resistance 145–8

predatory culture 6

'pressure-can' environment 101–6, 261

prison record keeping 89, 192

prisoner accommodation 69, 73–4, 80

prisoner classification procedures 79, 81, 82–5, 114–20

prisoner management, placement and privileges 87–91, 127

prisoner welfare 74–5, 79–80, 81, 108–10, 174

process for visits of family and friends 110–12, 174

programs and useful work for prisoners 74, 91–3, 105, 145–6

proposed inmates 20, 22, 78–9

protection prisoners 145

psychological control and coercion 63–9, 103–4, 106–14

psychological damage to prisoners 102–5

public response to opening 76–80

relations between prisoners 6, 25, 99–100, 121–2

relations between staff and prisoners 6, 25, 90–1, 93, 121–2, 135–6

renamed K Division 5–6, 95

self-imposed loss of privileges 135, 146

staff to prisoner ratio 74, 80

staff training and experience 81, 88, 89, 238

technological malfunctions 80, 88–9, 225

transgression and resistance in 134–45

troubled beginnings 80–2

see also Challinger Report; Downie, Sean; Jika fire; Jika fire Inquest; Jika five; K Division (Pentridge Prison); Williams, John

Jika Jika Revisited (collected prisoners' letters) 140–1

Johnson, Elliott 181–2, 184–5, 188, 206

Johnstone, Graeme (Coroner) 183

Jolly, - (prisoner) 125–6

Jona, Walter 74, 76, 77, 78

Jones, - (Senior Prison Officer) 152–3, 160, 207, 208

K Division (formerly Jika Jika, Pentridge Prison) 5–6, 95, 211, 235, 240

Kane, Dennis 33–4, 35

Katingal Special Security Unit (NSW) 16–17, 53, 61, 65, 75–6

Keating, - (Prison Officer) 155, 159, 160

Kennan, Jim
on brutality inflicted on prisoners in Jika 101
closure of Jika 4
labels Jika 'dehumanising electronic zoo' 6
views aftermath of fire at Jika *xii*

Kerr, Stephen 210–11

King, - (Chief Prison Officer)

his account of events surrounding death of Sean Downie 159–61, 177, 208

and official version of events surrounding death of Sean Downie 155

prison officers accounts of his conduct 163

prisoner allegations regarding his involvement in Sean Downie's death 164, 165, 166, 167–8, 212

prisoner and prison chaplain's allegations regarding his conduct 147

King, Michael 2–3

King, Wayne 105, 236, 245

Ku Klux Klan 57

landscapes, sanitisation of 8

Lapidos, Jeff 6, 121, 151

Leeburn, Eric (Prison Officer) 239

Liebling, Alison 10

Light, Richard
account of Jika fire 2, 4, 236, 237
allegations against prison officers 107, 121, 146, 147, 165, 198, 224, 226
discrediting of his evidence at Jika fire Inquest 236, 237
Jika fire Inquest findings 245

Lindgren, - (Senior Prison Officer) 48

Long Kesh H Block protests (UK) 137–8

loss of privileges (LOP) 54

Loughnan, James (prisoner) viii, 194, 217, 245

Lynn Report 212

Macdonald, Iain (Prison Officer) 153, 162, 210

McGauley, David

death in custody viii, 194, 217, 245

escape from Jika 125

protest action 138

McGauley, Ella 248

McGeechan, Walter 75, 76

Mackie, - (Chief Prison Officer) 2

management problems 6, 7

management structures, unaccountable 61

Maori prisoners 57

Marion Penitentiary (Ill, US) 68

Marten, - (Prison Officer) 160, 161, 163, 177

masculinity, hierarchies and cultures of 27

Mayne, Garry 45, 48

Melaleuca High-Security Unit (Vic) 256

Metropolitan Fire Brigade (MFB) 3, 156–7, 202, 210, 215–16, 236, 246

Minogue, Craig
  allegations against prison officers 121, 122, 146, 165–6, 196, 236
  anti-prison activist 128
  discrediting of his evidence at Jika fire Inquest 236–7
  documenting allegations 56–7, 141–2
  Downie Inquest 167, 195, 196–8, 207
  experiences of Jika 106, 107–8, 109, 110, 139, 142–3
  hunger strikes 144
  Jika fire Inquest findings 245
  on prisoner classification 115–16, 117–18, 119, 236
  protest action 1–4, 224, 226
  on purpose of Jika fire protest 226
  'resistance writing' 56–7

  on role of Ombudsman 54
  Russell St bombing 97, 196, 236
  transgression and resistance in Jika 134, 135, 136
  as 'troublemaker' 155, 236

Minogue, Rodney 97, 141, 142, 146, 164, 198, 224–5

Mooney, Ray 37–40

Morgan, Steve 39

Morris, Richard
  allegations against CPO King 147
  death in custody viii, 194, 217, 245
  hunger strike 144

Morton, - (Prison Officer) 162

Mountbatten, Lord 66

Mountbatten Report (UK) 66, 144

Mulgrew, Terry (Chief Inspector) 249, 250

murders 6, 80, 94–5

Murdon, Ian 141

Murray Inquiry 200, 211–12, 251–2, 256

Murray Report 251, 252–7

Murray, Tony (QC) 211, 251

Nagle Report 17, 53, 75

Nathan, Justice 240–1, 242

Neville, Timothy 125–6

New South Wales Corrective Services Department 75, 76

New South Wales prisons see Bathurst Goal; Goulburn High-Risk Management Unit; Grafton Intractables Unit; Katingal Special Security Unit; Nagle Report; Royal Commission into New South Wales Prisons

New Zealand, prisoner protest actions 41

Norden, Peter (Prison Chaplain) 151, 166, 174–5, 199

obstructive secrecy 28
Office of the Coroner (Victoria) 187, 204
official research, function of 80–1
'official truth-making', power of 48–52, 189–90
official violence, in prisons 26–7
Oikawa, Mona 8
Ombudsman (Victorian)
  prisoners' complaints to 140, 141, 143, 147
  review into public accountability measures of OOC 249, 250
Ombudsman Act 1973 (Vic) 36, 53–4
O'Toole, Colin 48, 51
Overcoat Gang (H Division, Pentridge Prison) 64

Parenti, Christian 28
passive resistance 135, 138
Payne, Dennis 79–80
penal policy 66, 69, 126
penal reform 49, 53, 54, 256
Penter, Edgar (Prison Governor) 3, 119, 156, 159, 163, 216, 222, 224, 225
Pentridge Prison
  baton charge in D Division 41, 48
  decommissioning and closure 7
  industrial strife by prison officers 40
  prisoner disturbances in 1970s 20, 40–1, 67
  public criticisms 41
  see also Jenkinson Inquiry; Jenkinson Report
Pentridge Prison high-security units *see* H Division; Jika Jika; K Division

Pentridge Village (housing estate) 7–8, 258–9
Peterhead Prison (Scotland), prisoner protests v–vii
Physicians for Human Rights 103
Pickering, Sharon 10–11
Pilger, John 262
Police Association 126
political activists, imprisoning of 35
political agitation by prisoners 35, 39
Port Phillip Prison 256
power and resistance 22
  as institutional text 126–30
predatory culture 6, 99
prison culture, and hierarchies and cultures of masculinity 27, 99
prison officers
  allegations of misconduct and brutality 6, 7, 26–7, 29–30, 35, 45, 46, 53, 54–8, 104, 199–201
  industrial strife 40
  'mind games' by 106–14, 120, 145–6, 174
prison rape 28, 46
Prison Reform Group (PRG) (Vic) 119, 140–1
prison riots 20, 36, 41, 53–6, 67
prison violence 25–8, 63, 99–100, 120–4
prison-industrial complex x
prisoner allegations
  against prison staff 29–30, 199–201
  corroborating and documenting 141–2, 146, 200, 224
  power of unauthorised accounts 37–40
prisoner campaigns 6, 17, 47, 61, 131–2, 140–5
prisoner evidence

documenting 141–2, 146

official discrediting of 194–9, 235–8

treatment of 50–2, 55

prisoner grievances, making public 140–5

prisoner militancy 41, 47–8

prisoner noncompliance and resistance 13, 19–20, 124, 127–9

bodily resistance 130, 132–3, 137–9

official discourse and responses to 28–30, 60–1, 98–9, 127, 145–8

passive resistance 135, 138

'resistance writing' 56–7

tactics 127–30

and transgressive acts 130–1

types of 130, 131–2

prisoner protest actions 6, 17

in Britain 20

international trend 41

prisoner rights ix–x , 9, 16, 19, 35, 42, 127, 260

prisoners

with AIDS 223, 225

'dangerousness' of 18–19, 20, 22, 63–5, 127, 244, 261

physical and psychological control over 13

political agitation by 35, 39, 127

racialised violence against 57

radicalisation of 35, 41, 61

see also Aboriginal prisoners; Maori prisoners; women prisoners

Prisoners Action Group (PAG) 6, 76–7, 94, 121, 248, 260–1

prisons

origins of 24

privatisation of x

see also high-security prisons; names prisons in each state; supermax prisons

psychiatrically ill prisoners 82

psychological control and coercion 15, 61, 63–9

public accountability of state agencies 180, 183, 184, 188–94, 249, 250–1

public safety 60, 63

Pugliese, Joseph 24, 25

punishment, of the body and mind 23–5

Queensland see Woodford Correctional Centre Maximum-Security Unit

Quinn, Barry 94–5, 218

racialised violence, against prisoners 57–8

radicalisation of prisoners 35, 41, 61

radio 141

Ranson, David (Dr) 201–3

rape see prison rape

Rapke, Jeremy (Counsel for OOC) 34, 236–7, 238, 243

Ray, Ross (Counsel assisting coroner) 244

Read, Mark ('Chopper') 64, 153, 169–71, 172–3, 195, 198–9, 207

Reed, Peter

allegations against prison officers 120, 122, 146–7

classification of prisoners 116–17

documenting allegations and grievances 141, 194

experience of Jika 97–8, 103–4, 106, 107, 108, 109, 134, 136, 137, 142–4, 260

Rees, Peter 236

rehabilitation 69

rehabilitative programs 61

remand prisoners 82, 84, 97, 106, 142-3, 153-4, 157, 193

resistance

exacerbation in high-security 22-5, 100, 126-30, 148

threat of 22-3

see also prisoner noncompliance and resistance

Review and Assessment Committee (R&A)

composition and role of 83-5

operations of 114-20, 154, 192, 222

riots *see* prison riots

Rippon, Tom 126

Risdon Prison (Tasmania) 18

'risk', discourses and concerns about 21-2, 263-4

Roberts, Gregory David 37

Robertson, - (Prison Officer) 155, 156, 158-9, 160, 163

Robinson, John 193

rock breaking 33, 44, 54

Rodriguez, Dylan 21, 62

Rohypnol 150

Royal Commission into Aboriginal Deaths in Custody (RCIADIC) 181-2, 184-5, 188

Royal Commission into New South Wales Prisons (1978) 17, 53, 75, 206

Russell Street bombing 97, 196, 236

Ryan, Michael (Deputy Director of Prisons Division)

actions during Jika fire Inquest 234-5, 238, 239, 242-3

classification of prisoner Robert Wright 221, 222

on Downie's mental state 158, 191

on mind games by officers 112

on 'real' cause of Downie's death 211

regarding Downie's placement in Jika 175

Sinfield affair 242-3, 252

Ryan, - (Prison Officer) 158, 162

Said, Edward 264-5

Santos, Michael x

Schein, Edgar 112

Scott, - (Prison Officer) 126

Scraton, Phil vi-vii, viii, 24, 27, 29, 49, 189, 193, 194, 251, 264

Scullin, Richard 51

security 5-6

and institutional polarisation 13

intensification and escalation of 13

segregation principles 66, 67, 69

self harm (acts of) 6, 25, 46, 80, 82, 132-3, 144

sensory deprivation 61, 68, 76, 77, 82, 86, 90, 102

sensory deprivation coffin experiment 102

Shaylor, Cassandra 15

Sim, Joe, vi 21, 24, 25-6, 27, 29, 63, 114, 263

Sinfield, Desmond (Prison Officer) 215, 216, 217, 238-9, 242, 247, 252, 254, 255, 260

Singh, Charandev 17-18

Skidmore, Paula 24, 29

'the slot' 38, 45

'smearing' *see* 'bronze-up'

social isolation 61, 68, 82, 102-3

Social Welfare Act 1970 (Vic) 41, 54

Special Training and Rehabilitative Training (START) behaviour programs 68

Stanford Prison Experiment 26

state power, legitimisation of 21

Stillman, - (Prison Officer) 216

suicides 46, 166, 182, 183, 185

supermax prisons vii, x, xi, 14, 20, 61, 138-9, 262

surveillance 5, 61, 70, 71, 72, 80

Tasmanian prisons *see* Risdon Prison
Tate, Teresa (Prison Officer) 226, 254
Taylor, Angela 97
Taylor, Laurie 98, 102, 130
Taylor, Stanley 51, 97
terrorist activity 18, 19, 64
Thomas, - (Counsel) 196–8
Thompson, Colin (Prison Officer) 245
Thorpe, - (Chief Prison Officer) 2, 3, 246
Thorton, Gareth 141
Tipping, Walter 90
Tognolini, Joseph 51
Toner, Pauline 95
transgressive acts 130–1, 134–45
Tyne Report 253

unauthorised accounts (by prisoners), power of 37–40
United Kingdom *see* Britain
United Nations Minimum Standard Rules for the Treatment of Prisoners 77, 82
United States
  Attica siege 20
  behaviour modification techniques for prisoner control 66, 112–13
  drug aversion therapies 68
  prisoner protest actions 20, 41
  Stanford Prison Experiment 26
  supermax prisons vii, x, xi, 14, 20, 61, 138–9, 262
Uniting Church Report 227–8

Van Oosten, - (Prison Officer) 126
ventilation 2, 5

Victorian Government 250
  see also Cain Government
Victorian Office of Corrections (OOC)
  conduct during coronial investigation into Jika fire 239–45
  conduct during Downie Inquest 176–7, 178, 179, 208
  confidential internal inquiry into Downie's death 211
  crisis of legitimacy 179, 218–221
  criticised in findings of Jika fire Inquest 245–6, 247–8, 249, 252
  discrediting of Prison Officer Sinfield 217, 238–9
  discrediting of prisoner evidence at Jika fire Inquest 234–8
  escape from accountability 7, 9, 28, 256
  further investigation of Downie's death 210
  independent review of fire and emergency services capability 249, 250
  inquiry into conduct during Jika fire inquest (Murray Inquiry) 20, 211–12, 249, 251–7
  internal investigation into Downie's death 176–7, 209–10
  Lynn Report 212
  obstructive actions during Jika fire Inquest 219–20, 247–8, 252, 253–4
  Ombudsman's review of procedures for public accountability 249, 250
  reported incidents in Jika 121
  response to Jika fire viii–ix, 223
  responsibility for problems in Jika 7, 218

suicide audit report on Downie
case 210–11

Tyne Report 253

Victorian Prison Reform Group
(PRG) 119, 140–1

Victorian prison system 83

calls for a Royal Commission
227, 244, 247–8, 249

investigation of allegations of
corruption 249, 250

lack of accountability 53–6, 218–
19, 227, 247

Lynn Report 212

need for reform 227

privatisation of 256

program to improve conditions
77

state of crisis 41

see also Victorian Office of
Corrections (OOC)

Victorian Prisoners Action Group
(PAG) 6, 76–7, 94, 121, 248,
260–1

Victorian prisons see Barwon
Prison Acacia Unit; Fairlea
Women's Prison; Melaleuca
High-Security Unit; Pentridge
Prison, Port Phillip Prison

Vietnam War, conscientious
objectors 35

violence

practice of researching 11–12

in prisons 25–8, 63, 99–100, 120–
4

Visiting Justice system 49

Wales, - (Prison Officer) 152

Wall, - (Senior Prison Officer) 149

'war on terror' 14, 18

Warburton, Sean (prisoner) 153,
171–2, 207

Ward, Shane 172–3

Western Australian prisons see
Casuarina High-Security Unit

Williams, John

death in custody viii, 6–7, 109–
10, 137, 141, 148, 149–52

Inquest into death 150, 151, 163

Woinarski, Brind (Counsel for
deceased Jika five) 234–5, 244

women prisoners 83, 256

in high-security 9–10

Woodford Correctional Centre
Maximum-Security Unit (Qld)
18

Wright, Ian 112

Wright, Paul 28

Wright, Robert

death in custody viii, 4, 194, 217,
245

escape from Jika 125–6, 221

experiences in Jika 105, 119–20,
138, 221

protest action 1–2, 138, 146, 221–
2, 226, 243

re-classification case 139, 140,
221–2, 243, 244

Yorke, Alan 79–80

Youlton, David 125–6

Zimbardo, Phillip 26

RECAPTURING FREEDOM
Issues relating to the release of long-term prisoners into the community
By Dot Goulding

This book is about the prison experience. It relates the stories of several long-term prisoners from the days leading up to their release from prison and through their struggles to cope with life on the outside. Most of these men and women do not successfully reintegrate to wider society and are returned to prison for one reason or another.

Using a combination of the prisoners' narratives and academic accounts, the book explores the notion of institutionalisation and the ways in which prisons strip individuals of their prior social identity in order to mould them into controllable 'inmates'. The book also explores patterns of surveillance and control in prisons, the role of prison staff, the duality of prison culture, and prisoner resistance to institutionalisation. Violence and brutalisation in prisons are also a central focus of the book. In this respect, it addresses the gendered nature of violence in prisons, the prevalence of sexual violence, and the participants' accounts of violent incidents and their claims of officially sanctioned violence against themselves and other prisoners.

The title of the book, *Recapturing Freedom*, alludes to the participants' experiences of 'freedom' out in the wider community. Since most of the participants were returned to prison for one reason or another, the reader can conclude that freedom, for these men and women, was not easily recaptured. Instead, many of the prisoners were recaptured by the system. The text, then, reflects on the participants' descriptions of life outside of prison, however brief the experience may have been.

Dot Goulding is a Postdoctoral Research Fellow at the Prisons Research Unit, Centre for Social & Community Research, Murdoch University. She was instrumental in setting up and running the Prisons Research Unit. Dot's background is in justice activism, prisoner advocacy and prison reform. She has been an Independent Prison Visitor at Bandyup Women's Prison and Casuarina Prison on behalf of the Office of the Inspector of Custodial Services WA. Dot is also a spokesperson for the Prison Reform Group of WA and is Secretary of the Institute for Restorative Justice & Penal Reform (WA Inc).

Institute of Criminology Series No 24
2007 • ISBN 9781876067182 • $49.95
Contact Federation Press to purchase *Recapturing Freedom*
www.federationpress.com.au

INTERROGATING IMAGES
Audio-visually recorded police questioning of suspects
By David Dixon and Assisted by Gail Travis

Police interrogation attracts debate and controversy around the world. Audio-visual recording is widely regarded as a panacea for problems in police questioning of suspects. *Interrogating Images* presents the first empirical study of the routine use of audio-visual recording anywhere in the world, focusing on New South Wales, Australia where such recording has been required for more than a decade. Its introduction is set in a historical account of disputes and concerns about police questioning of suspects. There is a detailed study of the participants in the interrogation process.

Various styles of police interviewing are identified, showing that many assumptions about the nature and purpose of interrogation are inaccurate. A chapter assesses the impact in NSW of 'investigative interviewing', a questioning style very different from that used in the USA. The penultimate chapter examines the experiences and perceptions of criminal justice professionals – judges, defence lawyers, prosecutors, and police. *Interrogating Images* concludes by pointing to some dangers of misusing audio-visual recording. If the complete questioning process is not recorded, confessions may be rehearsed and unreliable. A second danger is the misreading of images, particularly by those who overestimate their ability to identify deception from a suspect's 'body language'. Audio-visual recording can be a useful tool, but it must be one part of a broader process of effectively regulating investigative practices.

Interrogating Images is informative and thought provoking reading for lawyers, police investigators, academic researchers, policy-makers, legislators, students and those with an interest in police interrogation and its implications for criminal justice processes.

David Dixon is Dean of the Faculty of Law, University of New South Wales, Sydney. Also by David Dixon (ed), *A Culture of Corruption: Changing an Australian police service*, 1999, Institute of Criminology Series No 11.

Institute of Criminology Series No 23
2007 • ISBN 978 0 9751967 4 8 • $49.95
Contact Federation Press to purchase *Interrogating Images*
www.federationpress.com.au

REFUGEES AND STATE CRIME

By Sharon Pickering

In the aftermath of World War II, in the shadow of the Holocaust, the countries of the world signed on for a Convention giving rights and safeguards to refugees. Forced migration was a humanitarian not a criminal concern. Being a refugee involved discussion of human rights and protection rather than developing processes of criminalization and law enforcement.

Sharon Pickering documents how this has changed. Refugees and asylum seekers are dressed in the clothes of criminals, and national sovereignty has become the focus of the response of the Global North to forced migration.

Pickering adopts a State Crime framework, emerging out of a critique of law and order refugee politics, to explain policy responses. The roles of the administration, the justice system and the media are analysed to highlight the discourses of criminality which have come to dominate discussion of refugee and asylum issues.

She shows how the spectacle of the refugee as criminal allied to the rise of transnational policing, has led to the opening up of extra-territorial, extra-legal spaces, how contradictions have emerged as to national "borders" and how the rule of law has been debased.

Sharon Pickering lectures in Criminal Justice and Criminology at Monash University, Australia. She teaches and researches in the field of refugee law and policy, criminology and human rights.

Also by Sharon Pickering, with Caroline Lambert:
Global Issues, Women and Justice, 2004, Institute of Criminology Series No 19.

Institute of Criminology Series No 21
2005 • ISBN 9781862875418 • $55.00
Contact Federation Press to purchase *Refugees and State Crime*
www.federationpress.com.au

THE PRISON AND THE HOME
By Ann Aungles

Ann Aungles clearly demonstrates in this book the nexus between prison and home life. This analysis spans across a range of modern societies to show how forms of social control have been established between these two spheres. The relationship between the home and the prison is examined and many areas of intersection are exposed. Prison populations have increased significantly over the last few years, leading to other measures of detention becoming necessary, such as day leave, work release, home detention, and so on. This situation creates many contradictions as the home may then become the prison, and puts the burden of penal surveillance and care intake home sphere. A frequent consequence of this is that the prisoners' families and those who care for them bear the brunt of this contradiction.

This oft cited text continues to be relevant and thought provoking.

Institute of Criminology Series No 5
1994 • ISBN 9780867589030 • $32.95
Contact Federation Press to purchase *The Prison and the Home*
www.federationpress.com.au

DOING LESS TIME: PENAL REFORM IN CRISIS
Institute of Criminology Series No 2 1992 ISBN 0867585668
By Janet Chan

Doing Less Time provides an in-depth account of the development and implementation of the release on licence scheme and of the theories of prison reform, decarceration and social control which lay behind its introduction into New South Wales prisons. Interviews with those involved with its day-to-day operation record the story of the scheme itself - one marked by high expectations and deep disappointments. Dr Chan also examines the reasons for its failure and the implications for penal reform in the years that followed.

RESHAPING JUVENILE JUSTICE: THE NSW YOUNG OFFENDERS ACT
Institute of Criminology Series No 22 2005 ISBN 9780975196731
Edited By Janet Chan

Reshaping Juvenile Justice examines reforms in New South Wales under the Young Offenders Act 1997. The Act institutionalises a fresh approach to juvenile justice – one that regulates police discretion at the gate-keeping level, emphasises diversion as a principle, introduces restorative conferencing as an intermediate intervention, and relegates the use of courts to the last resort.

Reshaping Juvenile Justice brings together the most up-to-date research evidence and analysis of the Young Offenders Act. It details the history of the Act's development and implementation. It describes the working of the Act and evaluates its effectiveness and impact on young offenders, victims, and juvenile crime. In discussing the strengths and weaknesses of the Act and in identifying the critical success factors and barriers to implementation, the monograph lays the groundwork for future debates on juvenile justice in Australia.

Janet Chan is a Professor at the School of Social Science and Policy, University of New South Wales. Janet's research interest has been in reforms and innovations in criminal justice, policing and, more recently, creativity in the arts and sciences. She has published extensively on criminal justice policy and practice. Janet is also a part-time Commissioner of the NSW Law Reform Commission and a Fellow of the Academy of Social Sciences in Australia.

Contact Federation Press to purchase these titles
www.federationpress.com.au

INDIGENOUS HUMAN RIGHTS
Edited by Sam Garkawe, Loretta Kelly and Warwick Fisher

"*The language and concept of rights is one that Indigenous people turn to more and more. We all hold these rights by virtue of being human even if we have a different cultural construct of what those rights might mean in practice. This book makes a valuable contribution to those debates by providing a platform for the injection of perspectives from Indigenous and non-Indigenous Australians, as well as a number of overseas Indigenous lawyers and academics.*" Professor Larissa Behrendt, Director, Jumbunna Indigenous House of Learning, Professor of Law and Indigenous Studies, University of Technology Sydney

Indigenous Human Rights is an edited selection of proceedings of the Australian Indigenous Human Rights Conference, organised by members of Southern Cross University in February 2000. The collection covers a range of issues relating to Indigenous human rights including: racial discrimination and 'special measures'; removal of children; law and order; access to the United Nations; and prospects for the use of international law. One of the most important aspects of the book is the range of Indigenous and non-Indigenous contributors from Australia, the Pacific, north America, and Europe.

Institute of Criminology Series No 14
2001 • ISBN 9781864874099 • $33.00
Contact Federation Press to purchase *Indigenous Human Rights*
www.federationpress.com.au